THE
INTERROGATOR

THE
INTERROGATOR

AN EDUCATION

Glenn L. Carle

NATION
BOOKS
New York

Published by Nation Books,
A Member of the Perseus Books Group
116 East 16th Street, 8th Floor
New York, NY 10003

Nation Books is a co-publishing venture of
the Nation Institute and the Perseus Books Group

Books published by Nation Books are available at special discounts for bulk purchases
in the United States by corporations, institutions, and other organizations. For more information, please contact the Special Markets Department at the Perseus Books Group,
2300 Chestnut Street, Suite 200, Philadelphia, PA 19103, or call (800) 810-4145, ext.
5000, or e-mail special.markets@perseusbooks.com.

Typeset in 11.5 point Bodini Std Book

Library of Congress Cataloging-in-Publication Data

Carle, Glenn.

   The interrogator : an education / Glenn Carle.
     p. cm.
   Includes index.
   ISBN 978-1-56858-673-1 (hardcover : alk. paper)—ISBN 978-1-56858-675-5
(e-book) 1. Carle, Glenn. 2. Spies—United States—Biography. 3. United States. Central Intelligence Agency. 4. Military interrogation—United States. 5. War on Terrorism,
2001–2009. I. Title.
JK468.I6C358 2011
327.12730092—dc22

                                                                        [B]
                                                              2011012548

10 9 8 7 6 5 4 3 2 1

To my father and mother, who taught me to question everything, to accept nothing because others do, to be willing to change my mind—and that right and wrong are independent of authority or convention

CONTENTS

PREFACE: LYING, HONOR, AND THE GRAY WORLD

I was a spy. I broke laws. I stole. I lied every day, about almost everything: to my family, to my friends, to my colleagues, to everyone around me. I almost never was who I said I was, or did what I claimed to be doing. Sometimes I was not American. I exploited people's deepest hopes, won their deepest trust, so that they provided me what my government wanted. I was an angel who made men's dreams come true, but my name was Faust.

I healed a father's desperately ill child, helped a frustrated employee do in his boss, or the organization that slighted him. I was sometimes a revolutionary, nodding my head as some worked to overthrow oppressive governments; sometimes I sympathized with racists; sometimes I suppressed insurgents. I was suave, intellectual, and sophisticated, talking over sparkling glasses in salons with elegant women in low-cut designer dresses, appetizing curves, and high heels, smiling at banalities as we looked past each other. I bounced around mines in a jeep, carried a weapon, wore a *keffiyah* over my face to conceal my identity and offer a less obvious Western target to snipers, spat, swore a lot, scratched my crotch, slapped my buddies on the back, and almost got shot.

Some were ruined from what I did. Some were saved; others died. Few of the living, and none of the dead, knew I had anything to do with their fates. I burgled. I listened in on men's whispered and rustled secret lives, to what they did and hoped and feared behind closed doors—the inner lives, revelatory pettinesses and quirks we all mask during the hours of light and company— so that I could manipulate them, and perhaps help them realize their private perversities. I was faceless, all-powerful, and impotent: I was unknown but could destroy people's lives or cause an international scandal, and yet often I could not even control minor details of my daily life. I held babies and soothed their fears, wiped their tears, burped them, and kept them safe.

Desperate and good men looked to me in hope. I was a shoulder to cry on, and a spur for quiet action against injustice. I was a cynic, helping near socio-paths act upon their amoral and destructive impulses. I laughed at and took advantage of dignified officials willingly abasing themselves naked on their hands and knees, wearing collars around their necks and leashes as they crawled on the floor, barking. I paid people off. I deluded men and convinced them they were acting against the United States, or one of their personal en-emies, when in fact they were serving me and my country, so that we could undermine the causes in which they believed. I was a bureaucrat, and face-less, and powerless, and confused.

I made it possible for American children to sleep safe at night, and for American adults to ignore that I existed or to disdain or hate me, and to forget or never learn that the world was full of men and forces that would harm or destroy them, and our way of life. I have been called "war criminal" and "hero" to my face. I thrived in ambiguity, saw through others' eyes, saw every color of the rainbow, and realized that all the colors are just slightly different shades of gray.

All the while, to all but my colleagues I was just a wholesome, stereotypical New England Yankee, a former athlete struggling against middle age, someone always with his nose in an abstruse book, assessing, say, obscure pseudo-philosopher René Guénon's eighty-year-old musings about the death of God in modern society and how Guénon inspired Muslims to fly planes into sky-scrapers. I would often seek refuge while alone somewhere—in a garret in the red-light district of Paris, or beside a latrine outside Kabul, or in the CIA cafeteria during lunch—in my New England roots, with Emerson, say, and then realize that Emerson was an echo of Buddha and Siddhartha, their ideas brought back to Boston and New Bedford by missionaries and traders much as the West had been reborn centuries earlier from the returning Crusaders, inseminated by their Muslim adversaries, and betters. Carle? He's a nice guy. Normal. He likes the Red Sox. Hockey player. He lacks focus. Reads a lot. Smart. Arrogant. Unsure of himself. Both? His kids play baseball and ride horses.

It is hard to be a spy. I was one for twenty-three years. Yet, my colleagues and I share a devotion to mission, to ideals larger than ourselves, that inspired us to join the Agency, and then to serve for our careers. America is better served than it knows by its intelligence officers. Reflective people will usually seek meaning in actions and a framework for life larger than one's self. Many find fulfillment in the military, social service, or teaching. I found a direction, a way to get beyond myself, in public service, as a spy. I loved my work, even when I was bored, and even when I failed. Intelligence officers fail often, while successes come slowly and sporadically. And through it all, over the decades, many of them far away and alone, I always honored my oath, acted with integrity, protected and defended the Constitution of the United States, and never lost sight of home, or of human decency.

And yet, sometimes one finds more than one seeks. I sought mental, substantive, policy-relevant, moral, and physical challenges in my career. The Agency hires its case officers in part for their ability to thrive in ambiguity, to see clearly what decision to make, where all decisions contradict one's values and obligations; it chooses officers who will make the honorable and right decision beyond one's chain of command, when one is out of sight of anyone else, and when no decision is "right."

I love the "gray world." It is multifaceted and complex, obscure—and hard. It transcends the lie of moral purity, of good and evil, of a simple world. This is our daily challenge, if we are honest: to accept doubt, to realize there is no certainty, and yet to act with principle, finding meaning and purpose in confusion. Inhabiting the "gray world" with clear eyes has often fulfilled me.

And then I was "surged" to become an interrogator in the Global War on Terror. I traveled to a far and dark place, where I found the limits of human endurance, that zeal can blight integrity, and that with a "terrorist's" life in my hands—and perhaps the lives of many Americans—alone I had to decide how to fulfill my mission, what was legal, what was right . . . and at what point I had to oppose the orders of an administration whose actions corrupted the flag I had sworn to serve.

INTRODUCTION:
WHICH FLAG DO YOU SERVE?

"Joe, I don't do nuance."
—President Bush, *Time*, February 15, 2004

Il n'y a que les fous qui soient certains et résolus.
(Only fools are certain and resolved.)
—Montaigne, *Essais*, I.26

My involvement with what some will consider torture began as I was working at my desk on the second floor of CIA Headquarters, about 9:15, a normal Indian Summer morning in 2002. My papers, interview notes with senior officers about how to improve leadership behavior and skills among the CIA's Directorate of Operations (DO) officers, were strewn about my desk.

The chief of my component poked his head inside my office.

"Glenn. Good morning."

This was a surprise. Rob Richer, then the Directorate of Operations Chief of Human Resources, and later Associate Deputy Director of Operations,

1

never came back to my end of the office suite. One of the only other times he had done so I had asked him, "What are you doing here, slumming?" He had smiled after a moment, at first bemused, thinking my comment had made no sense whatsoever.

"Good morning," I said, looking up.

Rob never spent more than five seconds on small talk and was always in hurried, if good-natured, highly focused motion.

"How's your language? It's about a three level?"[1]

Three level in a language, according to the CIA's language scale, is supposed to be that of a university-educated speaker, who makes some errors and has a distinct accent, but can conduct a professional or a social meeting. A Foreign Service or CIA officer will not be assigned overseas to a designated "language use position"—a slot that requires language ability to perform one's job successfully—until he or she attains a three level or above.

Something was up. Why was he at my office, asking me about my language ability? My language skills had nothing to do with my current assignment. This was not the time to make some wiseass or self-deprecating remark that shaped others' perceptions of my abilities or character. I looked him in the eye and spoke calmly, with as much matter-of-fact authority as I could muster.

"No, I speak the language very well. I'm really a five. It's very good. Depending on the circumstances, sometimes I am taken for a native speaker."

Five level in a language is what a university-educated native speaker of a language with no or almost no accent speaks. By the Department's standards, Henry Kissinger might not receive a five in English. I had a very slight accent and made occasional errors; sometimes native speakers recognized me as foreign after the first word out of my mouth. My language was not perfect, but it was outstanding. Certainly I was one of the best speakers of the language in the DO, although I decided not to say this just yet to Rob. I did not want to come across as over-eager and boastful.

"Can you go TDY?[2] There is an urgent need for a case officer who is an excellent linguist. It would be for thirty days, as an initial deployment. It could

---

1 The CIA redacted which language was mentioned.

2 TDY: temporary duty. This is the ubiquitous CIA, military, and Department of State acronym for any official trip.

extend well beyond that. How would a TDY affect your family?" Rob was alluding to my wife's serious illness of the previous couple of years.

"Well, I'll have to call Sally. I think it would be fine."

He looked at me. "Call your wife. Let me know before noon. I'm not promising anything, but I'll let you know. This is important for the Agency, and it could be important for you, too."

Rob didn't have to tell me it was important for me. The DO had been running flat-out all around the world since 9/11, in the biggest series of programs since the Vietnam War, if not in its history. Almost all operations allowed some lead time to prepare. This one did not. Obviously he was debating taking me out of my nonoperational, Headquarters assignment and "surging" me into a sensitive, important operation for the Global War on Terror (GWOT in Agency parlance). He was also giving me an assignment that would begin, perhaps, the long, tentative process of rehabilitating me for operational work, a year after I had made a career-harming mistake in the field and been brought back to Headquarters to work for him. That was why he had added the assignment "could be important for you, too." But, for anyone this was the kind of opportunity every officer hoped for, and that came one's way only once or twice in a career, if ever. Almost no one wants to work at Headquarters, especially during a time of national crisis. The whole point of signing up was to try to be the pointy end of the spear. I sensed a sharp edge ahead.

This would be my third opportunity to become involved in a war. I had been deeply involved in the Contra-Sandinista operations early in my career, working for a time on a special project for Alan Fiers, Chief of our Central American Task Force. The job was fascinating, and a superb opportunity for a very junior officer. Most career trainees do interim training assignments that consist of filing, reading the flow of traffic to learn the ropes, doing "scutt work"—menial tasks like photocopying, or looking up phone numbers—around the office or, if they are fortunate, conducting traces—file checks—of individuals of interest. I worked directly for the chief, in the task force's front office. While most of my fellow trainees were rooting about the file room in the bowels of Headquarters, looking for records to establish whether the Agency had ever met a particular individual prior to that week and, if so, whether the individual was of "operational interest" or had "derogatory information" in his file that the field would need to know about, Fiers sent me on TDY assignment to Costa Rica and Honduras, and on various errands down to the Office of the Secretary of Defense or the West Wing of the White House to hand-deliver a document to National Security Advisor Admiral John Poindexter.

Among the reasons I won such a significant assignment was that Fiers wanted a case officer (C/O)[3] with strong academic credentials who, in theory, could write better than the average C/O and who had Spanish skills, too; this proved to be one of the few times during my career in the DO that my degree obtained something for me other than good-natured (and sometimes not so good-natured) ribbing about being a "Harvard man," witticisms along the lines of "*What* are you doing here? Couldn't you get any other job?" or "You *are* a throwback to an earlier era, aren't you? Those days are done now. . . ." It is not especially career-enhancing in the DO to appear too cerebral, to read too many books; in this way, at least, I was always a slightly different-colored horse in the DO. I spent twenty-three years trying, but failing, to mask my reading habits from my peers.

I had a presage of this nascent hallway reputation my first day in San José, Costa Rica. I knew no one in the station and had sent only a routine one- or two-sentence cable from Headquarters describing the reason for my visit and requesting Chief of Station (COS) approval for my TDY:

C/O SPORTINK[4] REQUESTS PERMISSION TO TDY TO COSTA RICA AND HONDURAS ON SUCH AND SUCH A DATE, TO MEET WITH COS AND OFFICERS INVOLVED IN [the issue I was working on] . . .

Midway through my first meeting with a second-tour C/O close enough in age and rank to speak with me as a peer, we took a little break and chatted

---

3 In DO usage one generally writes "C/O's" for the plural, rather than "C/Os," a senseless legacy, I think, of the days when the DO's cable and encryption system was transmitted by radio, and perhaps typed in by someone who did not distinguish possessives from plurals.

4 SPORTINK is a pseudonym. We always used our pseudonym, never our true name, in cable traffic. At work, I was never known as Glenn, always by my pseudonym. Mine was a somewhat strange-sounding name, similar to SPORTINK, which made me sound vaguely ethnic, a little irony for the quintessential WASP. Of course, this led to colleagues calling me from time to time, "Hey, Rinky-Dink!"

over coffee. The ice had been broken, and our initial business conversation had established in his eyes my bona fides as a legitimate and solid C/O, not as some ferreting and unwelcome outsider. He told me that he and his colleagues had been wondering why Headquarters seemed to be sending some "professor" down to the station to pry into their work. I still have not figured out how my simple, one-sentence, declaratory cable could possibly have given that impression. I think that there must have been a back-channel cable saying that I was coming to interview people, and that must have created the "professor" impression. We got on fine, conducted our business, and I had a successful TDY. Establishing a fellow officer's bona fides in direct conversation— measuring him or her personally and not relying on formal, guarded, and largely bloodless traffic or authorizations—is standard DO culture. Yet, this business of somehow conveying a slightly more intellectual character than the norm in the DO was to recur over the years. It helped me with the brighter of my peers (of whom there are many), and from time to time did not help me so much with a few of my knuckle-dragger colleagues. All groups have their cliques, tribal allegiances, and thumbnail judgments.

And yet, having a nature (and hallway reputation) that crossed the culture line from the quasi-military "can-do" approach of the DO into the intellectual bent of the Directorate of Intelligence (DI) was a major factor two decades later in my appointment as Deputy National Intelligence Officer (DNIO) for transnational threats (i.e., terrorism) on the National Intelligence Council, one of the three seniormost officers for terrorism analysis in the intelligence community (IC).[5] My career as a C/O in the field and as DNIO for terrorism was highly unusual, as few officers can cross or are interested in crossing from one career specialization to another, particularly at such a senior level, coordinating and shaping the work of the sixteen agencies and for years writing many of the National Intelligence Estimates on terrorism.

---

5 I was Acting National Intelligence Officer for transnational threats for four months, then Deputy for the remainder of my tenure on the National Intelligence Council. There was one other deputy with me most of my time there; thus, I was one of the three most senior officers for terrorism analysis in the U.S. government. We had a third deputy with us for the last six months or so of my time there.

In the end, Fiers was one of the victims of the Iran-Contra scandal. On July 9, 1991, years after I had moved on to subsequent assignments, he pleaded guilty to two misdemeanor counts of withholding information from Congress about secret efforts to aid the Nicaraguan Contras. He was later pardoned by the first President Bush. A number of our officers were indicted from the fallout of the CIA's involvement in Ollie North's schemes, several of whom had been my colleagues or superiors (everyone was a superior of mine at that stage of my career . . .). I had had a stroke of luck when Iran-Contra exploded: Still a trainee (CT in DO parlance) during my time working for Fiers on the Central American Task Force, I appeared on no manning tables. I did not formally exist. I could feel anonymous compassion from a distance for the travails of my erstwhile colleagues and superiors, finish my training, and get on with my career without becoming involved in the after-fiasco investigations and commissions.

The second "surge" situation that had come my way was during the war in Bosnia, in late 1995. I was offered the chance to work in the Bosnian war zone in the wake of the Dayton Peace Accords. In standard surge practice, the DO was going to rotate officers through the assignment for several-month TDYs. Such assignments can make a career, as well as be the most challenging and meaningful assignments one can find. Standard DO advice on how to get promoted has always been to "go where the bombs go off." When promotion panels sift through our files and compare an officer who did a solid job in Beirut, say, with an officer who did a solid job in a city in Europe, the inclination is invariably to reward the officer who has filled the more dangerous or arduous assignment. This is one of the reasons that NE officers—officers from the DO's Near East Division—have for decades been the cocks of the walk in the DO, with faster promotions on the whole, and more senior assignments.

The psychiatric evaluations for prospective case officers when you apply to the Agency harp on stressful situations, to see how stable we are, I suppose, and to measure our respective ways of perceiving and handling stress. "Would you mind sleeping in a jungle without any soap, for days on end?" This question and variants cropped up over and over in the long written psychological questionnaire. Most questions were straightforward: "Do you like crowds? Rate how much on a scale of 1 to 4. . . . Have you ever been institutionalized?"

and the like. Of course, for the soap questions I checked the box indicating that no, I would not mind, or that I would love a situation like that. I think most of us trying to get into the DO figured that this was a wimp test of some sort. Twenty questions later it was back: "If you had no soap, and were in the jungle, and had to sleep, for weeks at a time, and it was rainy season and rained for weeks on end, and there were lots of bugs, and your partners snored or you were alone for weeks, and you had no tent, and you were alone, and you had no soap, would you mind having no soap?" We all tried to game the system one way or another, but the foolish questions were relentless, and were clearly designed to wear through our attempted manipulations. A few questions further on it was back: "Suppose you were alone, in the rain forest, on assignment, and had an open-ended assignment, and it was raining, and you had no shelter and were alone, or you didn't like your partners if you were not alone, and you had no soap . . . would you mind?" Further on in the test it came back, and back: "Suppose you had soap, but no water. How would you feel about having no soap?" Jesus Christ. Over twenty-five years later I still think about these bloody questions and wonder what the hell is going on every time I pick up a bar of Ivory soap. They got in my head after all.

The shrinks never told us what they were getting at with those questions. I suspect they were assessing us for flexibility, to identify personalities that enjoyed or at least responded well to unplanned and disorienting circumstances, did not mind discomfort, improvised, and took initiative. Surge assignments like my travels to Central America, or the prospective assignment in Bosnia, by definition called for these qualities. Surge assignments had few fixed structures or routines. Many contained a degree of danger that most assignments did not have, and concerned an issue of at least momentary interest to policy makers. This was why promotions came to those who "went where the bombs go off."

I would have had a stimulating, great time in Bosnia. It would have made a difference in my career. I would no longer have been a pure EUR officer; my résumé would include M-16s and combat pay, not just having worked the salons of Europe for the previous decade, clinking glasses with elegant, thin, and charming women in low-cut gowns, and listening politely to sophisticated men in suits cut a little too tight, sometimes condescending to the naive American official, but almost always presuming to explain to me how politics really worked in America.

I turned the Bosnia slot down. Going would have meant leaving my wife on her own with our four-week-old baby girl and two-year-old boy. I would have missed the first six months of my daughter's life. Too many of my colleagues accepted these assignments in these conditions; sometimes they found themselves alone when they returned. But it was the prospective time lost that was decisive for me. It was irretrievable. My daughter would never again be an infant; my wife would never again need my help coping with two very small children. She was drawn and tired. She had begun on occasion to snap, it seemed to me, without reason, driving off into the night with a curse for I did not know what. I thought my work as a CIA officer was straining the family. I was irreplaceable at home. Other officers could do Bosnia.

Now, a half dozen years later, here was a third opportunity. I could sense from Rob's urgency and from the general frenzy that was the DO in the months following the World Trade Center attacks that what had brought him back to my office was likely to be unusually challenging.

Let him know by noon! I had three hours to arrange a key moment in my then eighteen-year career. It was typical of Rob to set nearly absurd deadlines, but it was also clearly a sign of the importance of the issue. I needed to speak to Sally. I called home, hoping she would be there. I believed she would understand the importance of the opportunity even in complete ignorance of what it entailed and, more important, would feel strong enough physically and psychologically for me to accept it. Sally was particularly supportive of the frequent unexplained departures typical of a case officer's life. I had to leave for three days? That's fine. No questions. No insecurities on that point. "Okay. See you when you get back." This job was going to call for a bit more than a typical one- or three-day business trip. My stomach tightened as I called, though. I wondered if I should refuse the assignment, as I had for the Bosnian War. Much had gone wrong for us recently, no matter what I had tried. My superiors knew of Sally's recent terrible illness, and that her recovery was fragile, but almost no one knew the full scope of our struggles. Would Sally be able to cope if I disappeared totally for months? Could I afford to leave the family?

She was home. I explained the situation, that I had been asked to go on an important assignment, for the organization, and especially for me. Our conversation was to the point.

"Is it important?" Sally asked.

"Yes."

"Is it good for you?"

"Yes."

"Well, then, of course you need to go."

The conversation took about three minutes. Sally, as always in significant or stressful moments, responded in a straightforward, down-to-earth manner. Sally's feet have always been planted on the ground more firmly than mine. She does not get lost in meanders of overly intricate thought. Issue, response, move on. That's all. This is one of the characteristics that attracted me to her years ago. What a relief she had felt strong enough to react as she had and as I had hoped she would. Now, if Rob gave the final green light, I was set.

I waited almost an hour before going to Rob's office. I did not want to appear too eager, or anxious. I worked, took a walk to the cafeteria, bought a coffee. I poked my head in Rob's office a few minutes after 10. He was studying papers on his desk. He raised his head as I called his name from the doorway.

"Rob. It's go. I've spoken with Sally and it's okay."

"Good. Thank you. I'll let you know."

He returned to his work, dismissing me from his attention. Rob never engaged in wasted words. He was cordial, but always focused and crisp. He always was setting deadlines a bit ahead of what one could conveniently accomplish, so that his staff always had to hustle. He cut you off at the knees if you failed in your duties. But he also supported his staff if they worked hard. And he appeared to have a flexible mind, and to judge people on their present actions, rather than defining people once and for all based on previous successes or failures. He seemed to be fair. I'd seen his leadership style in others, all of them shaped by their years in the military. Rob was a former Marine. The Marine approach to leadership had so impressed me with its inculcation of values from top to bottom of the hierarchy—"Every Marine a rifleman" is their slogan, meaning that every Marine must embody the same standards of comportment and leadership, regardless of rank or function, and cannot advance without demonstrating these leadership attributes—that I was basing the leadership program I was designing for the DO on it. Rob was hard to work for, but was an unusual leader for the DO, which is not known for good leadership, perhaps the best leader I had worked for in my career. I returned to my office to continue work on my project. While waiting, I sent him a short e-mail—e-mails to Rob always had to be extremely short:

> Rob:
>
> My language abilities:
>
> ████████: 5 level. I have interpreted for the U.S. Secretary of State, the ██████████ Foreign Minister and other members of cabinet. As noted, I am sometimes taken for a native speaker of ████████.
>
> *Spanish:* 4, 2+, 3+
>
> *Portuguese:* I can understand some Portuguese and can read the gist of newspapers.
>
> *German:* Ten years ago I probably had a 0+, 1 level. I expect that I have lost that now.

The Portuguese comment was a bit of a stretch, although it was true a decade earlier. The Spanish assessment actually understated my abilities. The point was to show my eagerness to go by using the pretext of a note on my language skills, to demonstrate an acceptable aggressiveness in my desire to go, not to cross his eyes with irrelevant background. Rob would understand what I was doing, in any event. He knew the ways of the DO as well as I.

At about 11, Rob appeared at my door again.

"I'm going to launch you." It was an unusual expression. "Thirty days or more, to start. See if you can get out there tomorrow. Go see the people in CTC.[6] They're waiting for you. I called them and told them you're coming. This is a good opportunity. It's a good opportunity for you. Come see me once you've spoken to them."

That was it. He left.

---

6 CTC—the CIA's Counter-Terrorism Center. I had started my career some twenty years before in ██████████, CTC's small predecessor, what I will call the "Counterterrorism Office."

It took me four days to leave. I had to arrange my ███████████ passport, get my travel orders, process my air tickets, arrange to have bills and pay issues addressed during my prolonged absence, all the small details of a trip overseas for a clandestine operation that would never make it into the movies. Just as laymen think "strategy" about great battles while professional soldiers think "logistics," so laymen think "derring-do" about spying while professionals think "administrative details." Much of a C/O's career consists of hustling down the long hallways at Headquarters to cajole as winningly as possible one harassed, low-on-the-totem-pole woman or another in a cubicle in some windowless underground Headquarters office to *please* dredge up your particular form from the huge pile on her desk, or from the endless queue of e-mails lit in green on her computer monitor, and to process it ahead of the other officers who have not hustled fast enough to get to her first. Experienced C/Os have learned how to maneuver amid the unwritten rules and ways of the DO, while respecting the formal procedures enough to avoid getting in trouble with the regulation mavens. If you always follow the procedures strictly, though, too often you will end up finding yourself on your way to the cafeteria to stand in line for greasy food, while your colleague walks past you in the hallway, smiles, says, "How ya doin'?" and claps you on the shoulder as he heads off to pick up his passport and catch his flight to Ulaanbaatar or somewhere. Experienced Headquarters support officers—in particular the long-suffering, unglamorous, and crucial women in the cubicles—know what C/Os are all about, of course. They can see us coming before we round the corner to their cubicles. "Don't *case officer* me," they'll warn, if a C/O becomes too transparently phony in his efforts to beguile them to do his bidding.

Everyone was efficient and helpful to me as I did my latest hustling around the building; we all shared an even stronger sense of mission than usual in the months and years following 9/11. But I still could not leave in twenty-four hours, as Rob had wanted.

My first stop was the CTC branch chief Rob told me to go see. CTC always looked improvised and ramshackle and looked even more so since the arrival of hundreds of additional officers post-9/11. Task force and surge offices always looked as though a bunch of guys had thrown together rows of cloth-divider cubicles in a large open pit lit by bloodless fluorescent light, commandeered a few rooms along the pit's edges for senior staff, and then plastered the dividers with photos or witticisms related to the mission the office handled,

$10 MILLION DOLLAR REWARD FOR USAMA BIN LADIN. SEE YOUR LOCAL LAW ENFORCEMENT OFFICIAL FOR DETAILS . . .

DO NOT WORRY.
WE ARE HERE TO HELP.
WE ARE FROM THE GOVERNMENT.
(written below a photograph of a U.S. soldier, M-16 raised, standing over cowering Taliban)

ZAWAHIRI AVENUE . . . A TALIBAN-FREE ZONE.

I knocked on the door of the branch chief's small, cluttered, antiseptic, and windowless corner office, closed the door behind me, and sat down to learn what I was getting myself into. The chief and I started with a couple minutes of the standard chat and pleasantries about mutual acquaintances, serving both as social ice breakers and as a beginning way to size each other up.

Keith was a slim, measured man in his mid-fifties, more formal in manner than most in the DO. He always wore his suit coat, yet never struck me as stuffy. He had originally worked in the Directorate of Intelligence, had been seconded to an assignment in the DO years earlier, and had stayed. We would occasionally jog past each other on the weekends, puffing our ways past one of the remaining Civil War forts that still ring Washington. I invariably embarrassed him the next time I saw him at work and mentioned that we had crossed paths, because he never once recognized or noticed me on the street. "I was working too hard just to keep going," he would say. In my experience, Keith never became agitated at work. He gave the impression that he was playing chess and knew what moves to make, while some other colleagues (and perhaps I, from time to time) gave the impression we were playing football and were scrambling sometimes to fill holes in the line. Some surely considered him a stuffy WASP, notable for his conservative, understated manner even amidst a DO full of Organization Men. He was considerate to others through his poise and self-control. Expressions of unbridled emotion were unprofessional, base, and perhaps insulting, although he would never mention this to anyone. Crowing, posturing, and backstabbing were alien to and beneath him. C/Os thought highly of him. A WASP myself, to me Keith was a gentleman of understated professionalism.

Keith turned to what my assignment would be. In his quiet way, he told me that CTC and NE, which shared control of the case, needed an experienced C/O with excellent linguistic capability.

"We want you to provide linguistic support for the interrogation team for CAPTUS. He is [very important in the al-Qa'ida network]."[7]

Keith briefed me on who CAPTUS was, why we had "rendered" him— kidnapped him off a street in a Middle Eastern country—only a few days before, and where we believed he fit into al-Qa'ida's network. They were sending me out to take part in the interrogation of one of our small number of "High Value Targets," always referred to as HVTs—the most important al-Qa'ida detainees we had. He was a very big prize. The task force in CTC that had run the operation was chuffed at the coup they had just pulled off. It was raising them to the big leagues, among the stars, in the competitive world of the components in CTC, the CIA, and the military services that conducted operations against our enemies.

The Agency and U.S. military had detained and taken prisoner many hundreds of jihadist or Taliban foot soldiers in Afghanistan when we crushed the Taliban and routed al-Qa'ida in the last months of 2001. These were, overall, low-level "men with guns," with little intelligence to offer about the high-level plans and intentions of al-Qa'ida or other jihadist groups. They were initially the useful flotsam of the GWOT—although, in subsequent years keeping them, and apparently intending to keep them *forever*, in specially built Camp X-Ray in Guantanamo, with no due process, and no realistic prospects for release or trial, would prove a lasting sore to the administration and raise serious questions about American policy, principles, and law as the GWOT became defined by its actions and not the fears that justified it.

---

7 I will, of course, use euphemisms and occasional distortions to protect sources and methods. The code name used, CAPTUS, is fictitious, but does convey the general way the DO masks the identities of individuals. CAPTUS was, indeed, "very important in the al-Qa'ida network," but I will not describe his specific functions, nationality, the location in which he was rendered, or other details that would identify him, or CIA operations.

HVTs, however, were top priority. We hunted them. They were the most senior al-Qa'ida members and terrorists on the planet. They could provide information on the inner workings of al-Qa'ida's leadership, plots, financing, strategies, personnel, organization, even the whereabouts of Usama Bin Ladin or Ayman al-Zawahiri.

Excellent linguistic capability. That was the first question Rob had asked me when he stuck his head through my door. I was a C/O. It was a bit surprising to send me TDY to provide linguistic support. I wondered what was going on but was not about to question the apparent basis for my involvement in a very important case.

Keith continued, "You may become involved, as COS decides, in the interrogation of CAPTUS, and in the substantive work of the team of analysts, officers, psychologists, and support staff dedicated to the case. You will work with the host country's intelligence service. Liaison is always delicate, and is particularly important because [the country] is taking some political and security risk by agreeing to take CAPTUS at all, and allowing the CIA to hold and interrogate him on their soil."

"As COS decides . . ." The COS did not know me. It was normal that he would want to vet a new arrival who was becoming involved in a sensitive operation. He could restrict me to linguistic support if he decided I was a no-load; heck, he could send me packing; or he could use me more if he decided I was competent. He would decide if he could entrust anything substantive to me after he had had a firsthand opportunity to size me up. It did not matter that Headquarters was formally in charge of the field and had notified him that it was sending out an experienced C/O. He had formally agreed to accept someone for linguistic support only. That way he would continue to control the case and me, and everyone would save face if necessary.

"The COS can't continue to run this case. He's too overstretched and can't assign one of his officers to the case, or to managing the interrogation team. He needs someone out there right away. Liaison is being polite for the moment and is dedicating their people to the case, but it is supposed to be ours. They are helping us out, but it is of secondary interest to them, unless we somehow get CAPTUS to tell us something that directly involves them. COS is concerned that our relations with them could deteriorate quickly. They are a little irritated that we have dumped a delicate and time-consuming case on them, and aren't running it at a level commensurate with the favor they're doing us, or the significance we told them we give to the case. For now there is CAPTUS and a bunch of our guys filling up our liaison partners' days, but not giving a lot of value to them. The case and the interrogation team have no C/O in charge, so COS is doing it for now, while the case is being run de facto by a DI officer, with no experience handling anyone, or with dealing with liaison."

Here Keith looked at me a moment, and then away, typically polite and reticent of the challenge and intimacy that comes from looking someone in the eye, particularly when concerning important points,

"That's why COS wants you there now. To provide linguistic support."

I understood. This explained Rob's surprising visit to my office, pulling me off my assignment, and the hurry to dispatch me halfway around the world. The station was overburdened—no station liked having to handle long-term "temporary" burdens beyond its normal duties when there were rarely enough hands available to do the regular work of the station—the case was very high-profile, and a DI officer or general lack of management on the case was fraying the all-important relations with liaison. The COS must have sent in a zinger demanding that Headquarters send out an experienced officer to run a case that COS did not have enough time to run, and to keep relations good with liaison. I would learn in a few days that the COS had done exactly that.

The case needed adult supervision, if COS decided I was up to it, although the formal traffic was that the case needed only linguistic support.

I spent the day getting briefed by various officers on the background of the case, on general principles of interrogation as applied to jihadists, meeting with representatives from all the offices involved in the elaborate handling of CAPTUS and the information he could provide. Some advice was more enthusiastic than reasoned. "You've got to speak to Muriel,"[8] one young, overeager colleague told me. "She *broke* one of the detainees!"

That sounded important; if Muriel had an approach that stood out, I needed to learn it.

---

8 A pseudonym.

Muriel was working in another component of CTC. We had never met. When I tracked her down a couple hours later, I found that she was straightforward, an experienced C/O. She was about thirty-five years old, athletic, attractive, neither overplaying her feminine charms nor suppressing them in order to be taken seriously by her male peers. She impressed me; she was confident enough to be frank, without puffery. There was no inappropriate, obtuse glitter in her eyes or manner about having interrogated or "broken" a member of al-Qa'ida. She spoke soberly, professionally, of a hard job.

When we sat down to talk a couple hours later she said with some derision, "Broke? You can say I broke him if you count making someone cry. I spoke about his family. He cried because he wanted to be with them. So what? This had nothing to do with how responsive he was."

"Did he provide better FI[9] afterwards?"

Muriel looked at me with admirable honesty, and hardness. Her expression indicated that she had just addressed that point and was weary of hearing crying and breaking a case conflated, but appreciated that my question showed that I did not see the two as necessarily going together.

"No."

Muriel told me that most of the time she had been straightforward when interrogating. Women sometimes had advantages in interrogating Muslim detainees, sometimes disadvantages; females could be disorienting, reassuring, or deeply insulting by their presence. Her remarks were my first indication that interrogation would call for exactly the skills, and approaches, of being a good case officer: Somewhat perversely, the *bond* one can establish with the individual being interrogated is the most important element for success. Of course, there are all sorts of bonds, ███████████████████████ ██████████████████████████, as in every operational relationship a case officer develops. No comment is ever innocent, and no bond straightforward. A case officer—interrogator—sitting one-on-one with a detainee has no special techniques. But the detainee is helpless nonetheless, and a C/O has ██ ██ ██████████████████████████, and all the resources of the CIA and the U.S.

---

9 Foreign intelligence, the term of art used for "intelligence."

Intelligence Community, that he could use in the interrogation to support his bonding. The detainee has nothing but his wits, fear, arrogance, or insecurities. ██ ██████████████████████████████. Everyone is vulnerable; all of us, however secure, however powerful, however pure. But this was all the normal work of a case officer; the difference in an interrogation is that the target is literally your captive, not a social or professional acquaintance.

Keith had explained that I needed to meet with one of his deputies, Terrell Wilmington,[10] whose branch was running the CAPTUS case at Headquarters. Wilmington would provide me with the case files and more detailed instructions on what to do once I got to post. I caught up with him a day or two later in one of the cubicle hallways in his branch. It was always quiet in these cubicle pits, most officers hunched over their computer screens, or perhaps sprawled in groups of two or three, one officer sitting at his work station, the others standing and leaning on the cloth dividers, discussing a case or shooting the breeze and telling tales to one another. With the surge, in CTC most officers, male and female, tended to be twenty-five to thirty-five, on the whole athletic, a federal-employee version of a Gap or L. L. Bean catalog photo.

I did not know Wilmington, but he was an old hand in the DO, a decade or more my senior. I sensed immediately that he was one of the DO's journeymen, who rattled around from office to office, division to division, too often had limited perspectives, the kind of officer area divisions allowed to be "surged" to other assignments and components because they would not be missed too much—the kind that for many years had filled the slots in CTC, always a poor sister in the DO—and who had found a meaningful job in CTC at the end of his career, almost surely just before retiring. I suspected that he was solid enough, but not very creative or driven. Experienced, but not particularly talented. He might be someone to watch out for. Officers like this sometimes could possess a sullen, selfish, latent hostility; they might not hesitate to hang you out to dry. I did not sense collegiality in his manner, as one could with many officers. I did not know yet. We always got on all right subsequently, but he kept me at arm's length throughout my involvement with the case, like

---

10 A pseudonym. Almost all names used are fictitious.

two-dimensional hired help. Keith had spoken to me as a peer, getting ready
to go to an important mission, which was true, and took time to speak with me
unhurriedly, clearing his schedule, deferring calls, and focusing on me entirely, and calmly. His job *was* me for the few minutes we spoke. It was that
way every time he and I met. Wilmington, one level of management down,
spoke to me as though I were keeping him from doing what he really wanted
to be doing, whatever that was. He always seemed to be attempting to mask
intellectual superficiality by sternness and a vague self-importance. It was a
frequent way I had seen officers act to keep—or imagine that they kept—the
upper hand on younger, more talented, or unknown officers. Leadership by
vaguely hostile posturing.

Wilmington's main point to me, made tersely and without a smile, was that
CAPTUS had important information on al-Qa'ida and that I was to do whatever
was necessary to obtain it from him. CAPTUS had frustrated our officers since
we had captured him ███
██
██████████████████████████████████. Wilmington explained that
our liaison partners were running the interrogation because it was occurring
on their turf, even though the case, and CAPTUS, were ours. It was a matter of
sovereignty. Our hosts were willing to help, not do our bidding. I could not
tell as I stood there listening whether Wilmington was projecting hardness
because he was hard (although I suspected not), because the job of managing
interrogations was a dirty business and called for it, or because, as I suspected, he was a slightly pompous lightweight and was playing the tough guy
to demonstrate that he was a leader.

I felt a flash of guilt as we stood there, for having judged Wilmington
harshly when he had spoken to me for only about two minutes—maybe he
was a good guy and a solid officer who was highly focused on a tough and
stressful job—but I also knew that one could size someone up accurately, over
90 percent of the time, within the first minute or two of conversation.

"So we work through them?" I asked.

"Yeah. They'll ask any questions you want. But they hold him, and they
do what they want with him. He's there, so he's theirs."

I had never worked with liaison before. For twenty years I had been undercover. A number of other services over the years had surely worked out that I was an intelligence officer—this was the normal progression of one's career—but the CIA had never officially informed anyone of this fact.

The service I was going to work with had a reputation for ██████████ when it suited them. ████████████████████. Americans did not torture. The CIA did not torture. We did not make people "disappear." We obeyed the law and strived to embody our country's principles in all our operations, the disbelief, hostility, and condemnations of some Americans notwithstanding (even my own mother did not believe me when I assured her that we obeyed the laws and did not kill people). Our job was to break other countries' laws, to thrive in the gray areas of policy, going to the limits of what our laws allowed. We were created to do hard tasks, but to act always within strictly defined parameters, and to be accountable for our actions before our political leaders, and the law. As individuals we signed on to serve and protect our society and its laws, not just to have adventures overseas. Interrogating a terrorist, with a host foreign service suspected to ████████████████, might well take the CIA—take me—farther into the murky gray of licit and illicit behavior than I believed the Agency had gone during my career, farther than it had ever gone in treatment of detainees, or in pursuit of information, so far as I knew. At the least, my colleagues and I were entering new territory, of that I was sure. We were case officers, not torturers, not even by trade interrogators.

I had been interrogated years before during my training, to prepare me for what could happen to me overseas. The experience was harsh, even under controlled conditions and knowing that it was an exercise. The DO had not done anything like this for decades, so far as I knew. The parameters for our actions were unclear to me, yet what I had been hearing made clear that we were now using measures that contravened our prior training and practice, and skirted up to the edge of the obligations and oaths that had guided us my whole career. *9/11 has really unleashed us* and *So this is what happens in war* were my first thoughts as I listened to my colleagues' briefings of what we were doing, and what was to be expected of me.

"We're going beyond SERE training?"[11]

"We're interrogating him."

That, and what I had heard already, constituted a clear yes.

"Suppose our partners do something to CAPTUS that I consider . . . unacceptable?"

Wilmington looked at me, his face a blank, then taking on the slightest hint of irony.

"Well, then, you just walk out of the room, if you feel you should. Then you won't have seen anything, will you? You will not have been party to anything."

Our conversation was quiet but had become intense. I did not want to appear out of phase with what our mission was. The case was well en train. Officers did not arrive and immediately challenge what the field, the branch, the division, and the DO had signed off on, particularly on a case that was so obviously top priority and approved from on high. I did not want to, and did not know enough to do so in any event; any decent officer first learned what was going on, and slowly developed some credibility to speak of a case, by working it and coming to understand its parameters and past. An officer needed to become involved and assume responsibility for a case; only then could he earn the authority to weigh in on how the case was being run.

Our mission, our existence in the DO, was to do the hard jobs. At least, we all hoped so; far too often, our jobs were bogged in bureaucracy, official refusal, and the failure that defines so much of our profession. The DO is a very prudent, cautious organization. The DO is aggressive but acts only after carefully considering the ramifications of the proposed action.

The challenges now before me were different than the normal work of a C/O. This was fundamentally different than seeking to obtain information on the workings of a foreign government concerning an arid diplomatic issue. We were at war. Thousands lay smoldering in New York, the Pentagon, and Penn-

---

11 SERE training—Survival, Evasion, Resistance, and Escape—is a long-standing program designed by the U.S. military to train individuals how to survive and resist the enemy in the event of capture. The techniques are largely based on the experiences of past U.S. and allied prisoners of war. A component of the training covers how to prepare for and resist interrogation. The SERE training, through a manual called the KUBARK manual, became the de facto basis of interrogation techniques in the Global War on Terror.

sylvania. My wife and I had known several of the 9/11 victims, one crushed at the base of the first World Trade Center tower as it collapsed, two young women trapped and then incinerated in the Windows of the World restaurant on the top floor of the World Trade Center. Every American—and perhaps we in the CIA more than anyone—was outraged and determined to destroy the jihadists who had killed our countrymen and had been attacking Americans for years. I was being sent to the front lines, as it were. I was going to be part of the avenging and protective hidden hand of the CIA, striking al-Qa'ida for us all. I *wanted* to interrogate the S.O.B. and play a key role in our counter-terrorism operations. We all did.

I had signed on to the Agency to test the limits of my intellect, knowledge, experience, physical ability, psychological strength, and moral compass. I did not want a "normal" job; I had resigned a nascent career as a banker to challenge all my faculties and capabilities. This was why I had walked away from much more money than I had ever made, or would make, as a spook. I sought and found a sense of achievement, meaning, stimulation, and purpose from seeking and meeting meaningful challenges, dedicating myself to causes and principles larger than self-interest. Our response to 9/11 was shaping up to be one of my generation's defining moments, our chance to rise to the challenges of our careers and our time. I could sense that becoming involved in the CAPTUS case was likely to be one of those rare moments I had hoped for—that tested *my* mettle, to make the right decisions, to embrace the hard duties and choices. This was what had brought me to a career in the CIA. I had sought challenges for which there was no right answer, which were impossible.

But acting hard-bitten was simplistic, no way to respond to a professional issue fraught with ambiguity, that involved moral and possibly legal questions. False toughness of that sort was easy, crude, and thoughtless. I was not going to act tough to appear to be up to the job—that was an unthinking and unworthy response to a situation defined by conflicting obligations. Machismo was neither courage nor judgment. This conversation—this case—was clearly one of the key moments in my career; I needed to *get it right*, to exercise refined judgment, to see and act clearly where values and goals conflicted, in the murky areas where there might be no right choice, but one had to choose and act nonetheless.

I had paused just a heartbeat. Wilmington waited.

"We don't do that sort of thing," I responded, registering a little surprise.

"We do now." Wilmington's voice was flat. The conversation remained quiet.

"What about EO12333? We've never done that sort of thing. The Agency'd never do that. We'd need a finding, at least."

My mind was working fast, although we were speaking in controlled undertones. Executive Order 12333, referred to in the Agency as EO12333, was the main regulatory and legal reference point for what the Agency could and could not do, what was legal and what was not. It was passed in the wake of the Church and Pike Committee revelations in the late 1970s of CIA assassination attempts, and of CIA operations concerning American citizens, including spying on them. It outlawed assassination, any espionage conducted against American persons, established congressional oversight of the Intelligence Community, and set up the requirement to obtain a FISA warrant before conducting a range of surveillance or surreptitious activities against "U.S. persons."[12] In particular for my current discussion, EO12333 established the requirement that the CIA obtain a presidential finding—a written executive authorization—that a covert action was found to be in the national interest, legal, and ordered by the president.

Findings were among the most highly classified, restricted documents in the U.S. government. The CIA would never conduct a covert action without a finding. They required the president's signature and were the highest guidance, on the most sensitive actions of the United States, with the CIA carrying them out. These were founding, guiding documents for all of us in the CIA. Our obligations under EO12333 were mother's milk to the DO; adherence to it was inculcated from the first days of an officer's career training. Neither the Agency nor its officers freelanced. One could go to jail if one did so. As we talked, Iran-Contra and the ordeals of my erstwhile colleagues were just jump-

---

12 The Foreign Intelligence Surveillance Act (FISA) court sits in New York and grants or denies warrants to conduct intelligence operations against U.S. persons, if the requesting agency—usually the FBI, CIA, or NSA—demonstrates to the court's satisfaction sufficient indications of illegal or espionage activity.

ing at me in my head. The whole characterization of the CIA as a rogue agency was absurdly wrong; we could be condemned for what we did on a number of levels—the role of intelligence and its limits are legitimate areas of public debate—but we always, always acted under orders from the president, and within the parameters of the Congress and the law, as best as the Agency could determine them. Having to square the policy and legal circles guaranteed that we would regularly act in the gray areas of legality and policy. But we never acted on our own. Colleagues and I would comment to one another, sometimes in frustration, that a C/O in the field "could not sneeze without prior authorization," even for our work that did not require a finding. But we took EO12333's parameters very seriously; it arose frequently in our operational discussions and shaped our actions. And yet, even with findings, it was usually the Agency and its officers who were left holding the bag when a covert operation went sour. Although they provided legal authorization, policy instruction, and some degree of legal protection, findings did not eliminate many of the risks for either the Agency or its officers involved in covert actions.

"We have it." Wilmington's manner brightened a little. "We have a letter from the president. We can do whatever we need to do. We're covered."

I was surprised, relieved, found it sensible that there be one given what we were talking about doing. Of course. We had a finding. This sanctioned what we were doing. Matters were in order. I was keenly aware as Wilmington spoke that being involved with a project that required a finding was deeply serious business—it had been a rapid shift from thinking about my leadership program for the Directorate of Operations to preparing to interrogate an HVT whom we had just kidnapped off a street in the Middle East. I did not focus closely on Wilmington's description of the finding as a "letter." I thought in passing that a letter from the president must have the same practical effect as a finding, and perhaps the president had had the letter written because it was administratively faster, and probably more restricted, than wrestling a finding through the interagency policy coordination process; the point was that the president had formally authorized what the Agency was doing.

I saw the letter before I left for my assignment. It was the "do what you want; what the President says is legal is legal" letter drafted by John Yoo in the Justice Department that subsequently would become the subject of a tense political and legal argument between the administration and Democrats (and citizens concerned with civil liberties, and the rule of law). It was described to me as coming from the White House and from the attorney general. I recall thinking when I read it (a view shared by many colleagues at the time) that it was tendentious and intellectually shoddy, an obvious bit of hack work, a bit of legal sophistry to justify what the administration wanted done, not a guideline and interpretation of the spirit and intention of the laws and statutes that had guided the Agency for decades. This was simply clear to those of us who had lived under EO12333.

Challenging a finding, though, was, as the expression goes, way beyond my pay grade, and in any event, would be viewed as presumptuous and out of place at that moment, in that conversation, given the narrow and specific assignment with which I was becoming involved. Legal issues were for the Office of General Counsel, the Seventh Floor, the White House, and politicians . . . that had been the case in virtually every other circumstance in my career, or in the careers of my peers. One of the CIA's and DO's mantras is "we do not do policy." Ah, but we do, we do. *Iran-Contra, Iran-Contra*, I thought: Standard procedure was inadequate for extraordinary circumstances. How we carry out our instructions makes policy. The higher one rises in the organization, the more directly implicated in policy issues one is. And whether I was in the bowels of the DO at that moment or not, *this* task was not like every other circumstance in my career, or in the careers of my peers. . . .

Our authorities and mission had expanded; that was appropriate. Changed circumstances and threats called for changed authorities. But that did not alter our underlying obligations and principles. My thoughts bounced from one side to the other as we spoke. Wilmington had assured me that we had a finding; who was I, just arriving on the case, to challenge or question something sight unseen? What did I know? I was hearing the briefing on the case for the first time. I was just getting started. It would have been unprecedented to challenge instructions in those circumstances, to challenge a presidential *finding*, while standing amidst cubicles and hearing a briefing in calm, low, intense tones; in just about every circumstance, doing so would have been taken as amazingly arrogant, way beyond the line, and a sign of incompetence, of not understanding where a C/O fit in the DO, Agency, and intelligence business.

At that moment I had not read the letter, and had been somewhat reassured by Wilmington's statement that we were acting under direct presidential authorization. *Well, then,* I thought. *Okay. So this is part of the new rules, how we are waging our part of the war.*

"We do?"

"Yes."

We were all subordinates in the CIA—certainly I was, in a windowless room of CTC, amidst the flotsam of a federal office space, being read into a case on which I had as yet held no responsibility. And yet it was insufficient to salute and execute; these extraordinary tasks called for careful weighing of our obligations, even at my operational level—perhaps especially at the operational level. Even a presidential letter did not alter our obligations to the law, to think critically, and to act with honor. The letter itself could undermine the laws and heritage it claimed to defend. Authority established no right or certainty. It was not clear at all to me how to resolve the conundrum of interrogation in an environment in which "we can do whatever we need to do" with our deepest obligations as officers, certainly not at that moment, at the beginning of my involvement in the interrogation of HVTs.

Case officers live in the gray world of ambiguity, duplicity, and lies. To obtain information clandestinely, serve our country, and help protect it, present irreconcilable intellectual, policy, and moral demands. The whole profession consists of winning others' deepest trust, conspiring with them to reveal their most intimate secrets, based on their love of you, and then manipulating the intimacies and individuals for one's own professional ends. In that gray world, too, is the hard and sometimes cruel duty to stop men who had killed, and who wished to do so again; and somewhere in the murk, deeper than necessity and threat, also reside the meaning and constraints of the society whose values my actions ultimately had to embody. We are hired, in part, because we thrive in ambiguity and doubt. I had faith that my colleagues in CTC were men and women of integrity, even though I was just starting to work with this particular group of officers.

But it was clear that my actions now, that *this* case, would be one of the supreme moments of my colleagues' and my careers—in the gray world, where there were no clear answers, no obvious right and wrong. We were talking about what some, what I, might consider the torture of a helpless man—that is certainly how I construed the conversation. Perhaps he was a killer, or had information that could save lives. Did this justify what our society long had determined was cruel and unusual punishment? What was torture? Sophistry and euphemism now were cheap and demeaning. A president's or attorney general's facile stroke of the pen could not erase the hundreds of years of labored effort embodied in the Constitution, lest we become a nation ruled by men of power, and not by law. Our first obligation was to protect our citizens, and to our oath; our first obligation was to the spirit of the laws, and of our oath. Of all Americans CIA officers had to have faith in and obey the system of laws and command that we served; of all Americans CIA officers, hired and trained to act in the world of gray, had to know when to challenge practices and orders that eroded the principles they claimed to serve. . . .

This was a classic ends-versus-means dilemma. In extreme circumstances, almost all points could be rationalized. But could they? This was what I had been trying to weave into the DO ████████ Program I had been developing until the day before: that the essence of leadership, expected of all officers irrespective of rank or function, was to exercise *judgment*, to associate one's immediate duties with one's higher obligations to one's colleagues and institution, and to exercise this judgment with and for one's peers, not simply for oneself. At some point in the near future I might decide I needed to "walk out of the room," decide at that moment what my obligations and duty were, not just follow orders. I was not at that point yet, standing there, but it had quickly become imaginable.

So, I figured, of all moments in my career this one called for me to risk being a pain in the ass.

Wilmington had briefed me on who I was to work with, what we were to do, generally how we were expected to accomplish it, what I needed to do as the officer running the case, that we had presidential authorization. This was all the guidance an officer could normally expect. He had been straightforward and competent.

I hesitated just a moment.

"What about the Geneva Convention?"

International law was not a usual point to address when planning or conducting operations. The DO existed to *break* every other country's laws.

Wilmington regarded me with a sudden hint of disdain. Interrogating terrorists was no place for goddamn candy-asses. He had finished his briefing and was not there to engage in a seminar, rolling operational problems around in feckless intellectual discussion with a new arrival to the team. We were at war. We had our orders. The president had authorized and ordered us to interrogate al-Qa'ida members and to protect the homeland. I was onboard and deserved to be there, or not. He bristled a little, grew colder still, and made his last substantive comment to me:

"Which flag do you serve?"

We stared at each other for a second or two. To end the moment, I nodded my head slightly once in acknowledgment and said a noncommittal but vaguely positive "mmm." Wilmington said flatly that several officers would address my logistical needs, and then walked away, leaving me standing alone amidst the silent and empty cubicles.

I flew out of Dulles two days later.

PART I

Everything can be explained by one's beginnings.
—Alexis deTocqueville

WHO'S OLLIE?

History turns no sharp corners.

—Anonymous

Summer 1985: Gray cigarette smoke filled the office. Files stacked a foot deep on every desk teetered and spilled over onto the adjacent floors. Every desk was crowded in against another, and jammed up against the walls. The incessant clatter of typewriters made conversation oddly confidential; one could hear someone speaking directly to you, if he or she was nearby, but conversations even ten feet away were lost to the rat-a-tat-tatting of the secretaries or desk officers. Phones rang off the hook. Fat middle-aged women in stretch pants sat intensely typing, while trim men in white shirts, suit coats off, moved from desk to desk, or came and went into the hallway. The contrast was striking with the silent, windowless, intimidating linoleum hallway I had just stepped out of, hundreds of meters long, door after shut door stretching in each direction, impassive and unmarked, receding almost beyond sight.

I was reporting to my assignment in the Counter-Terrorism (CT) Office, the Agency's action branch for countering terrorist attacks worldwide, and in particular, the rash of kidnappings in Lebanon by Hizballah and of plane hijackings. Only a few months earlier I had been writing my last paper for my master's degree from Johns Hopkins School of Advanced International Studies, an analysis of Raymond Aron's critique of Jean-Paul Sartre's reflexive anti-bourgeois attitudes and moral anarchism, which led Sartre so consistently to defend totalitarian governments or movements of the Left. Aron had noted, wielding typical stiletto-like irony, that "the polite smiles of the genteel, under the tutelage of Sartre, were deformed into grimaces" and that, stripped of condescension and fad, Sartre callously sanctioned mass murder. Now, at last, I had begun my career with the Central Intelligence Agency and had a chance to play my own part in the struggles pitting ideas, ideologies, and countries against one another, and not just read about them in a library.

The secretary looked up as I stood in front of her desk and blinked from the smoke and controlled chaos.

"Glenn? Welcome to the CT office. Let's go back and I'll introduce you to your boss."

We walked back from the hallway through a series of windowless rooms, with maps carelessly tacked or taped to the walls. We stepped into the last room, more a vault than an office. There were a couple of desks, a television, and a computer, one of the only ones in the CIA. It showed that the CT office was on the cutting edge and could obtain whatever equipment it needed to conduct its operations. A thin man in his fifties stood in the middle of the office, a cigarette in one hand, a cup of coffee in the other, reading a cable. He picked up a telephone on his desk. An officer's sword hung on the wall behind him. It was the only personal item in the otherwise nondescript office. He paid no attention to us.

"John, I'd like to introduce you to our new CT,[1] Gle—"

John stormed past us, electric, and erupted, "I have no GODDAMNED TIME for a GODDAMNED PISSANT, SNIVELING LITTLE CT! There's been a GODDAMNED HIJACKING. Get him the hell out of my way!"

The secretary and I stood there, nonplussed.

"John, I . . ."

John was waving his cigarette and coffee mug, his face red. "I have NO TIME FOR A PISSANT LITTLE SHIT. Get him out of here!"

---

1 CT—Career Trainee, the officer corps in training at the Agency.

We turned around without another sound and retreated to the secretary's desk in the front of the office suite.

The secretary had me wait a few minutes in the entryway and then sat me down unobtrusively in John's—and now my—back office. My boss settled down enough to meet me an hour or so later, but remained standing, and smoking two cigarettes and drinking two cups of coffee simultaneously. He always did.

John looked at me. "A CT? Harvard?"

"Yes."

"What the fuck are you doing here?"

So was I welcomed to the Counter-Terrorism Office, where as the most junior officer there, I was immediately accepted as number thirteen, on a staff of twelve.

John Carpenter was a former Marine captain, wiry, high-strung but cool about the use of lethal force—I remember him laughing in glee when recounting to me his involvement in a particularly outrageous operation in an especially remote and dangerous part of Africa, in which numbers of people died—nervous around superiors, with an incisive mind and, once he decided he liked you, a gentle soul who got a thrill from taking you, after a morning of planning covert operations, on a wild, careening drive through suburban Virginia, to the imported cheese section of the Gourmet Giant. I identified with him over time, for he never quite fit the standard molds; he was more action-oriented and antsy than analysts, and more intellectual than most ops officers.

John gave me two assignments: desk officer duties, which meant monitoring and answering the basic cable traffic from around the world that concerned terrorism, and manning the secure real-time communications computer—what is now called an instant messaging system—that linked us with all the U.S. government agencies that had a role in our counterterrorism work: Special Forces, the National Security Council, the State Department, the Marines, the NSA, and so on. From this perch I learned about Islamic radicalism, kidnapping, hostages, renditions, and how we went about counterterrorism work. Having a computer showed how cutting-edge we were in the CT office. No one else in the DO had one. I sat long hours, surrounded by John's cigarette smoke, listening to him curse behind me, staring at the orange monochrome screen, reading and responding to the messages from throughout the counterterrorism community.

I enjoyed the CT office, even though I was a little incongruous there, hockey player or no; "the Harvard guy" who read abstruse books, with a bunch of behind-enemy-lines kinds of specialists. The CT office in the mid-1980s was an offshoot of the Special Activities Division (SAD), the Agency's action branch, a version of what laymen see when watching derring-do in the movies. Most of the officers were former Navy SEALs or Special Forces officers, or had some military background. They were the ones who conducted the Agency's paramilitary operations: sabotage, training insurgents or intelligence officers in one godforsaken Third World country or another, using special-shaped charge explosives, clandestine exfiltration of people from countries . . .

One of the big efforts during my time at the CT office was to locate and free the Americans whom Hizballah had taken hostage, among whom was our COS Beirut, William Buckley. Hizballah had kidnapped him as he left his home in 1984, just as I was starting my career. He had rammed one of the cars trying to kidnap him with his own—I distinctly recall silently cheering him for this when I learned the circumstances—but they had caught him despite his resistance. Our SAD guys considered going into West Beirut black—a covert operation, their very presence unnoticed by anyone—across the Green Line, to rescue the hostages from their Hizballah kidnappers; a small unit of elite, clandestine commandos operating in exceptionally dangerous circumstances, with no possible support. In the end, the CT office chiefs and the Seventh Floor decided that the operation was simply too risky—who could back up the team that would go in?—and our intelligence too imprecise, to give the green light. These are the kinds of operations that our SAD officers conducted. Our CT office teams could deploy anywhere, with no notice, go in black, and often get to within meters of a target unknown to any local authorities.

My jump instructor at the Farm—the Agency's vast training facility where I spent a good part of a year learning various dark arts—was an SAD officer, and representative enough of their sometimes amazing abilities. Typical of many of them, he combined confidence, modesty, and a lack of pretention. He taught us how to jump from 2,500 feet using a static line; he himself was a HALO jumper—high altitude, low opening. He had my fellow CTs and me wait on the landing field after our own jumps one day. He took the plane up to 35,000 feet—seven miles high. The plane was totally lost in the distance and altitude. There was no plane, so far as we were aware. He then free-fell at terminal velocity of 150 to 200 miles per hour and flew himself many miles to the landing zone. We had no idea he was anywhere near until he opened his chute perhaps a thousand feet above us. He landed standing up not more than thirty yards away and walked calmly over to us, as we stood whooping and amazed.

My jump instructor and I crossed paths again many months later in the CT office. We were chatting as we changed in Headquarters' locker room during lunch hour, having just worked out. He had just returned from a TDY to meet with a liaison partner and to train for potential joint operations.

"Those guys were crazy, man," my old jump instructor told me, describing what he had experienced in a country where I had already worked myself, although not with the liaison service.

For once, he seemed nonplussed. I cocked my head.

"Oh?"

"You know what they had us do? They had us all get out on motorcycles and ride around practicing drive-by assassinations!" I gaped at him. "Crazy guys. It was crazy. We had to back out of any operations with them."

The CIA I had entered and served did not commit or engage in human rights violations or, of all things, assassinations. This was a hard-and-fast principle— right out the centrally important Executive Order 12333—and one rigorously taught to all officers.

John invariably referred to SAD officers like my jump instructor as "the methane breathers." He told me that he called them that because "their offices are so deep below ground here at Headquarters that no one ever sees them and the atmosphere consists only of the heavier gases" and "besides," he said, his cigarette flaking ashes and smoke puffing from his mouth, "these guys are so incredibly primitive that they breathe methane to survive, anyway."

I laughed, and forever after referred to SAD officers as methane breathers, earning my own laughs over the years. Of course, their and every other DO officer's sometimes not-so-complimentary moniker for officers from my ultimate home division was "Euro-weenie."

The CT office was developing a special action team, too, during my time there, that opened my neophyte's eyes wide, of foreign agents, dispersed in various countries, who could perform the same black, in-hostile-territory, muscled interventions to rescue hostages, or "render" dangerous targets who were beyond the reach of our laws or where we did not want to show any American hand. These foreign CTC agents stood ready, in response to a simple clandestine communication, to rendezvous and enter into action anywhere in the world. Once together, they would form a highly trained rendition team, theoretically not attributable to the United States, and possessing more operational flexibility ████████████████████████████████. The reasoning was that foreigners could travel to places and take certain actions that American CIA officers, and people who looked American, could not. As the creator of the action teams, CIA officer Dewey Clarridge, characterized them in his book, *A Spy for All Seasons*, they were "chosen for a wide variety of special skills, including use of weaponry. . . . The foreign national-staffed action team came primarily from the Middle East. . . . I wanted to surround [our officers] with heavy countersurveillance—preferably with sawed-off shotguns under their raincoats."

Developing such a capability in the CT office was controversial in the DO, however. A number of officers argued that the DO could not control the actions of this foreign action team at all times, which contravened a cardinal principle of tradecraft and sound operations; that they were ███████ and would act in foreign countries; that the risk of death, to one of them, to one of their targets, or to a third party, was high; and that the "blowback" potential—the risk to the Agency and to U.S. policy interests—far outweighed any supposed gain from having a team of foreign assets engaged in kidnapping terrorists for return to the United States.

I observed this high-stakes debate play out, lacking at that point sufficient professional knowledge to know whether the concept of using foreign action teams for operations was foolhardy and out of control or creative and appropriately aggressive. I recall one of my superiors, whom I admired, commenting during the internal wrangling over how, or whether, to deploy this team:

"What? We're going to arm some foreigners, with their own hates and axes to grind, and send them to kidnap people they are hostile to, in a foreign country, beyond the control of any CIA officer?!"

As I grew in experience and competence, I became less wide-eyed and I came to share the views of the action team's critics. At the time, however, I observed, played my minor support role as a junior officer, and tried to learn how the DO functioned, what were the guiding conceptual issues one needed to apply to operations, and what went into sound, reasoned, and prudent tradecraft.

The project was shut down, after the team had been set up in various countries overseas, but before they were ever issued any action order. The men were disbanded and sent back to their respective normal lives.

I had been working at the CT office for a number of weeks. The day was routine, quiet. We had no operation ongoing. I sat, as I did every day, before my amber monochrome screen and monitored the exchanges on deployments, requirements, meetings, occasionally answering a request for information or confirmation from the CT office. Usually I did not dare take part in the electronic banter that appeared on the screen between formal messages from the officers manning their own screens in the various branches of the intelligence and military counterterrorism community. I was too green, too junior; who was I to make a flippant comment to someone in the Office of the Secretary of Defense, or the Marines at Quantico, whom I did not know, when I did not know what I was doing or how things were done? The one or two efforts I risked were, it seemed to me, condemned by silence. I was not a full member of the tribe yet, and perhaps had not learned how to sound like one.

A message from the White House appeared on the screen. It said something like,

I'd like everyone in the Community to know how much we here at the White House appreciate your efforts in the recent operation. It was a great job. We really appreciate it. Keep it up. Good work.

Thanks,

Ollie

I swung my chair around to the left to look at John as he stood before his desk on the other side of our little windowless vault.

"Hey, John," I said. "Who's Ollie?"

John wheeled on me. His eyes bugged out.

"Ollie? Ollie?! That's Ollie Fucking North! You mark my fucking words. That fucking North is going to fuck up this fucking government!"

I thought John was, typically, a little overexcited. I just nodded and said nothing, my eyebrows raised. This was the first time I had heard of Ollie North. John had been so vehement, though, his remarks stayed with me.

I was green, but I was learning fast about the political, legal, and constitutional dangers of zealotry and of too passively accepting orders from superior officers. Formally, the CT office was the lead agency in the counterterrorism community, but over the ensuing months it became clear to me that the CT office and the CIA were being kept out of the loop on various operations run by the White House and Ollie North. We could tell there were operations going on but did not know what they were. I felt at the time some frustration but figured that the White House was the boss, and that it could conduct its business without involving the CIA if it wanted to.

Eighteen months later the Iran-Contra scandal exploded, nearly bringing down President Reagan's administration, and ultimately showing Ollie North to have bypassed the normal checks and balances on intelligence operations, in the belief that he was right, as his secretary Fawn Hall said, to "go above the written law." A number of my colleagues, one of whom had been among my superiors at the CT office (everyone was my superior at the CT office), were caught up in North's (and William Casey's) machinations, had followed orders from the White House, and were indicted.

John had known exactly what he was talking about.

Working in the field over the succeeding years, or managing operations from Headquarters, the terrorist reports one saw, and the work in which I was sometimes involved, created the impression that al-Qa'ida and Islamic terrorists posed a coherent, serious, and growing threat. In the 1980s, as a desk officer on the Lebanon and counterterrorism branches, our work occurred in a context of kidnapping, torture, and bombings of Americans and American facilities. On the Lebanon Desk and in the CT Office, I literally saw what Hizballah and Islamic Jihad did to our colleague, William Buckley, simply to spite us and to enjoy his agony. It was sadistic, and perverse, acts of domination and humiliation perpetrated by callous men, serving a twisted organization, unconsciously exorcising a culture of failure. I worked with colleagues who had survived the 1983 bombings of our embassy and our Marine barracks in Beirut. They told me of what they had experienced, of floors falling from under their feet, of walls falling on top of them, of rubble, smoke, cries, spurting blood, and shockingly white bones jutting through torn flesh—the results of our terrorist enemies' operations.

From 1997 through August 2001, I worked the Afghan target, which meant, as far as the CIA was concerned, trying to detain or, eventually, kill Usama Bin Ladin, and to disrupt and destroy al-Qa'ida. During these years the Agency substantially increased the pressure on him and his organization. Largely ignored by the public, the tensions and lethal maneuvers steadily increased. The Agency, from DCI George Tenet on down, was highly focused on the Bin Ladin threat. To its credit, so was the Clinton administration, which fully appreciated the risks al-Qa'ida posed.

In 1998, Bin Ladin issued his fatwa calling on "every Muslim who believes in God and wishes to be rewarded to comply with God's order to kill the Americans and plunder their money wherever and whenever they find it." Later that year, al-Qa'ida blew up our embassies in Nairobi and Dar Es-Salaam, while we broke up a similar plot to our embassy and personnel in Tirana. In December 1998, DCI Tenet sent to all CIA officers involved in counterterrorism work a message "declaring war" on al-Qa'ida. He sought, and obtained, authorization for the Agency to take much more aggressive action, including the use of lethal force if necessary. Late in 1999, I worked on the Millennium Bombing plot, in which an alert U.S. Customs officer, and subsequently the FBI, stopped a plot to set off a bomb in Times Square that New Year's Eve.

Like most, my attention to the issues was sporadic, a series of disjointed perceptions among a large range of unrelated cases and challenges, and so, as we all do, I relied on two-dimensional characterizations that were short on distinctions, mental shorthand that lumped together dramatically different Islamic societies, and the challenges they posed to the United States.

But after fifteen years of observing, and periodically working on, terrorist cases, it appeared to me, as it did to most of my colleagues in the DO, that Islamic terrorists posed a serious, coherent threat to the United States and the West, and that Bin Ladin and al-Qa'ida were the key to our problem.

THUNDERCLAPS
AND GROWING LEAVES

Resolving never to despair . . .

—Samuel Johnson, *Rasselas*

My contact and I had arranged to meet for lunch on September 1, 2001, on the plaza at the base of the World Trade Center towers. It was a spectacular early autumn day, with low humidity, the temperature in the eighties. We sat surrounded by thousands, and I watched over her shoulder the incongruous sight of country music singer Carolyn Dawn Johnson leading forty or fifty jacketless businessmen and -women of lower Manhattan in a line dance. "I never thought I'd see this!" Johnson shouted out over her band.

My contact and I discussed a terrorist case I was working. We needed to establish a relationship with a man who restricted himself to a narrow routine and rebuffed any approach by anyone outside his circle of associates. But I knew three things about him that made me confident he was for the having: He jogged every day, he spent a lot of his free time chasing girls, and he did not discuss his skirt-chasing with the people he worked with. My contact was a sophisticated, beautiful young woman. Men turned their heads to admire her as they walked past us. Her dress was refined: gray skirt, white blouse, and heels; yet her clothes hugged her body, her heels were high, her back straight, her regard direct. The slightest, appraising smile briefly hinted at the corners of her lips as I spoke. She evoked strong, momentarily controlled sensuality.

"Of course I'll do it. I can take care of myself. It'll be fun." She looked at me with an expression combining irritation and amusement. "You are all so predictable."

I told my contact when and where the man we wanted would be jogging, and arranged for her to jog the same route every day, in tight shorts and a tight T-shirt. I told her where to stop and stretch from time to time.

"Got it. This'll be easy. I'll let you know."

Our business concluded, my contact left to take a cab back to her normal life. I smiled slightly myself as I watched her cross the vast plaza, walking with purpose, her white blouse bright in the sun. She stopped about one hundred yards off and crouched to retrieve something, remaining motionless for a moment. At last she slipped from view behind the throng of men and women hurrying in every direction. I returned to Washington, enthused about the operation, confident that I was clandestinely controlling events.

Ten days later, the World Trade Center, Pentagon, and Flight 93 attacks caught me at the office, on the phone arguing with our Finance Department. I had not been paid for nearly eight weeks, which I had discovered only when my checks all started to bounce. When my officemate stuck his head through the door and told me that someone had flown a plane into the World Trade Center, I refused to leave my desk and join everyone else around the television in the front office. Nothing was going to distract me from browbeating Finance into straightening out my pay.

I still refused to go watch when the second plane hit. Then someone spread the news—later proven untrue—that a bomb had exploded in front of the State Department. The finance officer I was talking with apologized and said that he could not do anything for me with the confusion caused by the attacks.

My wife, Sally, was closer to events. An arborist had come to cut away some large branches that were scraping and damaging our slate roof. The arborist had just departed and Sally had made herself her morning cup of tea. She was sitting on the steps in our back patio, sipping from her mug and feeling satisfied that she could check off one item from the never-ending to-do list of home projects. The morning was magnificent, with bright sunshine and cool, dry air.

A deep, long rumble rolled over the rooftops. *Strange*, she thought. *Someone must be demolishing a building somewhere.* About a minute or so later, from every direction sirens went off; fire engines, police cars, who knew what. Now, that was very strange. Something was going on. She went into the kitchen to turn on the radio (we had no television in the house yet, as we were just unpacking from a move) and heard about the World Trade Center attacks.

She called me on the telephone to tell me.

"I know," I said, "but I can't talk. I can't talk. We just received the order to evacuate the building immediately."

"Take the side roads! Take the side roads!" she shouted as I hung up, not knowing if I had heard before the line went dead. I had. It was good advice.

Sally realized that the explosion she had heard was the plane crashing into the west side of the Pentagon, and the sirens the responses of all the fire and EMT units in every direction.

I drove home on deserted secondary roads in Northern Virginia, stopping at an intersection, the only car on the road in any direction, to listen to Dan Rather broadcast, himself largely stunned to silence, the collapse of the towers. I managed to get home before the roads all became virtually impassible with everyone in the city, it seemed, fleeing downtown.

I stopped at a Circuit City, determined not to have my life dominated by terrorists. The store was deserted. All the salespeople were bunched around one of the dozens of televisions on the wall, watching the ruin in Manhattan, the reports of a plane down in Pennsylvania, of the grounding of all the planes in the entire country, and of chaos in Washington. I interrupted a young saleswoman.

"I'd like to see some of the televisions."

She looked momentarily stunned, then returned to herself. "Oh! Of course. Yes. That's why we're here, isn't it?"

We examined the wall of televisions, all of them reporting on the terrorist attacks. After five minutes literally surrounded by dozens of moving images of smoke, fear, and rumor, I had to concede that my self-conscious effort at normality was hollow. To the woman's visible relief, I thanked her and returned to my car, the only one in the shopping center's parking lot.

When finally I arrived home, we picked our kids up from school and, like everyone else, watched and listened to the day unfold. I continued my project of the moment, with the radio on in the background: painting our house. "I will not have my life disrupted by these schmucks," I thought.

September 11 was our son, Spencer's, eighth birthday. "They've ruined my birthday," he said. That night, as we watched the news reports, he sat on the floor, made World Trade towers with his Legos, and flew his toy planes into them.

The country was in turmoil with the 9/11 attacks. A week later letters containing anthrax spores arrived simultaneously at a number of news media offices. The authorities and the public assumed that the letters came from al-Qa'ida. It was clear that our government was preparing to attack Afghanistan. But normal life continued, sort of. I took our children, Spencer and Margaux, to the adjacent Air and Space Museum, only to stumble upon police and men in bio-chem suits. I said nothing, and learned later that anthrax had been found inside the building, part of the anthrax attacks that everyone assumed to be a follow-on to the 9/11 attacks.

But what consumed my energies, and hindered my focus on work, was the terrifying and mystifying descent of my wife into what I feared might be insanity.

My home life had been in chaos in the months before 9/11, and I struggled to understand why. I did not know what had happened to Sally, or why, or what to do about it. She became shrill, capricious, hypersensitive. She slept for long, long periods, refusing to get out of bed. Yet, she was exhausted all the time. Everything I did was wrong. She was angry at my absences, irritated at my every word, and resented me when I was present. She stopped taking care of the routine tasks of daily living, such as the dishes, or grocery shopping, or making the kids' school lunches. And when I did them, she became angry with me. She would not go out with me, to the movies, or to friends. She stopped seeing her own friends. We could not have anyone over, as it was too demanding. I was at a loss. I assumed that her behavior toward me had to be due to my work. Being a case officer can place a huge strain on married life.

Often I worked long hours, and returned to find the kids in bed, but Sally passed out on the sofa, or half in bed. If I spoke to her, she lashed out, or became uncontrollably emotional: giddy, or despondent, or teary, or viciously, impossibly, irrationally angry. I tried to shield the children from these moods, while maintaining a normal demeanor with them. I tried to keep everything normal. I did a good job at it; our kids remained happy and trusting, from what I could tell. But it came to the point where my pulse rose every night as I approached my front door after work, and throbbed in my ears so that, literally, I could not hear anything else. What crisis would I find behind the door this night? I guiltily thought that if I came home later, there might be less to deal with. But of course I could not do that, however much work I had to justify staying late at the office; I had to take care of the kids. I had to be mother and father. I had to make home a loving, safe, and happy place. And I had to work.

But I started overlooking occasional minor details at work and in day-to-day life. I laughed it off, pointing out to anyone that "absentmindedness is a sign of genius, you know." I then added a typical self-deprecatory humorous coda, "Of course, my mother always replied to me when I told her that, 'I'm sure that is true, Glenn. But what, then, is your excuse?'" Always a sociable, friendly loner, I withdrew into myself. I spoke with no one about my concerns. I needed to handle this myself.

Sally was a highly successful fashion designer in Paris by profession. Blond, blue-eyed, feminine but strongwilled, she was in her element in the Paris fashion shows she organized or canoeing the coastline of Maine with me.

I married Sally in part because she looked me in the eye and spoke for herself, always. I wanted someone who would challenge me and support me. So her descent—our descent—into what appeared increasingly like madness bewildered me. I thought I needed to consult a psychologist, to learn what was happening, and what I should do. I had tried to cope on my own too long and had delayed past good sense. The situation was paralyzing.

At first, my errors at work were inconsequential. I often worked until the wee hours, sometimes to 3:00 a.m. I was working to the limit of my strength, and excelling—recruiting sources, providing important intelligence, and leading a "normal" professional life, too, so far as my non-intelligence officer peers could see, with all its own demanding responsibilities. I received several exceptional performance awards for my work during this period. I thrilled to my job to an extent I had never felt before and gave more than I had to give. I was determined to use all my abilities, and not to let any personal problem stop me. And, even though I often felt a knot in my stomach about my home crisis, and about work, I smiled, laughed, focused intently, and excelled. I compartmentalized well: one moment I would think of my personal issues, the next my work, the next my "public" life, and at each switch I would, so far as I was aware, simply put my other concerns out of my mind. I wore earphones at work as I wrote my reports and cables, listening to Shania Twain or Joe Cocker. The music blocked out distractions so that I could concentrate, and made me happy. Of course, I was alone in the office when I finally went home, and therefore was responsible to secure it, engaging the various systems, locks, and devices that protected the office from any kind of intrusion. All routine. I had done this many hundreds of times, for over fifteen years.

I was also frequently the first in to my part of the office, arriving about 7:00 a.m, sometimes only four hours after my departure. Last out, first in. I reversed the security measures, opening one thing or another, opened my safe, and opened up the office. One of these mornings I took each of these steps and, at last, came to my own safe. The safe was closed, but I found that the combination lock had not been "spun off." The tumblers were not fully engaged. I had forgotten to spin the dial as I had left. Despite the numerous other systems successfully engaged, and the certainty that there had been no compromise of security, I was in violation of security procedure. Irritated at myself, I reported my error to our security officer and received the standard "security violation."

But for all my compartmentation, focus, and intensity, I was distracted, stressed, and exhausted. I was also unlucky. Not too long later I secured the office again. One of the door sensors would not engage. I called the security office to report the problem. They could not engage it, either. I called the main security office at Headquarters to inform them. All other systems were engaged. We had a guard present. The system was faulty. After more than two hours of staying at the door, in the hallway, the security people and I decided I could do no more, that the office was not at risk of compromise, and that I had informed all relevant authorities. I went home. But, I received another violation.

A number of months later I had to secure a different door, in a different part of the office. I had never had to secure this particular door before. Officers in my category rarely went to this part of our office. But, this day, I was responsible for it. I was apprehensive about having received the violations, after a career without any. I asked a superior, who was also a friend, the deputy of the branch in which I worked, to secure the door with me. I wanted to be extra careful. We secured the door together, making sure it was secure. We both signed our names on the security check list.

But, we were wrong. There was an additional lock to spin off. We had not known. We missed it. Yet we were responsible for it. Again, no system was compromised, but we both received violations.

By this point I had become extremely nervous about securing the office, and had established a pattern of problems. Any further violations could be disastrous for me professionally. I never mentioned these accumulating problems to Sally. She and we were already overwhelmed by her own—our own—problems. I feared that they would simply anger her more, and that she would add painful criticism about these failings to all the other strains I was trying to cope with—even to understand—between us. No, I had to handle this myself.

I continued to work unsustainable hours, to excel, and I remained, at root, lost about how to help Sally and myself. Sometimes I wondered if I were burying myself in my work in an effort to simplify my life. I tried to pay extra attention to my security measures.

Then, at home, I had a revelation. Hanging up my coat one evening, I noticed a large, half-empty bottle of wine in the back corner of the closet, in

among the boots and shoes. I marked the level of wine. The mark did not help
me. The next day, the entire bottle was replaced with another, also half-empty
I felt obtuse not to have seen what was happening. But she did all her drinking
in secret. I felt a pang of recognition: My family's friend, Michael Dukakis,
had been pilloried when he ran for president in 1988, for supposedly not having been aware of his wife's substance-abuse problems. He was denounced
as cold and out of touch. How could such a brilliant man be so unaware? Now
I understood. I had been unaware, too.

I confronted Sally with the bottle I had found. I spoke to her about what I
at last knew was a serious drinking problem. Ignorant for so long, now I raised
the issue over and over, week after week. Of course, that had no effect, except
to make her resentful and to cause rancor. There was already enough of that,
with her mood changes. I did not know what to do. I started to arrange with a
psychologist to have an intervention. This was a whole new universe for me.
No one in my family drank. No one talks about these matters. At least, nothing
had registered on my consciousness. I kept telling the psychologist, "I want
to help my wife. I don't have a problem myself." He looked at me and did not
contradict me, but repeatedly explained how alcoholism was a family problem
and was affecting me as much as Sally. "I don't drink!" I replied in some exasperation. We scheduled the intervention for a couple weeks later. I started
calling family members and friends for their help. Everyone was supportive,
which was heartening.

But the horrors grew even worse. The psychologist and I were not fast
enough. One evening I was working on the computer in the bedroom, not
wanting to think about work, or home; I just wanted to turn off my brain.
Sally was cooking in the kitchen. I heard a plate crash. I paid no attention
and was barely aware of it. Ten minutes later I wandered into the kitchen
to get a soda from the refrigerator. Sally lay unconscious on the floor. I
was angry, disdainful. I decided to leave her there to sleep it off. I stepped
over her . . . into a huge and growing pool of blood. It covered half the
kitchen floor.

"Oh no! Sally! What have you done?" I crouched down to look at her head.
It was all bloody, and I saw a bright white bit through her hair. It was her

brain. "Sally! Sally!" I wanted to revive her, but not to awaken and terrify the kids with this scene.

I sat her up. She was breathing. What I thought was her brain was her skull. She had passed out and hit her head on the corner of the kitchen counter, the blow just missing her temple. She had been bleeding terribly since I had heard the crash. I applied pressure to her gash with one hand—I was afraid she had cracked her skull—and dialed 911. She came to vague awareness in the interminable time before the EMTs arrived.

Three hours later, when she had recovered enough to speak at the hospital, the doctor asked her, "Have you been drinking?" Sally denied it. But she looked at me later from her emergency room gurney and said, "I'll never drink again. I don't want to. Please. Please. Help me."

This terrible episode served as the intervention. I managed, with numerous painful disasters along the way, over a long period of time, to get Sally into an inpatient program. She drank herself into a stupor in fear and spite the night I drove her to the first inpatient program. When she came around in the car, she shrieked at me in anger that I was forcing her to do anything. First, she tried to jump out of the car as I drove us through the Lincoln Tunnel, heading toward Pennsylvania. Then, on the Pennsylvania Turnpike, she broke free. She punched me in the side of the head while I drove at sixty-five miles per hour. She opened the door and started to jump out of the car. She got one leg outside. I grabbed her by the shirt and yanked her back, the car swerving wildly as I tried to drive and hold her down. For the next two hours I bodily restrained her with one hand, while driving with the other. I got lost. I could not consult a map, hold her, and drive at the same time. I stopped to get my bearings in the middle of nowhere. She leaped out of the car and ran off into a cornfield and the freezing night. I found her after fifteen minutes of searching in the dry stalks and the dark. We made it to the facility.

At first my superiors were supportive. Then they decided my family problems were consuming me. A number of months after work learned of my crisis, the deputy chief of my unit approached me after a staff meeting. One always heard the best news, or the most revealing asides, or learned the true state of affairs, in the half-whispered exchanges with colleagues while walking out of staff meetings. "The boss wants you to know that you have to straighten out your personal life. You need to make a decision. Do you understand? Are you going to carry all your wife's problems? That's your decision. But he wants you to know you can't move forward with your . . . situation. It's your choice." I said that I understood. I was impassive. *What a disaster*, I thought. *What a prick*.

And then I made a ruinous mistake. One night I had an operational meeting, which had finished about midnight. The following morning I had a meeting in one part of town, and also had to be at a second meeting across town at the same time. I had my notes with me in my briefcase from the previous night's meeting. I would write them up when I finally managed to get to my office, sometime mid-afternoon.

The people at the first morning meeting were foreign colleagues, with whom I worked nearly every day, some intelligence officers like me. I left the first meeting early, saw that it was impossible to find a taxi, and literally ran about a mile across town to get to the second meeting in time to participate. I sat down and began to take part, totally focused on the issue under discussion, the previous night's, and the morning's first meeting, now completely out of my head. I was struck by the cool sensation of my sweat running down my cheeks in a strongly air-conditioned room.

Then, my nerves jolted down my arms and in my chest. I remembered that I had left my briefcase at the first meeting, with my foreign colleagues. I had forgotten to take it with me. It had my work notes and materials in it. This was a catastrophe. I was finished. Even without the accumulation of violations, indicating that something dramatic had been happening to me, which work could not ignore, this error was at least a tour-ending disaster. And I was responsible for it. I had done it.

I retrieved the briefcase in about two hours. But, for that period it had been out of the control of the responsible CIA officer (me), and in the control of what one had to assume might be a hostile party. My boss and I spoke about what happened about two hours after the event. He was terribly dismayed, for me, and angry. How could I do this? What was he to do now?

There was nothing I could say, or un-do. "I just forgot my bag," I kept repeating, bereft, staring obliquely away from his regard, seeing nothing. Of course, my boss had to take appropriate action. The wheels of the security establishment that turn after a "flap" like this started to turn. I knew they would grind me up.

I had to tell Sally about this one. Late the afternoon of the day I forgot my bag, she and I talked as we walked along a street near our office. She was horrified and angry when I told her—it meant almost surely a dramatic change in our lives. Unstated, but ever-present, was that this would add to our personal woes. Yet, this problem was of my doing.

"Do you have to tell anyone about this?" she asked. "Can't you just fix it and move on? There was no harm done."

There was nothing else I could do. "Of course I do. I did it. I've got to. There's nothing I can do. I did it."

She looked at me, realizing I was right, and that I was doomed.

Various offices with which I had been working formally requested that I be allowed to stay in my position, valuing the work I had been doing on critical issues. These were small, but ineffective, consolations as my disaster played out. The decision remained to bring me back to Headquarters.

I was moved out of my assignment, brought back to Headquarters, and given non-operational work pending a decision on what to do with me.

Then, in a cataract of falling disaster, we were buried in another crisis. For years, Sally had coped with severe ulcerative colitis. Now, it struck again. I had to rush her to the hospital emergency room. She was hospitalized for many weeks with serious intestinal bleeding. She shockingly withered to ninety-six pounds. Massive amounts of steroids finally stopped her serious internal bleeding. She swelled up dramatically, even as she weakened. Her colon had hundreds of precancerous polyps.

I tried to be positive at work, and to focus on my responsibilities, but there was no gainsaying the personal and professional catastrophes overwhelming me. My career and home life were intertwined, and both had spun out of my control, despite all my efforts. I was devastated that I was not playing as active a role in our work hunting Bin Ladin as I would have wished—I had worked this problem directly for years and I was now an officer with nearly twenty years' experience, no common thing; that I had been undone by simply forgetting my bag; that my concentration and career were affected by my personal woes; that I did not know what to do about them. I felt unworthy even to think of attributing any professional failings to personal issues. I was responsible for my acts, both successes and failures.

For six weeks while Sally was in the hospital I worked half days, hurrying home in my sporty red hatchback to meet Spencer and Margaux at the school bus stop. I explained to them that "Mummy has a bad boo-boo in the tummy," but she was getting better and would be home soon. Sally came home, over the worst of her intestinal crisis. But at first her moods were no better.

The bad events had come with thunderclaps and crises. The good news, when there was any, was like a growing leaf, so slow and slight did it come. But the help Sally received, and more than anything Sally's own struggle, gradually brought small bits of my wife back to me, and brought Sally back to herself. Her battles with the disease sapped what energy she had. Yet, after many months and many setbacks, one evening she smiled spontaneously at some inconsequential remark I made as we were driving somewhere. She did not realize it, but I did. It was something, tiny as it was. Once in a while there were other small, good signs: She took my hand as we shopped; the mood swings diminished; she could once again, progressively, offer me incisive advice. Her confidence slowly returned. My ears did not pound so when I returned home at night. But this took so long; there were so many contradictory and painful episodes that often in the moment it was hard to see much change.

Then Washington was rocked once again. In the beginning of October the Washington Sniper started to kill people as they walked to their cars in shopping centers and at gas stations. A couple of the victims were killed only a mile or two from our home. We were caught in the traffic jams after these shootings, as the police set up instant dragnets after each shooting, trying to catch the killer. Perversely, however, the sniper scare helped Sally and me heal a little bit more. We took to buying gas together, so that she could fill the pump, standing between the pump and the car for safety, while I sat in our other car at the edge of the station providing surveillance for security. So the fall of 2002 was a time of flickering but growing light, after a long period of darkness, as Sally slowly regained her physical health and showed signs once again of her true nature, as a generous, focused, witty, fun, and challenging woman. She was trying so hard, so desperately to overcome what had seized hold of her.

And then Rob stuck his head into my office. The assignment was important for the Agency, I had no doubt. It was also critical for me professionally and personally. It would put me back in my career track; it might begin my reha-bilitation. I thought of the comment the deputy had made to me about choosing my career or my spouse: My "choice" was to do my job as well as I was able to, and to help my wife, and myself, with all I had, imperfect as I was—and damn my boss and the Agency that spawned him.

Sally helped me pack my bags. She knew not to ask too much about work, especially this time. Just before I got in the taxi for the airport, though, she did say, with uncertainty in her eyes, "Can you tell me how long you'll be gone? And where you're going?"

These questions made me ill at ease, and I was worried about her reaction. "I'll be gone a couple of months, at least, I think." I paused a moment, and considered. "I'm going to Paris, to start. I'll see after that. I can't say, really."

I would pass through Paris. At least that much was true. Margaux wrote a little each day in a journal. She gave me her entry to take with me: "Daddys are a good thing to have. They love you." Spencer gave me a Yu-Gi-Oh card to take along. He had written on it:

"Daddy, this is your card it repesents [sic] you because it is strong and it can keep us safe!"

I worried about Spencer and Margaux as I boarded the plane at Dulles. What if Sally took another bad turn? They were only six and eight. I hoped Sally had regained enough strength to cope. But I had learned that she had to wage that fight herself. Sometimes one can help too much and contribute to bringing everyone down.

The plane surged down the runway, pushing me back into the seat. The rumble of the tires ceased and we angled up, starting a swing north around Washington. CAPTUS was my problem now. I would shortly be CAPTUS's problem. All my years of work on terrorism cases, all my years as a case officer, would now come into play. It was clear that this would prove to be one of the supreme moments of my professional life. I could not wait to look him in the eye, and get him to reveal the inner workings of al-Qa'ida.

An hour or two later I looked out the plane window and could see nothing, no stars, no lights below, not even the wing. The cabin lights were off. Most people were sleeping. It was cold. I pulled a blanket over my head.

PART II

The facts were nothing until they
became symbols; and nothing could turn
them into symbols except an eager imagination
on the watch for all that might embody their dreams.

—George Santayana

THE FIRST INTERROGATION

What are they? Wise men or fools? If wise,
why do you go to war with them? If fools,
what does it matter to you what they think?

—Epictetus, *Discourses,*
Handbook, Fragments, III.22.37

Dusty, hot, and dry streets, typical of so many I had known in the Third World during my career, surrounded our office. I flashed my passport to a guard at the first barricade. He nodded once, smiled slightly, and, his eyes continuing to watch the streets, quickly passed me through the entrance to the standard metal detectors, pat-downs, and heavy blast doors. Formal, fit, young officers, whom I always had trouble hearing, standing behind bulletproof glass checked my passport, glancing up at me, impassive and deliberate, to study my face. They handed me a badge and called my escort from our front office to come meet me. I had a short wait in a formal, largely empty reception area, staring at the overlarge, cult-of-personality and banana-republic-like portraits of the president and vice president on the wall. Then I was through the barriers and into the quiet, mostly empty halls, always a stark contrast with the turmoil and noise outside; without exception, wherever I was in the world, I ran into someone I knew from some earlier post or operation; this time it was a colleague whom I had last seen a decade earlier. We shared a moment of good-natured, flippant banter, and then the chief's secretary nodded me into the chief's office, and on to what I expected to be the standard positive, can-do discussions.

There was a twist to the pattern this time. This was a very high-priority, high-risk case. "Peter," the COS, a trim, impressive former military man, had a longer history of working the al-Qa'ida target than almost any officer in the service. There was no routine conversation with yet another TDYer this time. Peter wanted to establish his control, quickly get a sense as to whether I was up to the job, and make sure I did exactly as I was told. The leash was tighter on me to start, and his eyes were on me more than usual. This case had to be run right, it had not been well-run to date, by an analyst with poor social and psychological skills, and I had arrived to provide "adult supervision" to a delicate, complicated, labor-intensive case. And Peter did not know me yet.

There was no welcome or introductory conversation. Peter looked at me, peremptory and challenging.

"You are not a professional interrogator, are you?"

"No."

"You will take your lead from our liaison partners. This is their turf. We will go out together later today and I will introduce you. This is their turf. Understood?"

I understood and took no offense. The COS was harried, that was clear from my few minutes waiting outside his office with his secretary, and over-worked. The Seventh Floor was watching closely. He could not allow such a high-profile case to be messed up. The reins might loosen as I established my credibility. They did later, and I found Peter to be one of the best leaders for whom I had ever worked.

I was given the desk of an officer who had been surged for several months to ███████████ and parts unknown, in a small rectangular office cluttered with safes, maps, and three desks. One of my new officemates was in the field when I arrived. This proved to be the case most of the time, so that I rarely saw him. Various TDYers were to use his space during my time in-country.

The other new officemate was there when I arrived, though, and greeted me cordially. "Jack" was a young first-tour officer, strongly built ████████ like all the Irish kids with whom I had played hockey growing up. I found over the succeeding weeks that he combined the practicality of the street, the focus of an idealistic junior officer, and, when dealing with a more senior officer, the irreverence yet appropriate deference of someone with a well-centered and stable personality. Jack came to enjoy watching me fulminate about one frustration or another, and appreciated literally working alongside a much more experienced officer, to see how one could sometimes successfully maneuver the system and bureaucracy to get things done. I had, probably wide-eyed, paid the same attention, and felt a sense of privilege, many years earlier when I had been "number thirteen on a staff of twelve" on what was then the small CT office. Jack was to prove a good man to spend months with sitting elbow to elbow.

Jack showed me around the office and then took me down to the small cafeteria for lunch. I stopped in the men's room on the way. I stepped to the urinal and unzipped my fly, only to stop mid-action and stare, bemused, in front of me.

"Oh, for God's sake," I said, standing there, half undone. Whoever had installed the urinal had fixed it so high up on the wall that I literally had to stand on my tiptoes, lean back, and aim up to pee into it. This was absurd, and really hard to do. *Stupid Third Worlders*, I thought, in the end succeeding in the peculiar task imposed upon me. Fortunately, I was the only person in the men's room, so no one heard me cuss or saw me standing nonplussed, fly down, dick in hand, in front of a chest-high urinal.

Jack and I made the standard introductory small talk over lunch: sports, where we had worked and on what, who we knew, origins, and so on. Unfortunately, Jack was a Yankees fan, and immediately betrayed typical self-satisfied condescension to me, as ardent a Red Sox fan as one could be. Once we had established decent rapport and I had decided that Jack was a decent guy, I asked him, "What's with the men's room here?"

"What's with the men's room? What do you mean?"

I looked at him and reconsidered. I had just arrived and he did not know me yet.

"Oh, it was just sort of old and a little messy, that's all," I said.

Jack took my comment as a throwaway remark, maybe a little anal.

"Well, this is hardly Park Avenue, you know."

"Yeah."

The reasons I had been sent out started to become apparent on the drive through the city and into the countryside to the liaison service's facility, where the interrogations occurred. Roger, the analyst who had been running the case, insisted someone from the station drive him to the facility, because he was not comfortable driving in a Third World city, and he feared getting lost and finding himself left to his own devices. Only the COS and the interrogation team could interact with liaison on such a sensitive case; Roger's timorousness obliged the COS to waste his time on one case, often to act as chauffeur for someone who was always tense and sour, and to keep the interrogation team leader from totally alienating our liaison hosts.

The first "interrogation" I observed was a disaster. Roger knew more about CAPTUS than anyone alive, probably. This was why he led the initial inter-rogation team. But his knowledge consisted of the link analysis one does ▬▬

▬▬▬▬▬▬▬▬▬▬▬▬▬▬▬▬▬▬▬▬▬▬▬▬▬▬▬▬

▬▬▬▬▬▬▬▬▬▬▬ . . . while sitting in his windowless cubicle in the basement of CIA Headquarters. He had no social skills, or insights to human behavior, even of the man he had devoted his life to catching. He showed no interest in or knowledge of foreign cultures, or of how to smooth any interper-sonal exchange for personal advantage. Roger interrogated like this:

.[1]

---

1 The six redacted lines relate a generic question and response, and use an exclamation point. They do not describe what specifically we sought to learn, who CAPTUS was, what he had been doing before rendition—no "source" or "method" is revealed. Apparently the CIA fears that the redacted passage would either humiliate the organization for incompetence or expose its officers to ridicule; unless the Agency considers obtuse incompetence a secret intelligence method.

That was about it; ███████████████████████████████████. Roger disliked the answers he heard—they did not fit his preconceptions—while growing more and more dyspeptic.

As the CIA Inspector General's *Special Review: Counterterrorism, Detention and Interrogation Activities (2003–7123-IG)* would note two years later in its overall characterization of CIA interrogation practices, Roger's manner and assumptions represented the typical position of Headquarters and of Headquarters-based terrorism analysts, who found themselves involved in some part of the interrogation apparatus:

> The Agency lacked adequate linguists or subject matter experts and had very little hard knowledge of what particular Al-Qaida leaders—who later became detainees—knew. This lack of knowledge led analysts to speculate about what a detainee "should know," vice information the analyst could objectively demonstrate the detainee did know. If a detainee did not respond to a question posed to him, the assumption at Headquarters was that the detainee was holding back and knew more; consequently, Headquarters recommended resumption of EITs [Enhanced Interrogation Techniques].[2]

In short, Roger broke the most basic rule of interrogation, and of human relations, once again laid out decades ago in the KUBARK manual: "The assumption of hostility, or the use of pressure tactics at first encounter, may make a subject resistant who would have responded to . . . an initial assumption of good will."

Afterward, Roger remained angry and wrote that CAPTUS was stonewalling and a liar. ███████████████████████████████ ████████████████████████████. I was incensed. This struck me as absurd, stupid; it demonstrated a shocking ignorance and incompetence

---

2 The CIA Inspector General's *Special Review* also noted (paragraph 264) that "some participants in the Program, particularly field interrogators, judge that CTC assessments to the effect that detainees are withholding information are not always supported by an objective evaluation of available information and the evaluation of the interrogators but are too heavily based, instead, on presumptions of what the individual might or should know."

concerning human dynamics, personality, elicitation, conversation, and, I quickly determined, interrogation. But this "analysis" and the consequent instructions I received concerning the case would prove a recurring and growing point of tension between Headquarters and me throughout my time running the CAPTUS case in the field.

Roger was also ill, and broke down into uncontrollable spasms of wretched coughing and sweating, leaving CAPTUS—and all of us in Roger's presence— alarmed that he either suffered from tuberculosis or was infecting us all with some debilitating respiratory affliction.

At the same time, Roger ignored our liaison hosts and partners, or treated them in a surly manner, as though they, too, were the enemy. He was unable to speak to liaison directly, did not interact with them, refused to find his way alone through the city or to leave the office or his hotel, and largely ignored the entire multiagency interrogation team there to support him in the interrogation.

I left that first "interrogation" appalled. It was immediately obvious why the COS was so tense, why his control of the case had become so tight, and why I had been brought in.

The next day's interrogation was the same: chaperoning through the city, lack of interaction with and disdain for our liaison partners, interrogations consisting of denunciations of CAPTUS, Roger hacking and wheezing his way through any human interaction.

Between these sessions, I had of course started the "hallway" conversations that were so crucial to any operation, where one learned what was really happening, established one's credibility, protected oneself, or insinuated one's own positions into the web of rumor and whispered confidences. I began to learn who stuck up for whom, and who called whom a fool or a snake. I had coffee with an officer named Selma, a member of the interrogation team who had arrived with Roger. She said that in the very first interrogation of CAPTUS, Roger had wanted to put a heavy bag over CAPTUS's head and then sit there shouting at him. Selma looked at me wide-eyed as she related Roger's method, smiled ruefully, and exclaimed, "I mean, what was *that* about? What sort of crazy shit is that?" She said that the COS had been aghast. As Roger bellowed and belittled CAPTUS the COS pulled Selma aside and whispered,

"Can't you stop this? Do something!" She said that she replied, "I can't. I'm not one of you guys [CIA]. He's yours. You've got to." She laughed. "Then you showed up a few days later."

By my third day I decided I had to end the debacle.

I used one of Roger's coughing fits—our liaison partners wide-eyed in concern and growing irritation that Roger accomplished nothing, and did so rudely—to send him back to his hotel, to get him out of the way, and off the case. The COS was present, and visibly struggled not to explode in anger at Roger in front of our liaison hosts. Over Roger's croaks, rocking, and moans, I told our liaison partners that we were sending Roger home "so that he can die out of our sight," garnering a useful laugh; later, back at the station, I unkindly characterized Roger as "diseased," getting laughs there, too, but the COS was only too glad to act upon my larger meaning, and that was the end of Roger as a member of the interrogation team.

Peter had been impressed, relieved, really, that I needed only to be given the address of the interrogation location and took care of myself and that I did not need, or want, his involvement in the case, and he liked how I had moved quickly to remove Roger and resolve his corrosive effects on our work. He was pleased with the easy rapport I established with liaison. I deferred to them; I interacted with them; I asked them their views; I treated them as peers, who nonetheless owned the turf; I showed clear deference, without losing independence of action, to the senior liaison officer. I found this officer to be wary, aggressive, and sullen, but this did not matter. He was the man in charge, and so I made a point of having the best relations I could manage with him. As a result, Peter started to give me more independence in running the interrogation and our relations with liaison about the case. He was obviously relieved to have someone competent on the job, and to have one less task that he had to perform.

I had been struck in the first interrogation session I had observed to find that, as so often is the case when conducting operations, there appeared to be little or no plan about how to accomplish our task. On a typical operation in the DO, too, even if one managed to come up with a sound plan of action, time pressures, resource shortages, and competing operational demands often obliged officers to conduct operations on the fly, acting as coherently as possible in the swirl of events, but without being able to act according to a strategic "plan." Good officers improvised well, to unanticipated circumstances and without prearranged support, and realized that usually there was no higher structure guiding events.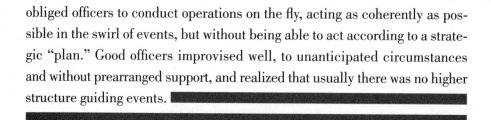

███████. The CAPTUS case was no different, for all the years of work that had gone into identifying and capturing him. The interrogation process for CAPTUS—as for all detainees, for that matter—was evolved on the fly . . . just as I had been pulled from my job one minute and the next had been sent around the world. CAPTUS was viewed, in my view simplistically, as a ████████████ detainee ████████████, who should answer questions when asked . . . and that was the end of it. Years before, I had had a conversation with my officemate of the moment, a former sergeant in the Army who saw through foolishness with the wisdom of having had to live amidst it for years. He had just come back from a staff meeting and was laughing about how typically it had gone.

"Well," he said, "the boss just told us the plan: 'Go get 'em.' . . . That was it. 'Go get 'em.' That's the plan? That's the plan?! 'Go get 'em'?"

That was the situation I stepped into: tubercular coughs, interrogation by denunciation, an overburdened, wary, and pissed-off COS, alienated liaison partners, Seventh Floor attention every day to our slightest action, the order to "do whatever it took to get him to talk . . . and to do so now," and the instruction to "walk out of the room if necessary" so that I would not see anything unacceptable according to U.S. standards in the treatment of prisoners during interrogations.

CAPTUS AND JACQUES

He who knows only his own side
of the case knows little of that.
—John Stuart Mill, *On Liberty*

"He has the social skills, the C/O skills, of some creature that lives in dark corners, snivels a lot, and fears people," I said.

I had waited several days after my arrival at post before telling Peter I wanted and needed to be running the interrogation. I spoke to him one-on-one the morning after I had undercut Roger by characterizing him as "diseased." I told Peter that Roger needed to go home—he was creating problems with liaison and was utterly incompetent as an interrogator.

Peter cocked his eye at my characterization, liking it, finding it amusing and colorful, almost inappropriate, but also agreeing with it and silently welcoming that someone spoke frankly and concurred with the way he himself clearly felt. Peter had by then assessed me to be a balanced, competent officer, although he was still wary.

He agreed to let me interrogate CAPTUS, impressing upon me the importance of the case, its sensitivity, and how careful I had to be to act appropriately toward liaison and to follow whatever guidance we received about the interrogation. I must keep him informed at all times of the slightest development and clear with him any step I intended to take, but I must *not* burden him with handholding issues and doubts. I understood. A good case officer, an experienced case officer, solves problems without taking them to the COS, but knows, too, when it is necessary to approach him. The COS needed this case off his hands. And that was why I was at post, anyway: Peter needed a solid officer to take over the case.

Peter looked hard at me. He was deadly serious and was clearly giving me an order.

"You will meet with me every morning to apprise me of developments. Got it?"

"Yes."

I was enthused that I was being entrusted with one of the key operations in our efforts to detect, disrupt, and destroy al-Qa'ida. *This* work was significant, had a real impact on our national policy and American lives. We had all lived 9/11. I had seen the huge number of threat reports that arrived from around the world every day. It was sobering, at first view, stunning. Being engaged on issues of national importance was why I had joined the Agency. Even as a case officer in the CIA, one's life and career often consisted of endless, insignificant routine.

The sunlight shone stark on the sidewalks and the sides of buildings, as we pulled out to drive to the first interrogation that I would conduct. The light whitewashed everything I saw. The tree leaves appeared a paler green than normal, the faded look objects have for me in the first moments of sight after I have had my eyes closed in the dark for some time. I have often experienced this perception of visual bleaching during intense experiences. I felt focused, alert.

I had thought about how I would interrogate CAPTUS from the moment I had been read into the case. Peter was right: I was not a trained interrogator. The CIA had none. We were case officers with various skills, but interrogating prisoners—"detainees" now in GWOT parlance—had nothing to do with our careers, until 9/11, and until our bosses poked their heads into our office doors on beautiful Indian Summer mornings. Then there was Wilmington's "guidance," which he had literally waved in my face, our new instructions from on high, from the White House and Vice President Dick Cheney, to "use any means at our disposal" and to "take our gloves off, if you will." We were in a war now; the circumstances differed, our orders were much more aggressive than anything the CIA had been involved in during my career, certainly since Vietnam. My work on the Sandinista-Contra war, and on the Kosovo war, even my work on Lebanese issues during the Israeli invasion of southern Lebanon, and on terrorist issues when on the CT office . . . we and I had done nothing like what we were now doing in the GWOT, and what I was about to do.

Many of the parked cars I passed were dusty. It had not rained for many days. I was glad that I was at the wheel and not being chauffeured. It gave me a sense of routine and control. Until today, I had been observing the interrogations, in forced passivity.

I would have our daily requirements to address: specific questions sent from Headquarters, or prepared by the interrogation team. That was straightforward, the same job I had been doing for two decades. I knew I would approach each session with the strategic objective of manipulating CAPTUS. My conception was that the conventionally accepted perception of "breaking" someone in an interrogation was probably misleading; I had almost never met a human who became abject, and completely surrendered all free will and any individual objectives. All human interactions, whether in negotiations, conversations with a child, or, I anticipated, interrogations of detainees, consisted of a dynamic that depended upon rapport and reading the other party's motivations. I would seek to manipulate our nascent relationship, of course, get inside his head in ways he identified, and in ways he did not. I would be willing to stress him and disorient him.

But causing pain to pry out information? Torture? Physical torture? I would not do it. Yet, what was physical torture? I would accept, perhaps, manipulating one's circadian rhythms, as I had experienced many years before in SERE training: disorienting and eliminating one's sensory connections and reference points to the world, one's sense of personal grounding. The unstated, operating assumption in our training had been that this contributed to making someone more willing to talk. But even about this I was uncertain. I had experienced it. It had very quickly made me confused, and frightened—I had rapidly begun to lose my sense of self, and of reality; it had not made me any more willing to cooperate with my interrogators. So did it serve its purpose? I doubted it did. But I did not know, and I found this treatment not to fall in the category of cruel and unusual punishment. Our formal guidance assured us that it did not. I thought often about this point, though. One could well consider that sort of treatment torture. The U.S. Code defined torture as "severe physical or mental pain or suffering." But this was broad, and disturbing, because "severe" was a relative term, and could authorize all manner of treatment, acceptable to some, outrageous to others. Even on issues that seemed clear—does one support torture or not?—one quickly entered the world of gray. Dividing lines and definitions blurred, legitimate objectives clashed. Physical acts beyond that which I had experienced, the express infliction of pain, or of lasting physical or psychological harm . . . *this* I could see clearly: I would not do it and I did not want to be part of it. Would this occur? Would I need to walk out of the room, or oppose it? I did not know. What would I do if this occurred?

Traffic was light. It was early in the morning; there was no discernible rush hour traffic this day. The drive seemed shorter than usual. We left the city behind, drove through the country for a while, and pulled up to the gate of the interrogation facility.

Twenty minutes later I passed from a dark hallway, my eyes still blinded by the glaring sun outside, into the wan light of the interrogation room. The walls, chairs, and floor appeared pale, drab, and drained of color.

CAPTUS glanced up with anxiety when the liaison officer and I opened the door and stepped in. A new face. What was going on? We sat down opposite CAPTUS in silence.

My liaison partner glowered. CAPTUS looked uncertain. I felt tense. I tried to project authority.

The liaison officer leaned forward, elbows on knees, then leaned back in his chair, paused to stare at CAPTUS, and introduced me in a cold voice.

"This gentleman is a very senior officer who has come to speak with you."

Another pause.

"You will answer whatever he asks you. He will not be pleased, and I will not be pleased, if you waste his time, and continue to waste mine. He came here because you have been wasting our time."

The liaison officer and I sat silent and dour again, looking hard at CAPTUS. "You have heard what I said?" the liaison officer demanded.

CAPTUS's voice was soft: "Yes. Yes. I understand."

He looked at a loss; terrified, uncertain, wanting to show his willingness to do whatever the "very senior officer" wanted. CAPTUS's emotions were real, I was sure of that already. I had no idea how sincere he was, though. He could be terrified, yet also devious and a liar. I did not know.

To CAPTUS's visible surprise and initial alarm I rose and extended my hand. He hastily half-rose in response but remained hunched, avoiding my eyes. Many years earlier, during my first overseas assignment, African peasants had treated me with the same trembling subordination. It had disturbed me then to see elderly men cower; in this instance, I supposed, we wanted CAPTUS that way.

I sat back down.

"Assalam'alaikoom"—greetings. "My name is Jacques," I said.

I told him my "name" to begin to establish a relationship with the man. No one else he saw had names. He did not know who we were (although he had figured out that Roger was an American). He had no idea where he was. By my first gesture and my first sentence to CAPTUS I had already strongly distinguished myself from the cardboard figures, hostility, and silence he had known so far.

I was so intent on CAPTUS, on establishing my authority and beginning my role as his interrogator, that in this first session I noticed almost nothing about the interrogation room. I looked intently at CAPTUS the whole time. I started with a brief recapitulation of what he had been telling my predecessor.

"We know you possess information that is very important to us. We know you have been involved deeply with al-Qa'ida," I said. "You have been involved in some terrible things, and know some people of great interest to me. Now you are here. And we will talk about these activities and people."

My liaison partner stayed motionless and silent. CAPTUS glanced at me but kept his eyes down most of the time. I was taciturn, unsmiling, and deliberate in my movements.

"Today we will continue with the subjects you were discussing with the man who was here before me. I will have other subjects later, and I may do things differently. I may treat you . . . differently. That depends on you. *Fahimt?*"

CAPTUS had settled down a little. I believe he had feared being taken away when I walked in. He remained frightened and uncertain.

"*Na'am*"—yes.

"*Hasan*"—good. "Yesterday you said . . ."

My interrogation of CAPTUS had begun. I spoke until my voice started to tire. *This is like a meeting with an asset*, I thought, *except that this one is petrified*. He was trying hard to give no possible offense, to be responsive and plastic. He did not know what to do, considered dangerous every question I asked and gesture I made, and so tried, without knowing how, to disappear.

I returned to the office much later, tired but exhilarated that I had come to grips with my assignment, interrogating an HVT, a senior al-Qa'ida terrorist.

FAHIMT ?!

It seems, in tragedy, that innocence is not enough.
—T. H. White, *The Once and Future King*

"*Fahimt?!*"

I sat staring at CAPTUS, my face affectless. CAPTUS held his eyes open wide, the whites showing around his irises. He kept blinking. So this was what one of the top al-Qa'ida operatives looked like. The iconic photographs of Usama Bin Ladin and of Bin Ladin's deputy, Ayman al-Zawahiri—scraggly hair, the dirty beard of a man who slept under a bridge covered in wet cardboard, gaunt eyes, slouched shoulders, effeminate lips—had conditioned me to expect the same offensive, deranged characteristics. Despite my poker face, though, I was surprised: CAPTUS was unremarkable, normal-looking with the gut of a sedentary man. ███████████████████████████████. He sat slouched on a folding metal chair.

The CIA and fellow agencies in the Intelligence Community had devoted years of painstaking work to identify who CAPTUS was, and then to find him. Colleagues had followed up endless numbers of vague, largely useless years-old reports. And yet, the officers dedicated to CAPTUS's case were astounding in their dedication and pursued every conceivable lead for years, analyzing concrete reports and vague reports, thinking big and thinking in precise detail,

as they sat in small, windowless cubicles and slowly, methodically checked
every conceivable way to identify and locate CAPTUS, whom they came to
consider one of the key individuals in Bin Ladin's worldwide network of operatives, financiers, sympathizers, cutouts, and allies. Eliminate CAPTUS,
the analysts came to feel, and CIA will have seriously crippled al-Qa'ida's
██████████ capabilities.

I was flabbergasted, as a Directorate of Operations case officer, to observe
such single-minded purpose in my analyst colleagues. For many years I had
recruited spies, and sent in my reports, and had little to do with the analysts
on the other side of the house. Like many in the DO, I often found them to be
immersed in minutiae that would drive an ops officer half-crazy.

Finally all the pieces had come together: The Agency analysts hunting for
CAPTUS, his network, and his links to Bin Ladin had found him. They had
found CAPTUS. The analysts' work had made me blink in amazement; it was
passing rare to see analysts produce critical, operationally relevant information. This level of success comes rarely in an officer's career. The Agency's
Seventh Floor had given the green light to snatch him, after weighing the risks
of a "flap" (of something going wrong) and the benefits of neutralizing a key
component of the al-Qa'ida ██████████ network and of having the chance
to interrogate him. There was a strong possibility that he could lead us directly
to Bin Ladin himself, the highest goal of the U.S. government in the Global
War on Terror. In any event, the time for finely weighing pros and cons had
ended with the attacks on 9/11. Now the approach was to act aggressively and
worry about consequences later, if necessary.

The Agency's officers in the field ██████████████████████ had "rendered" CAPTUS from a country in the Middle East—kidnapped him as he walked
along a sidewalk. The snatch took seconds to execute. The CIA's decades-old
guidelines on interrogation, the KUBARK "Human Resource Interrogation"
manual, which I had first seen twenty years earlier when I was working on Central American issues, recommends this be done in such a way as

> to achieve surprise and [cause] the maximum amount of mental
> discomfort . . . [so that the subject] experiences intense feelings of shock,
> insecurity and psychological stress. . . . [The subject should be] imme-

diately blindfolded and handcuffed. [The subject should never hear a word spoken] from the moment of apprehension to initial questioning.

██

██.

Only a few days later CAPTUS sat before me, ████████████████████ ██████████████ calculating what to say to try to get out of the terrible fix in which he found himself ██████████████████████████. He now knew the Americans had him, but he had no idea where. He knew nothing else.

My interpreter and I also sat on metal chairs. Otherwise, the room was bare, seedy, windowless, and silent. I took notes by writing on a pad balanced on my knee.

I leaned toward CAPTUS, locking my eyes into his wide and blinking ones. He leaned back slightly. I repeated:

"*Fahimt*?!"

My tone was commanding, demanding, a little too loud. This was Arabic for "do you understand?"

I assumed that he would always describe himself as an innocent man, perhaps a victim. That is what anyone would have done, sitting in his place. But I was not buying it. I thought he was being disingenuous.

CAPTUS did not answer.

██

██

██████████████████████████████████.

The KUBARK manual also cautioned that an interrogator must "have an exceptional degree of self-control, to avoid displays of genuine anger, irritation, sympathy, or weariness."

This moment, though, I was peremptory. My question had been simple. For a third time, louder, I demanded CAPTUS,

"*Fahimt*?!"

The silence continued as I sat staring at him.

We had rendered him because of his involvement in terrorism. Americans had died. My orders were to learn what he knew so that we could destroy al-Qa'ida.

I told him that I knew when he told the truth—and others were not as nice, or patient, as I was.

My tone was uncharacteristic. I thought CAPTUS grew uneasy.

Another moment passed.

"Na'am," CAPTUS said. "Ana Fahim."—Yes, I understand.

He answered my question.

It did not do him any good, though.

MANIPULATION, INTIMIDATION, AND RAPPORT

Man cannot so far know the connection of causes and events,
as that he may venture to do wrong in order to do right.
—Samuel Johnson, *Rasselas*, XXXIV.30

It was obvious from the outset, to me at least, that interrogation had to be founded on a human relation, which I would exploit, but which had to exist as a real, mutual psychological bond. It was absurd, to my mind, to think denunciations, or perhaps pain, sufficed to elicit or pry the information we sought from CAPTUS. One needed to play upon all aspects of a person's mind and personality, not reduce him in *our* minds to nothing but a guilty and frightened object, who was not part of the human interrogation dynamic. He was an enemy, perhaps. He had information we needed, perhaps. But he was surely a three-dimensional man, and I would so treat him during the interrogation, to the extent that I was able to do so.

I quickly found that interrogation called for the same skills and approaches as those of a good case officer: developing rapport, personal trust, a bond between the two individuals, and, of course, manipulation, sometimes seen, more often performed behind affirmations of purity and altruism. Interrogation, done right, was intensely intimate, far more than I had anticipated. I found myself developing a strong personal relationship with CAPTUS, and liking him, a man we considered so implicated in the horrific business of al-Qa'ida that we had seen fit to kidnap him.

The relationship a case officer (a CIA spy, to the man on the street) has with his "assets"—the men and women we recruited and convinced to commit treason, to provide us classified information, often at the risk of their lives—is the most intense personal relationship in one's life, more intense even than with one's spouse. Whenever you manage to meet, you look into the asset's eyes, demand and earn his total trust, hold his life in your hands, and manipulate his life for your government's own good purposes. Trust is critical, and we convince an asset to trust us with his life. Protecting your asset is a case officer's greatest responsibility. And we take that responsibility very seriously. Recruiting and running a spy is intoxicating, the thrill of the high wire, an experience of veiled power and intimacy that calls for uniquely controlled personalities, capable of deep, sincere emotional attachment and cynical intellectual detachment simultaneously. Convincing people to commit treason for a living calls for a bizarre mix of clarity of purpose and integrity, the ability to thrive in a world of duplicity, the recognition that morality is relative and can change from moment to moment, and yet that one must adhere to a firm moral (and legal) compass.

But we also make cynical jokes about our relations with our assets back in the office, for we know that our first obligation really is always to our country. This bizarre mix of devotion, love, and cynicism creates wearing emotional dissonance, too. Our first obligation, of course, is always to our country; policies change, relationships are sacrificed, and the requisite emotional detachment takes officers at times toward the definition of sociopathy: friendly and considerate, but these attributes are used to blind others to the agenda behind the officer's behavior. I've had to "terminate" an asset (cut off all contact), knowing that meant he would not be able to afford or obtain life-sustaining medication. I've worked closely with an asset, describing how my government supported his cause . . . to see us bomb his country not long afterward. Such calculating, obligatory personal detachment hurts and can take a toll on an officer over the years; if it does not take some toll, the officer is losing the humanity that makes him decent, and able to function as a good officer. Hard men can be great recruiters sometimes. But it takes compassion to win the most subtle targets' fealty and information. This was my view, although it was not one to mention in the DO; it was taken to be soft by the callous, and to be harmful to one's career if stated out loud. This was the job, and hand-wringing about it indicated professional unsuitability. It is easy to ask why one would put oneself in situations that wear so on the soul. For many, there is no compelling answer, they cannot handle the intimate compromises, and they leave the service to pursue more normal, humane professions.

To interrogate a High Value Target, or HVT, properly is a hugely labor-intensive operation. Run-of-the-mill detainees, like almost all of those held in Guantanamo, know little and are the grunts or "men with guns" picked up in any war. They may be committed and willing to die, but they pose more of a security problem than an interrogation challenge—what do you do with people who may be intent on killing you, but who may not fit the definition of "enemy combatant," and for whom you have little evidence that would stand up in a court of law? In intelligence, there are never more than a handful of targets, or "nodes," or individuals who have information that merits clandestine collection. High Value Targets, however, are among the few who have information about the senior personnel, plans, organization, and intentions of a terrorist organization. They hold, or are themselves, the keys to an organization.

An HVT interrogation team will consist of representatives from throughout the Intelligence Community, bringing their respective areas of interest and expertise to the interrogation process, including a psychologist and medical professionals, to monitor the detainee's mental and physical states and guarantee that he is stable, healthy, and compos mentis.

Then, with CAPTUS, there was the particular complication of having to work with liaison, who were not in my chain of command or under my direct control. But whatever happened, I was not going to "just walk out of the room," as Wilmington had coldly suggested.

I was going to fulfill my orders, though. The goal was to induce him to cooperate, not terrify him into blurting out anything. I wanted to get in CAPTUS's head, and convince and lead him to cooperate himself. Psychological pressures and manipulations were much more likely to be effective than physical intimidation . . . or pain, what I considered crude "enhanced techniques, involving physical or psychological pressure beyond standard techniques," as the CIA's declassified guidelines for interrogation put it. It was clear to me that this "enhanced techniques" jargon was transparent sophistry for a dirty business. Yet I *was* interrogating him, not simply debriefing him as though he were a colleague.

I was finding very quickly, just as the KUBARK manual advised,

although it is often necessary to trick a subject into telling you what you need to know . . . and to induce mental discomfort [the key to a successful interrogation was] understanding the emotional needs of the subject and relieving the fear which he feels when he is subjected to "questioning."

It was another irony that the maligned KUBARK manual was significantly more astute and sensitive psychologically than the procedures and approach taking shape around me post-9/11.

I had begun to establish a relationship with CAPTUS in the first session. This was central to how I intended to conduct the interrogation. It would take time. I believed it was the approach most likely to succeed.

YOU WILL TELL ME
THINGS WE WANT TO KNOW

It is not what a lawyer tells me I may do, but what humanity, reason, and justice tell me I ought to do.

—Edmund Burke, Speech on Conciliation with the Colonies

I acted sterner, more of a judge, or an accuser from the moment I walked into the interrogation room the following day. I wanted him to feel to his marrow the forces that controlled him, and how implacable they, and I, were. I let my anger build as I spoke—and found that I in truth became as angry as I had begun by simulating. I wanted to appear as ruthless as I could. CAPTUS needed to understand how he was linked to large stakes, in the grip of forces far beyond his power to imagine, and that he was in real danger of . . . of what? I wanted his imagination to work, imagining terrible things, but leaving them largely unspecified. Our imaginations are much stronger than our realities.

"Before we begin our questions today," I told him coldly, "I want you to know why you are here, what my government and I are doing, how important what you say is for you, and for any future you might have. I want you to know what might happen to you, and who I am. No one has told you these things clearly. Is that right?"

CAPTUS nodded his head warily. "I know nothing."

"CAPTUS, you know that I am American. Is that right?"

He nodded his head again. He held one hand inside the other on his lap.

"I am an American intelligence officer. I am from the CIA."

I looked at him for a moment in silence.

"It is the CIA that took you off the street and brought you here. Do you know what the CIA is?"

CAPTUS nodded his head.

"We had been watching you for some time. We know all about you. We know many things. We decided it was time to stop you from working with al-Qa'ida—we believe you are part of al-Qa'ida. This means"—I said this part acidly—"that you are in tremendous trouble. You are in very, very deep trouble. We have only begun with you, when we took you off the street. You saw then, already, that we can do whatever we want, wherever we want. We were easy on you, CAPTUS, because my organization, because the CIA, wants me to talk with you. You will tell me things we want to know. This will be good for you.

"That is why I am sitting here. CIA officers do not travel around the world to waste their time. You will not waste my time, for I will know if you are wasting it, and I will become very angry. You do not want to make me, or my superiors, angry."

I was working myself into a state. For one of the only times during my months interrogating CAPTUS, I stood up from my chair and paced back and forth in front of him, hands on hips from time to time, stopping to stare at him, pacing again, pointing my finger at him and raising my voice in concert with what I was saying. CAPTUS followed me with his head, slowly, but dared hardly move.

"We took you off the street and took you out of your life because we wanted to."

I looked directly at him, paused, and lowered my voice.

"We can do anything we want, CAPTUS. I can do anything I want. Do you understand? No one knows what has happened to you. No one. You have just disappeared. You are gone from the world. This is your world now. And we have just begun with you.

"Three thousand of my countrymen are dead, in part because of *you*. Some of my friends are dead. They were burned alive. Some of my friends were burned alive in the al-Qa'ida attacks on September 11. Others fell—jumped!—five hundred meters, from the top of the towers, so that their heads burst like eggs when they hit the ground. *No one* does this to Americans, CAPTUS. Our hand is now reaching out to find and to crush the killers who did this. The CIA hand is everywhere. I am part of it—and you are now in *my* hands—and I will do what I need to do to find the men who killed my friends.

"Now, you are in tremendous trouble. My countrymen are dead. They were innocent. But my colleagues and I are not innocent, easy men. You are mine now, but there are nastier men than me in the CIA. And so far as we are concerned, you are in part responsible for my countrymen's deaths.

"So what am I going to do with you? What will happen is this: I will ask you questions. You will answer me with the truth. This is what you can do: You can tell me the truth when I ask you questions. This is in your power. I will know, or will find out, if you do not tell me the truth. Things are bad for you now; you do not want to make them worse. And that is *your* decision. I will recognize honesty. I will appreciate it. It will help you with me and with the CIA. I will tell my superiors in America, in the CIA, if you tell me the truth. It will make your life here better; that is in my power, too.

"*Fahimt*?!"

I did not want to give him any hint that I could be flexible at this meeting. This meeting was intended to terrify him, and yet leave him some sense that he had free will on some crucial decisions. I sought to lead him where I wanted him to go so he would answer my questions truthfully. They had to come from him; I could not extract them by force. I knew that the personal relationship between detainee and interrogator was the single most important tool to ascertain the truth. But intimidation and fear could be useful psychological tools. I would use all the psychological tools I had.

"Yes, I understand" was all CAPTUS said, wise enough to perceive that he should not at that moment protest his innocence or engage at all with someone so furious. I did not want to talk to CAPTUS just then, either. I had worked myself up, and I wanted him to mull over what I had told him.

"I am leaving this room now. I do not want to see you. I am too angry at you. You are part of al-Qa'ida, which has murdered my countrymen. You have misled the man who was here before me. I think I have come around the world and that you will waste my time now, too. I will not allow you to do that to me.

"Think about what I have told you, CAPTUS. Think about it. I will come back later. I will have questions to ask you then. You will need to answer. So you think now."

OFFERING HOPE

Our patience will achieve more than our force.
—Edmund Burke

My main approach was to deepen his and my burgeoning relationship, not terrify him. Developing trust is more natural to me than intimidation. In any event, one can only be oneself. One's character will emerge eventually, even through concerted efforts to project certain attributes or attitudes.

Over the following days, CAPTUS became less tense. He showed what I came to find a likeable personality; a bit of the hustler and rough, but with bonhomie. It was unclear to me how clever CAPTUS was, and he was frustratingly incoherent. He reminded me of so many I had met in the Third World, who saw shapes and heard signs where I saw shadows and heard sounds, who often understood my words, but not my meaning. I supposed, too, of course, that I had my own delusions about what CAPTUS meant and thought. But how could I know what they were?

I tended to keep this sort of reflection to myself, or at least to be selective about to whom I shared my views on how cultural anthropology provided relevant insights to case officer operations—and interrogations. Many times over the years superiors had told me, one way or another, that "we don't do sociology

83

in the DO; we collect intelligence." This was not a moment to be the abstruse "Harvard guy." Nonetheless, each day I worked hard to know CAPTUS as a man. *Flies, honey, and vinegar,* I thought.

CAPTUS's and my worlds were so different. ████████████████████████

██

██

██

████████████████████████.[1]

The KUBARK manual had noted the usefulness of discussing ideology or religion to establish rapport and motivation, and to help the detainee reason his own way toward cooperation. It noted the merits of "discussing the principles of and offering valid alternatives to the ideology that motivated the subject . . . to provide him reasons which he can use to justify for himself switching sides." I considered this sound advice and assessment, and followed KUBARK's precepts.

The KUBARK manual was remembered by the public, if at all, only from the Agency's involvement with the Contras in the mid-1980s, for a few controversial passages concerning coercive methods in interrogation. But I was repeatedly surprised to find that KUBARK presented a remarkably accurate portrayal of a detainee's reactions and thoughts, and in a number of regards a subtle and even humane approach to interrogation. This was ironic on a number of levels: Two decades earlier, as I was beginning my career, the KUBARK manual was cited by many as proof of the Agency's involvement in torture and human rights violations. But this misinterpreted the objective of the KUBARK manual. I knew then that the Agency had worked hard to *stop* human rights abuses by the participants in the Sandinista-Contra war—I worked the issue specifically in my assignment as an assistant to Alan Fiers, the head of our Central American Task Force—and that the KUBARK manual, for all its debatable points and faults—was part of our effort to stop abuses of detainees. As the days and weeks with CAPTUS passed, I was consistently surprised to find that my reactions and the approaches to interrogation that I developed

---

1 The passage above describes how I used CAPTUS's and my cultural and religious differences to assess his motivations, actions, and truthfulness.

myself, on the fly—emerging from my intense determination to accomplish my mission, and to do so morally, honorably, and legally—frequently corresponded to the psychological approaches described in the KUBARK manual.

██

██

██

██

████████████████████████████████. Yet, I was no sucker that establishing good rapport and CAPTUS's willingness to discuss "safe" topics exonerated him from anything. I was interrogation team leader. The pressure to produce disseminable—operationally useable—intelligence *now* was intense. No one in the chain of command would care what I asked CAPTUS, or how I spoke to or with him, so long as I produced intelligence quickly. There was little time for what I knew would be considered irrelevant, soft conversations. An HVT interrogation team was a huge investment of precious officers, resources, liaison equities, and Headquarters support. The Agency had not spent years finding CAPTUS and committing huge resources so that a case officer could discuss comparative religion with a terrorist. And there was always the criticism against which I had to guard, that I was being duped into wasting my time by a clever opponent.

The days and nights ran together, and I always worked long hours, sending in my reports to a Headquarters waiting for the payoff from such a big coup. Sometimes I surged with frustration and anger at incomprehensible nonsense. I was not surprised to find that CAPTUS came to feel pleased to meet with me. I was the only world he had now; whatever my personal qualities or skills, the Stockholm Syndrome is powerful. Who else was CAPTUS going to identify with? Slow as the process was, the information he provided was useful. Al-Qa'ida member or not, CAPTUS knew things we did not, and needed to know. But my assessment started to challenge the official view that CAPTUS was a willing and critical member of the al-Qa'ida network.

WHAT PAPERS?

One thing only I know,
and that is that I know nothing.
—Socrates

I came progressively to believe that what Headquarters considered CAPTUS's willful obfuscation or lying was due to a clash of cultural perspectives. His mind functioned differently than a Westerner's. He did not reason linearly, or conceive the world in terms of subject, verb, object. There was no shortest line between two points. No question or subject had a straightforward answer. I thought of the English essays my brother showed me from the high school English classes he taught. Many of them were incoherent, yet they were from my own world. CAPTUS's mind was as illogical as theirs, and he was not from my world. We were in Plato's cave, I spoke of figures of men, and at his best CAPTUS described wavering shadows.

As the days went by, CAPTUS visibly relaxed with me. He was careful with each of his answers, for which I did not blame him. ████████████

██

██

██

██

———— .

———— .

———— what he imagined to be American power, knowledge, and sophistication. ————

———— . From a distance, back in Headquarters, many saw this to be disingenuous. I came to see this differently. ————

———— .

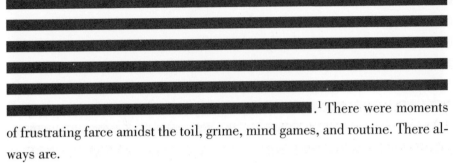.[1] There were moments of frustrating farce amidst the toil, grime, mind games, and routine. There always are.

My team and I made the trip out to the interrogation facility. I jockeyed at jammed intersections with motorcycles whose roars hurt my ears. None of us ever spoke too much on the drives. Eventually I turned onto a small, nondescript side road. It was hard to locate, and several times I drove past it unaware, only recognizing my error dusty miles later.

The trees were always pleasant and shaded on this little country lane, and I could feel the cooler air and breeze and hear the leaves rustle peacefully through my open window as I drove. But I always had the impression we were approaching what the locals knew to be a place of taboo and fear, and that they stayed away lest they saw someone or something forbidden and dangerous, and so found themselves pulled into darkness. Never once did I see any other cars or humans on this road.

"There's no one around," one of my teammates said the first time she drove with me there, as we descended into a copse of deeper woods.

"Yeah. Pretty, though," I replied, keeping my thoughts to myself. I always worked to be even-tempered, or pleasant, or to allow myself to become angry, but only when I wished to show it. Usually I succeeded. This was not detachment, as many thought; it was an effort—more often futile than successful—to control what was happening to me, and to protect myself. She kept looking out the window, perhaps unconvinced. I hoped that she was unconvinced.

---

1 The redacted passages above describe in generic terms how CAPTUS thought, how various levels of the CIA assessed his answers and manner, and how we often disagreed among ourselves. There is no legitimate justification to redact the passages, unless the CIA has decided that saying CAPTUS's ignorance of current events and that differences of opinion constitute intelligence "methods." The public, however, already might suspect CIA officers usually are not monolithic blockheads and do have internal debates. As with so many redactions in this text, the Agency has overstepped its bounds and made itself a fool.

We drove up to a gate, the attendants looking down impassively at me from inside their booth as I rolled to a stop beside them.

The guards were always taciturn. Once I told them, as I had to every day, that I was there to meet with "Mr. Muhamad,"[2] they passed me through to a spare, quiet waiting room. . It had a small transom, open to create an air current with the door on the other side of the room. Sometimes, for something to do while we waited, I stood in the door to look at the trees.

No car but mine that I saw entered or exited the compound during all the months I went there.

The factotum eventually received word that our hosts were ready to receive us. He escorted us to our next stop, disappearing as quickly as his pleasantness had been pro forma. This man was not a phony; he was simply dim and could manage to enact only a couple forms of learned behavior. I always imagined him sitting silent, stoic, motionless, and thoughtless until we arrived, whereupon he stirred, smiled his rote smile, and set to his task, and that he returned to passivity as soon as he had fulfilled his commission with us.

The door issued into an empty, dark service hallway. The only light came from a sole transom a couple dozen yards down the hallway. I was always blinded at first, passing from the day into the dark. My liaison counterparts met us standing just inside, silently shaking hands, at first only shadows to my vision: the chief, who wore ill-fitting, cheap polyester suits, whose looks were hard and ruthless, and who would leave us after shaking our hands; the thuggish officer with a craggy face who was usually in good humor, who enjoyed his work, and who in his simple mind revealed no apparent scruples, qualms, or thoughts beyond a willingness to do what his partner, or I, sug-

---

2 Of course, a pseudonym. Almost every name in the book is a pseudonym.

gested. I was happy that he and I rarely spoke. We would have had almost nothing to say to each other. The third, more intense and quick-minded officer was the counterpart I interacted with most of the time, more refined than the other. He always smoked intensely during our rare breaks, his hands and eyes restless.

We only ever knew the name of the boss, Mr. Muhamad. The COS and he had regular business together and I spoke with him from time to time when I had to arrange something with our host service. The officers with whom I worked would not tell me their names, so that for my whole time working the interrogation my team referred to them simply as "Big Guy" and "Little Guy." No one is anyone's friend in intelligence. Countries may have shared interests concerning specific issues and may work together, but no country, and certainly no intelligence service, ever has any friend. There is only each country's national interest, and each service's and officer's specific orders.

I came to like Little Guy a good deal. It was he and I who virtually lived with CAPTUS, who ███████████████████████. He was patient with CAPTUS—sometimes more than I—and he was patient with me.

The holding room in which we met with our hosts was disheveled: a couple sofas around a coffee table, dirty ashtrays, and empty peanut and chip bags lying on the table, an overflowing trash can, unemptied for days. The place became progressively grungy over the weeks. Stale cigarette odors, faded pistachio walls, and the general mess wilted the spirit; at least they did mine. Little Guy and I left my teammates in the holding room to go meet CAPTUS.

CAPTUS sat, as always, in his salmon jumpsuit as we entered, hands in his lap. The tan walls were bare and had not been painted in decades. A single ceiling light lit the room. A single transom high up on one wall, cracked open but well out of reach, hinted of the outside world. The glass was opaque, though, so CAPTUS could see nothing but his cell and his interrogators. The room was always stuffy, the air stale, the transom useless, an empty evocation of relief.

CAPTUS answered with his typical narrative incoherence, combined with precision on some details. As usual, I wondered as CAPTUS spoke whether his brain was that disordered, or if he was dicking Little Guy and me around.

I put my notepad down on the floor.

"Look, CAPTUS. Listen."

I leaned back in my chair. I dropped my conversational tone and spoke forcefully. ███████████████████████████████████████ .
███
█████████████████████████████ .

I could feel that my pulse had risen, and my breathing. I had become angry. CAPTUS saw my intensity, blinked a couple of times, and looked down at his hands. He became anxious. He absently fretted with the cuffs of his jumpsuit.

CAPTUS replied to each question, but he replied in general terms. Then he stopped, bewildered.

He told me that the information I sought was in his papers, which we had seized when we rendered him. All I had to do was look in his papers for the answers.

██
██ .

Well, this was news to me. What papers? I attempted to mask to CAPTUS that I had been unaware that we possessed his personal papers until he told me so himself. *Wouldn't that have been nice to know?* I thought to myself as he spoke, confounded and annoyed at the absurdity that he knew more about our rendition operation than I did. But I looked at CAPTUS with an expressionless face.

I did not mention my irritation to my colleagues when I left. As team leader, I did not want to come across as an angry cynic. Better to project calmness and confidence. They also had been unaware that we held CAPTUS's documents. I figured that Big Guy was too slow to perceive the little moment. But I thought I—we—had been made to look a fool to CAPTUS and to Little Guy. Little Guy noted my discomfiture even if CAPTUS might not have. We, not CAPTUS, were supposed to hold all the cards. We were supposed to know what we were doing, not waste our liaison partners' time.

I always liked smelling the fresh, flower-laden air when I stepped out into the fading light. I always liked leaving the ███████████ compound, driving back up the deserted wooded lane, seeing the first headlights and pedestrians on the highway, being surrounded by the neon and noise of the city, and finally finding once again my brightly lit, cramped, and cluttered office, and the dirty carpeting of the station. I liked if my officemate, or someone else, was there so we could trade good-natured insults.

That evening I cabled to our station in the country where CAPTUS had been seized to request that they send me CAPTUS's papers by immediate courier.

Back at the hotel, as usual I sat alone in the back of the lounge, listening for a long time to locals sing karaoke to the house band, which consisted of classically trained Latin American musicians, incongruously making their living by playing pop tunes in a Middle Eastern hotel lounge to hookers, drunken businessmen, and tourists. The two hookers who always worked the lounge had no business this night, so their good humor was unfeigned. I watched them as they sat and chatted together below me, by the band, smoking endless chains of cigarettes, their hands performing slow, delicate arabesques to the music. Later, back in my room, I lay on my bed, the air conditioner high up on the wall blowing cold air over me, and stared at music videos, silent, stoic, motionless, and thoughtless until almost 3 in the morning, when, at last, I fell asleep.

SEND A COURIER

*Those who work without knowledge will damage more
than they can fix and those who walk quickly on the
wrong path will only distance themselves from their goal.*

—Arabic proverb

The field station's reply awaited me the following evening when I returned from my session with CAPTUS: Not possible, can't spare anyone to courier them. Not possible to send them. The field station offered to send them to Headquarters, however. Headquarters could then send them on to me.

"Bah!" I said to the computer screen.

This was a useless proposal. It would take many weeks for the documents to arrive. It would take far too long. Headquarters was for all practical purposes as far away from me as the country where the papers now sat futilely—and I needed them here. For all practical purposes, as far as this aspect of the case was concerned, I was working in a pre-electronic and pre-aviation era.

The text on my computer screen was green. I tend to work with the overhead lights of my office off. My officemate had finished for the day shortly after I had come back from the interrogation facility. I looked around the cramped, slightly musty office, glancing at the stacked gray safes, the maps piled on a credenza, the drawn venetian blind of the window by my desk, and the one personal touch someone had put there: a wall calendar of scenes of small-town American life.

I knew how to resolve this little dilemma. I cabled my reply, the words floating green and disembodied before me in the near dark. Of course, I thanked the field for their explanation and expressed understanding for their resource constraints. I then cabled Headquarters, requesting that they send a courier from the United States to the station holding the documents to retrieve them and bring them to me, the interrogation team leader. Headquarters existed to manage and facilitate field operations. CAPTUS was an HVT, a high-priority detainee; his documents were critical to the interrogation. And with my request, I had just arranged for someone to get a trip around the world for me.

I stretched a moment, satisfied at my solution, and strolled to a different part of the station to chat briefly with a couple of colleagues who were also working late. One of them described his work briefly.

This colleague's operation was equally important as mine, but had an entirely different tenor, I thought. He had a lot to work with.

I was envious. My colleague had a straightforward case. He was interrogating someone who really did have blood on his hands.

"So my guy plays dumb, or we're stupid to have him," I said, sitting on the edge of a desk, "and your guy is an arrogant, benighted, little shit with a death wish."

"That seems to be about it," my colleague replied.

My operational cables, intelligence reports, trace requests, accounting reports, comments on field queries, requests for guidance and "requirements" based on information I had obtained that day, comments on intelligence reports and operational cables received from elsewhere in the world that were relevant to my work concluded, I shut down the computer, spun off the safe, secured the office, and left the focused quiet of the office to drive through sultry night air to a dinner party at a colleague's house. I arrived well into the dinner. He had been kind enough to invite several of us long-term TDYers for an evening of tall tales and American beer. The gathering was perfectly pleasant, amidst our host's collection of African memorabilia.

I enjoyed speaking for a while with one of the officers present, a former
career soldier named Josh. He was ██████████ rangy and fit ██████████
██ .
Josh was not an experienced case officer, but he struck me as a solid professional I would trust. He had spent many years in one dusty or dank Third
World backwater or another ████████████████████████████████████
██
████████████████████████████████████ . Josh spoke per-
fect Arabic. He spoke softly but was frank, and with understated amusement
and irritation noted people's self-deluding foibles. He made these observations
more from an instinctive inclination to pith cant than from malice. He spoke
simply and directly, and distrusted those who spun tales or puffed themselves
up. I found Josh engaging, confident enough in himself to acknowledge ignorance and to welcome help.

Over dinner, though, Josh found himself the somewhat unwilling star of
the evening. One of the dinner party guests prevailed upon him to relate the
astounding tale of one of his ██████████████████████ training exercises many
years earlier. He told us that he had been doing airborne training. Routine.
He said that he enjoyed the free fall directly out of the plane, as he had many
times before. At the appropriate altitude he pulled on the rip cord . . . and the
chute failed to open.

Josh said that he had not felt any particular fear, just irritation at the technical
failure. He wrestled with his chute for several thousand feet of descent, trying
to get it to billow and open. He twisted and turned, wrestled and pulled. Nothing.
Finally, with only seconds before he smashed into the ground, he said that he
suddenly remembered that he had a reserve chute. "I felt really stupid. That
was my main sentiment—that was all," he said. He hastened to pull the string
on the reserve but was too late. He crashed through tree branches, which broke
his fall to some extent, but he still hit the ground at high speed. The impact
broke his back. In an amazing stroke of luck, the break did not paralyze him.
He healed over the course of six months and was able to return to active service.

"I always knew as I was falling that I would survive," he said, matter-of-
factly. "Never doubted it. I was too busy to feel scared. I just felt stupid. A
tree limb broke my fall. My last words were 'Oh, shit!'"

The one other truly memorable twist to the evening was when our host, to his wife's good-natured chagrin and the consternation of the neighbors, insisted on wildly playing his bagpipes outside in his garden for twenty minutes, causing all the neighborhood dogs to bay and howl and yap and bark to the dissonant trills and wheezes of the "music."

AN ASSASSIN
COMING AFTER US

And ye shall hear of wars and rumours of wars:
see that ye be not troubled: for all these things
must come to pass, but the end is not yet.

—Matthew 24:6

The incessant work was wearing on me. I decided to take my first day off since my arrival. I drove for hours and hours through an empty landscape of hills, faded fields, and more and more baked stones and earth, to get away, to be alone, to immerse myself in the local culture, to become what the locals were, to shed being an American, to forget about interrogation, and CAPTUS, and cables, and *"fahimt?"*

I finally stopped at a far-off town and wandered through a medina with kilometer after kilometer of narrow pedestrian alleys. Burros were the only means people had of moving anything heavy. Thousands and thousands of people jostled together. I walked among countless spice shops, herb and scent shops, former harems, tanners' quarters, pottery ateliers, and mosques. The alleys were only an arm's span across, with high walls, the temperature many degrees cooler than just beyond the walls. I enjoyed having an endless series of urchins approach me, peddling themselves as guides, or curious what a Westerner was doing in their midst. I was charmed by the scenes of local life—a wedding procession weaving on foot through the thousands of pedestrians in the narrow alley, flowing by on both sides of me, the bride and groom looking about seventeen years old, slightly pimply, and nervous. My colleagues came to know me as the guy who always enjoyed going off alone, and to tease me about this idiosyncrasy.

I returned to the office refreshed, as I always did from my solitary explorations. "It's Lawrence, come back among us!" my colleagues would greet me after my trips. I half-smiled at these remarks but said little.

Shortly after my return we learned that the American diplomat Laurence Foley was assassinated in Amman, Jordan. Initial reports were that either one of Saddam's operatives had killed him, or more likely, one of Abu Musab al-Zarqawi's operatives, crossing into Jordan from their base in Iraq. At the time, some parts of the CIA thought Zarqawi's links with Usama Bin Ladin and al-Qa'ida might be tighter than we subsequently learned to be the case, and the administration, of course, was fully convinced of this (and remained so despite overwhelming subsequent intelligence that Zarqawi had *nothing* to do with the Saddam regime). This was a detail, in any event. Zarqawi was a rare, charismatic, competent, and aggressive sociopath, committed to jihad, which for him served as a means of becoming an important man, of justifying his hates, and rendering heroic his sadistic pleasure in killing. Over and over I would find in the coming years as I worked on the jihadist threat that most jihadists were actually ignorant punks who found imaginary justification for their sullen resentments and social hatreds, but who mostly used the rhetoric of jihad, without understanding, or caring, about the doctrines that so exercised Western analysts; or they were idealists and zealots, not unlike Robespierre, Lenin, or Pol Pot, who in good conscience could kill large numbers of people for an abstract "greater good." But whatever the doctrinal motivations or assessments, the fact was Zarqawi had just assassinated a fellow American official. Like all Americans, we were disgusted and angered.

We were electrified, however, ████████████ after Foley's death, by an urgent cable that arrived at the station. It cautioned us to take all possible se-

curity measures. We were under imminent threat, too. ████████████
██
██
██
██
███████████████████████████████████.

██. We redou-
bled our attention to our surroundings, █████████████████████████
to the extent we could. We were careful going ███████████████████
████████████ to and from the office. ██████████████████████████
████████████████████████████████I tried even more than normal to be
aware of my surroundings ███████████████████████████████████
███████████████████████████████████. I thought often as I drove or
walked about the city and its environs about the first time I had detected surveillance on me, many years before during my first tour abroad. My stomach
had fallen, then risen to my throat ██████████████████████████████
██. It was
one of the few moments in my career when I felt physically ill with tension. I
had successfully avoided a problem in that instance; I wondered how I would
react if I detected something unusual now that we had apparently reliable reports about two assassins or terrorists coming for us ██████████████
████████████████. We all carried on, a bit more on guard, but otherwise focused
on our work.

The reporting had been excellent. Our allies were active in our behalf.
██
██
████████████████████████████. The dénouement was anticlimactic: Jor-
danian officials detained several men and charged them with the assassination
of U.S. diplomat Foley. The brief surge of tension dissipated, and we returned
to our normal moods and thirteen- to fifteen-hour days.

I'M AN INTERVIEWER NOW

On ne peut pas employer de menteurs professionels
sans leur donner le monopole de la vérité.
(One cannot employ professional liars
without giving them the monopoly on truth.)
—Volkoff, *Le Montage*

A morning or two after the bagpipe dinner, I was sitting at one of the free desks in my office starting to write a cable about the previous day's interrogation before heading off to see CAPTUS. Jack, my burly, first-tour officemate, sat at his desk a few feet away. I was musing about what I was writing, slouched far back in my seat. We would have a staff meeting in a few minutes. I shifted screens to check incoming traffic. I started to read a general guidance cable that had arrived from Headquarters overnight.

I chortled derisively at the computer. Jack turned his head. He was becoming familiar with my habit of denouncing the computer as though it were alive, and was amused by it.

"I'm an interviewer now," I told him, deadpan.

Jack raised his eyebrows expectantly. He knew there would be some ironic twist to my comment.

"The DO is standardizing practices concerning all detainees. We have new procedures to follow. There's a new protocol. They say they're professionalizing our practices. No more ad hoc stuff. From now on, all cables concerning detainees—all my cables about CAPTUS—will refer to interrogations as 'interviews.'" Here I laughed. "We are not to use the term 'interrogation' any more. So," I concluded with a tone of sufficiency, "I am an 'interviewer' now."

It was obvious to all of us that the Agency wanted to avoid future problems, or accusations that our treatment of detainees had been as harsh as an "interrogation" might imply. In the staff meeting that morning, of course, I presented the change of practice in a relatively straightforward manner. The COS had a dry sense of humor, but subversive irony would have been inappropriate for a diverse group of junior and experienced officers; he was also no-nonsense and the staff meeting needed to set a tone of positive focus. So I betrayed my cynical amusement by my expression but remained professional and factual.

From then on, of course, some of us made jaded, acidic, and largely humorless jokes about this petty effort at cover-your-ass bureaucratic obfuscation, I more than most. I learned that this guidance came from some legal staff in the Agency, which was no surprise, concerned that the Agency act appropriately and not expose itself to criticism or challenge by subsequent investigators. I couldn't help but think of the scene in *Marathon Man* in which Laurence Olivier holds Dustin Hoffman strapped into a dentist's chair, and tortures him for information by drilling holes in Hoffman's front teeth without any Novocain, while repeating in soothing tones, "No pain, no pain. There is no pain." I also thought, of course, of *1984*, where words were assigned meanings opposite to the truth, so that events sounded benign, whatever the reality. After receiving this surreal cable I took to characterizing my involvement in this phase of the War on Terror to colleagues as "interviewing some of our most prestigious guests."

When the staff meeting had finished I asked Jack to go down with me to the cafeteria for a coffee. We stepped into the hallway to take the elevator.

"You go ahead," I told him, changing my mind a little. "I'll join you. I have to use the head."

I jogged down the stairs to use a men's room on the way to the cafeteria, instead of stopping in the one by our office. I entered and stepped up to the urinal. But I stopped in my tracks, before unzipping my fly.

"This is *not* possible!" I said to no one. This urinal, too, was located high up on the wall, just like the one by my office. I would have had to contort myself like before to conduct my business, and that surely badly.

I had been doing some thinking about my previous idiotic episode. I realized that, in fact, only authorized Americans were ever allowed into these ███████████ spaces. The fool who had installed these stupid things had actually been some American contractor with a security clearance. It wasn't the locals. At least, some American had run the show. I used a stall instead, and did so for the remainder of my time in country.

Jack and I chatted calmly in the cafeteria, a matter of starting the day as much as anything.

"Jack, you haven't noticed anything about the men's rooms here?"

"You look normal, Glenn, but I'm starting to think you are weird."

"No, really," I said through my laughter. "Nothing? You haven't noticed anything?"

"I do not think about our men's rooms . . . as you do."

"The urinals. The urinals! Doesn't anyone ever pee around here? The urinals are like five feet off the ground or something. You have to stand on your tiptoes and pee way *up* into the air to use the stupid things! They're all that way. It's completely retarded. You've never noticed that?"

"Well, no," Jack said, growing serious. "It must be just that you have a really, really short dick."

Of course, thereafter Jack occasionally arched his eyebrows at me when the men's room came up in conversation.

Over the days, a trend emerged: My assessments of the case consistently, and progressively, diverged from those of Headquarters. ███████████████

██

██

██

██████ .

I now had been involved in the CAPTUS case for weeks; it had become mine. From the first briefing I had received at Headquarters I had been surprised that we had decided to "render" CAPTUS, rather than try to penetrate his operations or turn him to our use. The rendition was like an excision; it would obviously shut CAPTUS down, but I thought it would almost certainly reveal our hand and show al-Qa'ida that we were onto this part of the al-Qa'ida network. Bringing a terrorist to justice had trumped our more classic penetration and collection work. I took it that the decision had been made to treat the CAPTUS case as a war-fighting and disruption operation, with the intelligence collected a useful but secondary objective. We wanted to destroy al-Qa'ida and save lives. At Headquarters, I was just being read into the case; I listened, tried to learn, and was in no position to say anything.

My initial case officer reaction and instincts returned strongly, however, as I came to know the case, and to assume fully the role of the field officer responsible for it. Having rendered CAPTUS, we could now obtain what he knew—perhaps. But CAPTUS would be replaced quickly; we would almost surely not have insight or access to this new individual and would have to develop it all over again. We had signaled our knowledge to our enemies of whatever CAPTUS had touched or been involved in by rendering him.

I was also coming to feel that CAPTUS's involvement with al-Qa'ida was because he had had little choice—he could cooperate or risk grave personal problems. It was safer for him not to ask too many questions. Al-Qa'ida used him, yes, but he was no terrorist, and his conscious complicity was questionable.

There was little chance now we could turn CAPTUS and use him as an asset, since his rendition had occurred weeks earlier. But I thought it still might be barely possible. It would be better operationally to have CAPTUS committed to serving us, and finding out new information, than to keep him indefinitely in detention. And freeing the man and running him in the field as an asset would be more just, given my assessment of him, than letting him rot in a cell. I was determined to explore whether I could turn back the clock and do operationally what I felt should have been done in the first place.

"Goddamn it! Blow me."

I was reading the morning traffic two days after sending out my request to Headquarters for a courier. Jack turned his head toward me, an expectant smile forming on one corner of his mouth.

"Do you always talk to your computer? It's inanimate, you know. And you are vulgar."

"Headquarters won't send a courier to pick up CAPTUS's goddamned documents. No courier available."

"Oh. That sucks. Good support you're getting there, Glenn."

I thought a moment, as I continued staring at the computer screen.

"Screw 'em. I have a whole interrogation team. I'll send someone myself to get them. I'll worry about it when I get back. For now, I gotta go see CAPTUS and Little Guy."

I shut down the computer and headed to the interrogation facility.

A FUTILE PROPOSAL

The definition of prayer: To ask that
the laws of the universe be annulled in behalf of
a single petitioner, confessedly unworthy.

—Ambrose Bierce

As always, I sat opposite CAPTUS in the folding metal chairs we used, about eight feet away, slightly to his left. Little Guy was to my left. CAPTUS was now at ease and answered questions freely. I assessed that he answered truthfully—most of the time. He continued to pretend ignorance on some topics where my colleagues and I believed he had information. I assessed that he spoke freely about 85 to 90 percent of what he knew. Headquarters, of course, wanted me to pressure CAPTUS to provide what must be the critically important 10 to 15 percent he seemed to withhold.

This was a major meeting. ████████████████████████████
██
██. Today I was going to make a critical effort to set the case on a course that would satisfy Headquarters, accomplish my mission, and fulfill my various obligations, in all directions:

"CAPTUS, ██
██

████████████████████████████████. This is what I would like to do. It would be dangerous."

I then described my operational plan, one I expected was, by this point, impossible. Still, I was determined to explore any possibility to run the case sensibly and successfully.

Naturally enough, CAPTUS perked up. I had never said anything like this before.

CAPTUS was frozen as I spoke. Little Guy was enthusiastic. I had planned with him what I would say, and he had liked my idea very much. I continued:

"Now, I want you to understand this, too: This will be ████████████████ ██ ████████████████████."

"So. Will you do it?"

I was intently focused on being as compelling as I could. I knew it would be an irresistible proposition. It was the *only* glimmer of a future CAPTUS was likely to see, and he would know this.

CAPTUS sat up, glanced quickly at Little Guy, and spoke directly to me ██. For the first time, CAPTUS looked determined.

"██ ██ ████████████████████████████████."

His eyes flashed.

"██ ██ ████████████████████████████████."

He looked around the small, tired interrogation room. In all the time I met with him, he never once looked at the transom high up on the wall, the only connection to the outside world ever within his sight. He did not do so at this moment, either. Instead, he looked at me.

"Yes, I will do it."

ROUGH HIM UP SOME?

If we imagine no worse of them than they of themselves,
they may pass for excellent men.

—Shakespeare, *A Midsummer Night's Dream*, Theseus, V.I.211

CAPTUS did himself no favors, however. ███████████████████
██
███████████████████████████████████████.
████████████████████████████████████
██
███.
██
██
███████████████████████. Not long after he agreed to my proposal he so irritated
me that I got up from a session and walked out. Big Guy was waiting in the hall.

Big Guy was not too bright and did not trouble himself with what CAPTUS
said. He always struck me as having been detailed to the intelligence service
as a jailor from some subaltern position in the army. He received his orders
and simply carried them out. If CAPTUS was a prisoner, Big Guy's service
must want him to be detained; that sufficed. He was uninterested in, indeed,

incapable of perceiving, any sort of psychological manipulation or game. For him, the issues were straightforward. He was the kind of man that Wilmington had tried to appear when briefing me back at Headquarters. But Wilmington was a white-collar, educated intelligence officer, projecting toughness, playing a bit of a false role. Big Guy was not playing. He had no guile. He was, at heart, a thug.

"Ah," Big Guy said with a slight turn-up at the corner of his mouth, because I seemed ruffled, and because he felt, at last, more in his element. He violently plucked out a couple of his nose hairs and casually flicked them off his fingers. "██ ██ ████████████." Big Guy looked at me expectantly.[1]

I was appalled. I had expressed frustration with CAPTUS, but ███████ ██ ██ ██ ██ ██.

I did *not* want this and would not allow it on my case. I was there to interrogate an al-Qa'ida member, not torture anyone.

I answered Big Guy with all the official force, command, and seriousness I possessed:

"No. No. Listen to me. No. ███████████████████████████ ██ █. Am I clear about this? █████████████████████████████ ██ ██ ██ ██."[2]

---

1 The deleted passage concerns what Big Guy proposed to do with CAPTUS.
2 The deleted passage concerns my emphatic opposition to what Big Guy had proposed.

Big Guy showed almost no emotion, but I took his stoicism to be a comment on my reaction, and detected a hint of disdain. He was professional, however.

"Yes, yes, okay. I understand."

He remained amused that CAPTUS had irritated me. Early that evening, Little Guy joined us for a wrap-up meeting about the day's work. Big Guy told him, half kidding me for having lost my temper, that I "wanted to have CAPTUS roughed up." I found nothing amusing about this at all and repeated to Little Guy that "I do *not* want CAPTUS 'roughed up.' I would not have anything to do with such a thing, and I in no way whatsoever said, implied, or desired that CAPTUS be touched. I do not want that at all. And I am speaking formally."

Little Guy understood and the matter ended there. But I had been apprehensive that a frustrated expostulation might lead to torture. It did not.

Our cases were always compartmented on a need-to-know basis. Frequently during my career, I did not know what my officemates were doing, or whom they were meeting, and they did not know whom I met. As one of the few officers involved in interrogation of HVTs, though, one heard things informally from time to time.

There were occasional murmured comments about terrible fog-of-war choices facing colleagues dealing with detainees.

While I was exasperated with CAPTUS, and heatedly telling Big Guy to do nothing about it, I heard a grim rumor, furtively mentioned by a colleague traveling TDY and passing through the station, that ██████████████████ ██████████████████████. I was shocked. I had to assume that if true, it must have been due to circumstances beyond anyone's control—battlefield situations, perhaps, like what had happened in the early days of our war in Afghanistan, when CIA officer Johnny Spann, and numbers of Taliban, were killed in chaotic conditions. It was inconceivable to me that there could be any other explanation. But my thoughts nonetheless recurred to the challenge, the impossible challenge, of seeing and deciding clearly in the "gray world," where there might be no good choice, and yet one must choose a course of action on the spot. It was so easy to cross a line, when one could not see clearly, where there might not be a line, where one had to decide immediately what to do, when historical guidelines had been repudiated, and when pressure was intense and relentless.

In any event, I had my own problems, rumors were always insidious, the echoes were distant, and no more substantial than the hot whispered air by which one heard them.[3]

"My guy" CAPTUS was in solitary isolation, but well treated otherwise. So far as I was aware, he had not been subjected to physical coercion.

Liaison informed us that we would have a several-day break in meeting CAPTUS. He had been sent away " ███████████████," according to liaison, to give the CAPTUS interrogation teams a short break. This happened several times. It was true that the interrogation was tremendously labor intensive and draining for all concerned. These visits " ███████████████ " disturbed me; I did not like what, to my ears, was too elusive a characterization. I did not know what liaison did to CAPTUS during these interludes.

But liaison controlled the asset, and the case, and allowed us to interrogate CAPTUS, whom they were holding for us. This was their soil, we were there on sufferance, and they had ultimate control, so long as we kept him in their country. ███████████████████████████████████

███████████████████████████████████████

███████████████████████████████████████

███████████████████████████████████████

███████████████████████████████████████

███████████████████████████████████████

███████████████████████████████████████

██████.[4]

I do not know any more about this element of the CAPTUS case—and I was the one running it. I knew that no one person actually ever ran any operations in intelligence, and I unhappily thought of my tense conversation with Wilmington at Headquarters, which seemed so long ago and so far away, when

---

3 I heard nothing more about the incident, or incidents. I learned much later that a detainee had died in Afghanistan, which was the subject of a formal investigation. It appears that the detainee died, unintentionally, from an aggressive interrogation gone hideously wrong. The man froze to death.

4 The deleted passage concerns my effort to learn about what happened during these absences.

he sneered to me, "Well, then, you just walk out of the room, if you feel you should. Then you won't have seen anything, will you? You will not have been party to anything."

Headquarters' pro forma response to my proposal arrived; it lauded my initiative but said that it did not consider my proposal feasible.

My plan had been forlorn from the outset, and I had known it before sending it in. It reflected my growing doubts that CAPTUS was the evil al-Qa'ida member we believed him to be when he was rendered, and ill ease that we had destroyed the man's life based on an error. And yet, I wrestled with my conflicting knowledge that he possessed information about al-Qa'ida operations that he appeared to avoid discussing. But then, I knew, too, that he was trying not to say things that he was sure would be misconstrued to his detriment. I thought this reticence understandable, and not necessarily proof of guilt. The stakes were high and the case was rife with contradictory impulses and information. So I knew my proposal was forlorn from the outset; believed that he was a victim of our misguided assessments and zeal; found detaining him to be inefficient, probably unjust, but now inevitable; believed, too, he was withholding information about certain aspects of al-Qa'ida operations.

And CAPTUS, because of some combination of unfortunate circumstance, his stupidity, his willful duplicity, the CIA's self-fulfilling yet erroneous assessments about him, the CIA's legitimate determination ruthlessly to pursue and destroy al-Qa'ida killers in a time of war . . . found himself rendered, trussed, isolated, manipulated, interrogated, and "sent to the desert."

The one consequence of my futile proposal was to put Wilmington and Headquarters more at odds with me on some aspects of how the case should be run, and on significant parts of the entire operation. They added this to my implicitly critical views on how the case had been and should be run, to my cables detailing my conviction that CAPTUS was not a member of al-Qa'ida and to my initial concerns concerning interrogation methods, however discreetly indicated during my initial briefing. But this was, and always remained, sub rosa. Tensions and disputes almost always play out sub rosa in the DO.

The cable from Headquarters closed by expressing Headquarters' support. It was the DO's version of a thin smile.

AL THYRIA

We are never tired so long as we can see far enough.
—Ralph Waldo Emerson, *Nature*

CAPTUS's absence freed me for a couple of days. I liked getting away from my American colleagues and going native. I liked hearing what the Arabs thought, and seeing how they lived. I always had found that the life of an American official was much more constricting than my years abroad on my own had been. I informed COS that I was going out of town, and flew to a distant place, far from the city and the embassy, and from the mind-set of my routine with CAPTUS and my ████████ colleagues.

I took my own trip "to the desert." The irony did not escape me. I rented a car and drove and drove. On the road, I spent time in cafés, barbershops, restaurants, and modest roadside hotels where I was the only foreigner, walking the streets and asking directions as a pretext to start a conversation with the locals. The hit tune *"Las Ketchup,"* by three attractive Spanish women, played over and over on the radio as the kilometers and dust blew by. Sometimes I presented myself as a Frenchman, sometimes as a German or a Spaniard, whatever appeared simplest and least obtrusive. I let people decide where I was from and then often agreed with them. Everyone was hospitable to me, the rare tourist in their part of the world.

Early one afternoon, far out on a lonely road on which I had passed no cars in either direction for many kilometers, I picked up a thin and retiring young soldier on leave hitching to his home village. He was surprised to have been picked up by someone exotic, from glittering America. He did not even have a stock of stereotypical images of American life picked up from movies. He had little to say about his own country, or himself, and he was not very bright. But he was gentle and good-natured, nodding and smiling shyly to my dwindling attempts at conversation. An hour into our drive together we had settled into a pleasant silence, with only the noise of the wind through the windows accompanying the unfolding emptiness of rugged, pebble-strewn desert. I spotted a man a hundred yards off to the car's left, crouching motionless on the ground. The sun still shone strongly. There was no cover anywhere near for him, and there was nothing whatsoever, from what I could tell, for miles in any direction except stones, dry earth, sun, and wind. He did not move.

"What is that man doing?" I asked my hitchhiking soldier, pointing my arm out the car window.

"He's waiting."

"Waiting? Waiting for what?"

"For the end of Ramadan."

I was nonplussed at this senseless answer. "But Ramadan is forty days long!"

The soldier shrugged. "He is waiting."

I drew in my arm. The lone man slipped from view, the car raised a billowing wake of dust behind us, and I drove with purpose through the desert toward some place I had never been.

Near the end of the day I stopped and approached a group of young men sitting on the side of the road, many kilometers from any place I could discern on the map, simply to see what would happen. They asked me to join them. They had gathered to break their fast at the setting of the sun. I spent a memorable hour and a half eating of their flat, doughy, salty bread, crouched on my haunches, saying almost nothing as we watched the growing darkness deepen on the sharp mountain peaks and the sky turn from blue to violet, then to black. They were mechanics, simple, guileless, and winning. I left them after it had become dark, three men placidly savoring the night air and calm around them, enjoying the warmth of silent camaraderie.

One innkeeper invited me after dinner for mint tea before a roaring fire. The two of us sat in plush chairs in the inn's den. I was the only guest. The only electric light was behind us in the dining room. The firelight lit our faces in the dark as we talked. The only sounds were our voices, and the crackling of the fire. Every so often, the innkeeper poked the fire and added another log.

"Our business has dropped 90 percent, 100 percent since 9/11. No Westerners come anymore. It is terrible. You are one of the only ones to come through in months. But we have nothing to do with any of this! It is terrible. I built this inn for Westerners. You must tell people to come here. I traveled to America once. I want to move there. But I cannot. My business is this inn. I built a pool, and now it sits, a hole in the ground. I have no guests, I have no money to finish it. I have no money. Islam does not support this terrorism. It condemns it!"

I left my host about midnight. I stepped onto the balcony of my room, staring into the night at the few buildings jostled together that formed the village where I was staying, small against the empty hills and mountains only a hundred meters beyond. Nothing moved and the only sound was the whistling of the wind through the eaves of the inn. I started to look at the stars, glittering and dazzling by the thousands. The Milky Way splashed across the sky. Stars have always had a special importance for me. They link us to the enriching and consoling myths of the deep past. They humble by their aching remoteness, so frail in an implacable black sky, yet hopeful, too, that at some points, at least, the light can prevail. Wherever I am they remind me of my father, who as a boy wanted to become an astronomer, who first turned my eyes to the sky and taught that the promise of the stars was always to ask critical questions, to realize that most questions had multiple answers, and in so doing, to move closer to a truth that can never be reached, and perhaps to lift one's spirit to the heavens.

I wanted to find several constellations. I studied the sky for a minute or two, and started with the Little Dipper and the North Star. But in the clear night the temperature was quickly dropping toward freezing. The wind whipped down off the mountains and I started to shiver. It was too cold for me to stay outside and search. I retreated to my room, closed the shutters, and went to bed disappointed that I had been defeated in my solitary stargazing, sad that I was the only tourist who had passed through in months, but pleased that I was the one who had.

My host approached me at breakfast.

"My friend. I am going to do you a service. I am going to ask of you a service."

I anticipated that he was going to suggest I visit someone to look at their fine rugs.

"I would like to offer you the hospitality of my brother. He works just down the street. Perhaps he will be able to help you to find something beautiful. He will wish to offer you tea." My host put his hand on his heart. "You will do this for me, yes?"

"Yes, I'll go, of course," I said, trapped by his hospitality and preceding night's melancholy kindness, but telling myself that I would stay for only five minutes and then be off on the road.

The innkeeper's brother was about forty-five, roughly the same age as CAPTUS, with a similarly thick middle and stubby, fat hands from soft living, and slow, gracious movements. He had a neatly trimmed beard, which he stroked reflectively as he spoke. He wore a *djellaba* of blue, its hood forming a high cowl around the back of his neck. For thirty minutes he did courteously and gently show me his Oriental rugs, which covered almost the entire floor of the shop. From a side room, his servant silently brought in large rugs, carrying them on his shoulder like a duffle bag. The servant tossed them onto a large pile of unfolded rugs on the floor. They landed hard, with a dull thud.

Finally the innkeeper's brother smiled in acquiescence to my persistent polite demurrals.

"Please, I would like you to come in the back for tea. Will you?"

We sat on piles of rugs in a windowless room. Rugs hung like tapestries covering all the wall space. The rugs isolated us from all sound or connection with the outside world. The only light was from an overhead bulb, hanging uncovered on the end of a cord from the ceiling. A ventilator hummed softly, blowing cool air from the top corner of one of the walls.

We spoke of our families. We spoke briefly of religion. He told me, as so many Muslims do, with unconscious condescension, that he respected and liked Christians, for "Christians are People of the Book." He asked me what I did for a living. I spoke vaguely about my work as a diplomat.

The tea tasted sweet, with a sludge of sugar covering the bottom of the cup.

"I am trying to go into the desert," I said.

The innkeeper's brother savored a last sip of tea, puckering his lips slightly to taste its sweetness. He thought a moment, stroked his beard, slowly set his teacup down on the pile of rugs before him, and placed one hand on each knee.

"You are my brother's friend. I am going to do you a service. I am going to ask of you a service."

I waited, slightly apprehensive that I was going to have to fend off another cloying sales pitch. The innkeeper's brother spoke softly.

"To find what you seek, you must go far beyond the road." He looked up from his hands, into my eyes. "You must . . . go to meet Hamid."

Another "friend!" I thought. They were sucking me in too far.

"I think I'll just drive on alone. Thanks. I'll jus—"

The innkeeper's brother quickly flashed anger at me.

"You think I am not to be trusted? My brother sent you to me. If you do not trust . . ."

His instantaneous surge of anger surprised me and I felt an immediate pang that I had unintentionally dishonored him by my fumbled attempt to extract myself from the web of obligation that had started the night before in front of the fire in the inn.

I decided as suddenly as he had angered. I could see that the man was honorable. This was an adventure. Just as Arabs stand closer than Americans when conversing, making us ill at ease, so their gestures of friendship or kindness can overwhelm, too intimate almost for American lovers to do for each other, even. The warmth and the anger were so sudden, so intense, so real, and, it seemed, so lasting. My New England Yankee reserve simply had to appear bloodless, shallow, rude. My detachment and effort not to allow partings to hurt too much, because they are so frequent, must appear heartless and selfish. What did such a man offer of *himself* to others? And if he did not, had the man no feelings? Such a man must be hollow, or ruthless. But sharing tea with the innkeeper's brother, seeing inside his and his culture's heart, feeling as others felt, was the *point* of my many years abroad, and of my career. I interrupted him mid-sentence.

"No, no. I do not mean that. I am sorry. I spoke poorly. Please excuse me. I am honored by your interest in what I am trying to do. Hamid can take me to the desert? Yes, how do I find him?"

The innkeeper's brother's anger dissipated as quickly as it had come, an expression of relief and pleasure crossing his face. He stroked his beard to calm himself, then folded one hand inside the other on his lap.

"You must drive very far. The service I do for you is to send you toward Hamid, in the desert. The service I ask of you is to seek for Hamid."

The innkeeper's brother rose. He took my hand and then placed his hand on his heart.

"You have a very long journey. You will find Hamid at the dunes. . . ."

I left fifteen minutes later.

I drove all day but stopped along the road a number of times. The people I met often talked of current events. Most spoke freely. I tried to listen and let the conversations go where they wished.

I stopped for gas and to stretch at a tiny oasis hamlet. I struck up a conversation with the two men working at the station. There was no traffic or business and they were happy to talk to a surprising stranger, appeared from nowhere and so far from where one usually would expect foreigners:

"No Muslim would do the September 11 attacks. Therefore, the American CIA did it to make Americans hate Muslims." "The Jews did the World Trade Center attacks, to justify and win American aid. The proof is that all the Jews had cleared out of the World Trade Center before the attacks." "No Arab or Muslim is really safe in America since September 11. We all had to leave." "The Jews control America. What difference is there between Israel and America? There is none. Therefore, the Jews control America."

I stopped for a late lunch many kilometers down the road. I struck up a conversation with the restaurateur, as I ate a salad. He, too, wanted to speak with the rare "European" tourist, and after standing over me as I ate, invited himself to sit down with me, apron on, but happy to converse with an American, come from the center of power and living amidst the latest trends:

"Usama Bin Ladin would never do the World Trade Center attack." "He is the creation of the Americans." "He works for the CIA, therefore the CIA committed the World Trade Center attacks." "There is no such thing as al-Qa'ida. It is propaganda by the CIA." "Whenever America wants to solve a problem, it does. But it does nothing in the Middle East. Therefore, America wants Israel to kill Arabs. Therefore, America wants al-Qa'ida and Usama Bin Ladin to exist, to justify American aggression in the Middle East."

These conversations were typical of what I heard during my explorations.

The roads grew smaller. The few cars or trucks faded behind me, so that I drove on alone, long past the last road or habitation, the last man on earth, racing the setting of the sun to reach my destination before I lost all sense of direction to the darkness. All vegetation had ceased long behind me. For dozens of kilometers the land had been a vast plain of scattered rubble and baked earth, extending to the horizon in every direction. Finally, just as the last light disappeared, as my senses lost the ability to discern depth or distance, direction or detail, and as total black covered the land, I found what I sought—vast dunes of sand rose before me, looming shadows in the gloom. My headlights shone on a lone figure standing before the first building I had seen in several hours. He wore a *djellaba* and a *tagelmust*—a turban and veil—which covered all his face but his eyes. I stepped out of the car into a stiff, cold wind and approached him.

"*Sabah al Khayr*," I said, my voice strong in the dark, which means "Good evening" but literally means "By the light of the sun."

"*Anta Hamid?*"—Are you Hamid?

"*Sabah al Nur*," replied the man in a voice almost lost to the wind, "Good evening"—"By the light of the moon."

"*Na'am, ana Hamid*"—Yes, I am Hamid. He was a nomad.

We shook hands. He was short, slight, quick-moving, and silent. The innkeeper's brother had pointed me to a rendezvous none of us had planned. With gestures and nods we arranged to travel deeper into the desert.

My camel and I cast a gray shadow against the sand in the moonlight, my body swaying with each step he took. On each side I saw sometimes evanescent glints of light along the crests of dunes, which soared massively hundreds of feet above me and on all sides rising, fading, undulating as far as I could see; where depths were hard to determine; shadows were dark, hinting at crevices to one's side, or perhaps simply a small fold of hard sand, but where it was impossible to fathom which was the case; where the horizon receded to nothing and land merged with sky; a world where the only certainty was the pommel of my camel's saddle, onto which I held tight as a proof against slipping completely into a world beyond principles, knowledge, or judgment. Hardest was descending the vast, steep dunes, the camel's knees locking and bending with erratic jerks, over and over, throwing me far forward each step, making me fear the humiliation of pitching into the sand and rolling down the dune. After hours of teetering unsure on the camel's hump, we camped in a depression amidst the towering mounds of sand, during a freezing night in a tent that kept out the sharp wind. The moon set, taking with it the last, ethereal gray. Hamid sat almost always silent, almost unseen. The only sounds were the sporadic wheezing rasps of the camels and the increasing howl of the wind.

We ate outside, on a rug the nomad had laid on the sand, by the light of a small lantern Hamid lit. "*Kel,*" the nomad said, pointing at my plate. Eat. He looked at me. I did not know what he had put on the plate. The nomad was stern. I ate. "Ehhh," he said, impassive.

We sat, silent and unmoving. He pointed to a constellation. Thousands of stars shone in the black, cold air, brilliant, glittering points that shimmered if I looked at them one by one. "*Al Thryia,*" he said. His voice was soft. "The Pleiades," I replied. He pondered my answer. "*Al Korsy,*" he said, pointing to another. "Cassiopeia." "Ehhh," he said. "*Baard,*" he said. "Cold." "Ehhh," I replied. "*Baard.*" We sat under the stars, silent once again, for a long time. "*Masa'al Khayr,*" he said, rising. "Good night." He walked into the blackness around us. It was freezing. I was alone. The wind howled outside my tent until I fell asleep.

I returned to the opaque, gray world of interrogation and espionage—so far from the sand, the stars, the wind, and the chill of a nomad's desert night—refreshed, and ready to carry on trying to handle the conflicting imperatives of the CAPTUS case honorably and effectively.

"You did what?!" the COS said upon my return, perplexed that I was always going off among the locals, out of town, alone, this time in the desert with illiterate nomads. He shook his head.

Miserable CAPTUS awaited me, in his starless cell, also alone.

I described my trip to my liaison colleagues when I met with them the day following my return to the capital. I related some of the comments I had heard about who had carried out the 9/11 attacks, fishing for their reactions. I did not expect much from Big Guy. Little Guy surprised me, though.

"We, too, have heard in the ministry that the Jews committed the World Trade tower attacks. We received reports that the Jews had been given advance warning to evacuate the buildings before the attacks. The Jews have great influence on your government; this is true."

Little Guy was open-minded and bright, but I realized as I listened to him that all of our thoughts are circumscribed by the perspectives of those around us and by what is conventionally considered "true" or "right."

I did not say much in response.

A RECURRING HEADACHE

Nos chimères sont ce qui nous ressemble le mieux.
(Our delusions are that which resembles us the most.)
—Victor Hugo, *Les Misérables*

The documents issue was a recurring headache and embarrassment.

Over the next several days, I started to make arrangements for one of my colleagues to travel to pick up CAPTUS's documents. She was enthusiastic. I was envious. The location was exciting, and hard to get to. The more different a location from my normal points of reference, the more I liked it. Taboos and social categories that define us recede; one could be a man made new. I had devoted my life to pursuing chances like this. But the arrangements fell through, as she was unable to travel before her return to Washington for another assignment.

I chose a second officer to send and went to discuss it with the COS.

"No can do, Glenn. She is supporting another case. I'm down a couple of officers and can't support you guys with PCS [permanently stationed] officers. We have to do our own work. Sorry, can't go. You'll have to work it out yourself. There is no one I can spare."

I selected a third officer to go retrieve the documents. Two days before he was to depart he, too, was suddenly recalled to Washington.

CAPTUS became at times slightly contemptuous of what seemed to him simple incompetence because I—as far as he was concerned, the CIA—was unable to provide his own documents. He asked me, " ███████████

███

███

███████████ ?"[1]

I had no answer I cared to give CAPTUS.

Our hosts, too, were bemused by my inability to provide something important to the interrogation. I sensed that Little Guy and his boss, Muhamad, were also starting to become impatient and frustrated, progressively skeptical about the CIA's claims about what and who CAPTUS was, ███████████

███

███████████████, but they remained tactfully silent.

And so the dance would repeat itself, and repeat itself.

Headquarters sent another cable. They had just rendered another al-Qa'ida operative, and I was to be involved in the case. ███████████

███

███

███

███

███

███████████████. I did not know much about this new individual, but I was distressed. I was having trouble reconciling my assessment of CAPTUS with that which had underpinned his rendition. I suspected the new man was a victim of a similar operational zeal and lack of nuance. Be aggressive! Take them down! Go get 'em! But I also understood the position that our enemies were ruthless killers and that we had to act aggressively to destroy them. If in doubt, err on the side of protecting American lives before that of protecting foreigners' rights.

I tried to go myself for the documents but in the end could not; if I went, the CAPTUS operation stopped; no one could deal with liaison on this case

---

1 CAPTUS asked an insulting rhetorical question.

in my absence; the COS could not drop his other duties to fill in; I had other duties the COS needed me for; traveling would take me away for a full week.

In the next "interview" session, CAPTUS pointed out in irritation again, while Little Guy squirmed, ill at ease, that he would be able to answer my questions, if only I would show him the documents he knew I had. . . .

I returned to the office late that afternoon to write my day's reporting cables, angry at the absurdity of the situation. A TDY member of my team rode back with me. He was unaware of the long saga of the absent documents but sensed I was in a bad mood.

"What was wrong with the interrogation today?"

"Nothing. It's a long story."

I was atypically uncommunicative. The TDYer tried again.

"You all right?"

"Ehhh," I replied. The TDYer looked at me as I drove, thinking I had simply made an incomprehensible grunt.

"It's a language of purity," I said, glancing back. "Everything's fine."

Jack was working at the adjacent desk. After a short while of typing in uncharacteristic irritated silence, to Jack's initial glee but then distressed surprise, I positively exploded to him about our feckless incompetence. I leaned back in my chair, away from my computer.

"Jack, I am simply embarrassed, mortified, horrified, *ashamed*, even to see CAPTUS. How fucked up is that?! The interrogator afraid to see the detainee? Jesus Christ. I just know he thinks we're idiots, as well as kidnappers and torturers, which, of course, we are. I feel like some stupid son of a bitch standing clueless at a formal cocktail party, his fly down, wearing no underwear, and his dick hanging out. God*damnit*! We ██████ some sorry sucker and need *three or four months* to get the documents necessary for the interrogation to the officer conducting the interrogation? Did nobody think that maybe having CAPTUS's documents with him for the interrogation, or at least in the hands of someone who could use them, made a little bit of sense? What am I to tell liaison? They already suspect that we're interrogating some poor innocent sap and that we have no idea what we're doing, that we're typical, culturally clueless American clods, stumbling about beating up Arabs, but they tell themselves that we simply must have information we are not sharing with them, which is irritating to them in its own right—for otherwise, what the hell are we *doing*?! It is inconceivable to them that the CIA could be so fucked up. Thank God they think we're the Wizard of Oz and always know exactly what we're doing. The front line. The front line. We're the front line?! Good God."

Jack enjoyed my periodic little frustrated riffs, but he sympathized, too. I then told him, laughing at the absurd situation and my own characterization of it, that I consoled myself on such occasions with the wisdom of an earlier officemate, who also used to laugh at my expostulations: "Just remember, Glenn," he told me, "things can always get worse." We laughed, but I was still irate.

PROPITIATE THE GODS

Indeed, I am more afraid of our
own blunders than of the enemy's devices.

—Pericles

"They want to know your thoughts about sending CAPTUS to Hotel California."[1]

COS and I were listening to a TDYer, just arrived from Headquarters to serve on my CAPTUS team. By this point, the TDYer constituted my entire team. There were not enough officers worldwide to accomplish all the DO's missions and operations for the Global War on Terror. The resource demands on the DO to wage the War on Terror made it difficult to sustain an intense HVT interrogation like the CAPTUS case for the entire length of the interrogation. It was difficult to staff such long-term, ad hoc operations as the CAPTUS case; there were few officers to go around, and fewer still able or willing to leave their normal assignments, lives, and families for an indeterminate number of months.

The resource issue was real. I had also kept my COS and Headquarters informed of liaison's growing conviction that CAPTUS might not be the critical

---

1 "Hotel California" is a pseudonym I have given a CIA detention and interrogation facility where some of the most dangerous and sensitive HVTs were held. I have altered some details about it.

individual in al-Qa'ida that we had told them he was. Liaison had resource constraints, too. And I knew that I was progressively at odds with Wilmington and Headquarters. The thoughts and frustrations echoed in my head, long before the CIA Inspector General wrote them: "If a detainee did not respond to a question posed to him, the assumption at Headquarters was that the detainee was holding back and knew more; consequently, Headquarters recommended resumption of EITs [Enhanced Interrogation Techniques]." Finally, I knew that Wilmington and Headquarters would prefer to run the case without having to work through liaison and worry about how the case affected relations with them.

Hotel California! I had heard a couple of whispered, furtive allusions to Hotel California, but even in the DO few knew of it. Its name evoked the Hidden Hand and Dark Arts of our Global War on Terror. It was rumored that it was where the hard cases went. Hotel California was run from our Point Zero Station—itself a place of legend, deeply engaged in the Global War on Terror.[2] I knew of it at all only because I was running an HVT case. I perceived it as a place for the most recalcitrant, most dangerous of all terrorist cases. I saw no reason to send CAPTUS there. This was a disturbing development, although not a surprise. Nor was I surprised to learn of Headquarters' thoughts via a TDYer, rather than by cable. One always learned the ruminations and critical atmospheric information needed in the DO by one-on-one meetings. Cables tended to formalize decisions, but the issues were worked out as much as possible in conversation first.

"I don't mind pressuring CAPTUS," I said, as usual perched on the edge of a desk, one leg on the ground, the other hanging free. "I think liaison is getting a little tired. But they're okay. They're okay. Hotel California?" I shook my head in doubt and ill ease. "I dunno. I don't think so. No. He doesn't need to go there. To accomplish what? Screw him over? For what? He's talking. He's talking to me. The case is moving where it should. On the whole, we're getting what CAPTUS can provide—with some exceptions. But he's putting out. He is."

---

2   Point Zero Station is a pseudonym I have given for one of our overseas stations, deeply engaged in the Global War on Terror. I have changed some details about it.

Peter, the COS, sat silently at his desk, listening. The three of us were cramped into his tiny office, the door closed. There was barely enough room for us. Maps covered the wall behind me, haphazardly tacked up and overlapping with each other. He pondered our comments a moment, leaning back in his seat, relaxed but in command. No meeting lasted more than a few minutes with Peter. He expected a short description of the issue at hand, solicited relevant comments and divergent views, decided, and then dismissed us.

"Sounds like you're running out of time," Peter said, looking at me, his hands folded behind his head.

"If he goes to Hotel California, the case'll be put on ice, basically. It'll have to start over, but no one will be able to do it. No one will do it. Instead of an officer who knows the case, he'll rot. I want to run it here."

"Go to it," Peter replied. "You run it. But it sounds like you're running out of time."

"Yeah."

There was much behind the TDYer's relayed query about my thoughts on sending CAPTUS to Hotel California.

As the case had progressed, my cables had stated more and more clearly my growing conviction that CAPTUS was not what we had assessed him to be. My offline remarks, as always is the case, were even more frank: that we had de facto, as I started to state furtively but intensely with colleagues in one-on-one conversations, and then more openly, "got the wrong guy." We had rendered the man we wanted to render; we had gotten our target. What I meant was that our assessment of the information we had was wrong, that we had erroneously inflated CAPTUS's importance and role, and that CAPTUS was not the al-Qa'ida operative we had taken him to be. I had become convinced that CAPTUS ██ ██ ██ ██ ██ ██ ████████████████ was more like a train conductor who sells a criminal a ticket; to me, this did not make him complicit or part of the al-Qa'ida network.

I was running the interrogation team in the field. I had been running the case now for a substantial period of time. Almost always, the officer in the field knows the facts of a case, can see more clearly than Headquarters or anyone else involved. This was certainly the case now. I knew I had a better picture than Headquarters or our analysts, who never ran operations, did not meet with assets, and were not well-equipped on the whole to assess an asset's psychological and human motivations, and who, frankly, often were conceptually constricted by a worldview defined by cubicles filled with middle-class white guys, few of whom had lived many years abroad and who had the default perspective of Omaha or Des Moines. Good officers, and good Headquarters managers, always tried to defer to the field.

But this time, my assessment progressively challenged the underpinnings of one of the premier coups and cases in the administration's War on Terror.

██
██
██
██
██
██
██
██
██ .[3]

When a case goes wrong in the Directorate of Operations and outsiders learn about it, it is referred to as a "flap." My assessment of the case shattered a lot of presumptions and erroneous decisions. No one wanted a flap.

I informed Headquarters a number of times over the succeeding weeks, orally via the returning TDYer and in my operational cables, that I believed the best way to run the CAPTUS interrogation was as it was being run, and that I did not see merit in sending him, at this time, to Hotel California. This was all conducted collegially, in the way that issues are addressed in the DO. Headquarters acquiesced, but I knew that it did not agree with my approach.

---

3 The deleted passage concerns my assessment of why Headquarters would persist in its conceptual and operational errors in the CAPTUS case. The passage is acidic. This is the only reason I can see why it would be redacted, for it reveals no source or method—other than contemptible institutional incompetence.

More than anything, CAPTUS was now caught in the bureaucratic dynamic I had experienced countless times before as a case officer: Once the institution settles on a perspective and a course of action, it interprets other views as proofs of error. Critical thought degenerates into rigid orthodoxy. If the premises and perspective are correct, all is well, and the system checks the excesses of officers who are inexperienced, or biased, or simply wrong. Any institution must have accepted views and practices. No institution can function like a college seminar, subjecting all issues to endless rumination. But the dominant paradigm will reject any challenge and becomes blind to error.

One risks excommunication to challenge orthodoxy, even if it maintains that the sun revolves around the earth, or that we must sacrifice humans to propitiate the gods, or, well, or that men are not quite what we believed.

YOU WILL BE TAKEN TO A
MUCH, MUCH NASTIER PLACE

All may be well; but if God sort it so,
'Tis more than we deserve, or I expect.
—Shakespeare, *Richard III*, II.iii.27

"My masters believe that CAPTUS continues to withhold critical information. So I am going to raise the stakes today."

As usual, Little Guy and I stood talking in the dark, run-down hallway outside CAPTUS's interrogation room. My interrogation team colleagues sat in the holding room a few feet away, but I tended to prefer to speak to Little Guy or Big Guy one-on-one. Direct discussions are always more frank and efficient than group meetings. In any event, my teammates knew what I planned to do. Little Guy listened intently, tightening his eyes a little as I spoke, assessing the likely consequences of my planned action, and trying to gauge my true objectives. Big Guy stood mute, as usual willing to take the Little Guy's or my lead, a satisfied expression on his face.

"You think he has information he has refused to tell us, but can? Raise the stakes?" Little Guy was serious, reflective, and, I thought, dubious. He turned a cigarette end over end in his fingers as we spoke.

"My Headquarters believes so. I think so," I replied, fully sharing Little Guy's skepticism, but trying not to show it. *"Inshallah"*—God willing—"he will speak today as he needs to."

"Yes, *inshallah*," he said. Big Guy idled off to one side, once again plucking a nose hair with a sudden, shameless jerk of his hand. Little Guy stepped outside for a smoke before we entered the interrogation room to face CAPTUS once again.

Physical coercion—torture—has nothing to do with a useful interrogation. Torture is simple, crude, obtuse, and immoral, and does not work. It is patently stupid, an offense to any understanding of how a mind works, independent of its illegality and barbarity, independent of how it corrodes the principles the CIA is sworn to protect and U.S. society defines itself as embodying. Torture is more a projection of an individual's or a state's arrogant, self-absorbed sense of power, and sometimes a symptom of fear, than a meaningful tool to extract good information. Legal casuistry can assert that torture is a vague term, that there is ample leeway for a host of "coercive measures," and that a moment of grave national danger justifies taking whatever measures are necessary for the national defense. In fact, there is almost no circumstance that justifies inflicting severe and lasting physical pain on someone to extract information, while basing a general practice and legal framework to authorize torture, call it what one will, upon the most extreme, unlikely case—the "ticking bomb" scenario—saps the foundation of our legal system. Such sophistry can justify any act for reasons of national expediency and urgency, erodes the foundation of the law, and attributes lasting power to those supposed to exercise momentary authority. We have seen liberties wither this way in other times, and other places.

A good interrogation, like a good "development" (cultivation) of a target individual by a case officer—like all good lies—should rest upon as much of the truth as possible. A good interrogation, or a good developmental operation, is like a successful seduction: You tell the truth, the part of the truth that serves your own ends. ███████████████████████████████████

██

██

██
██
██
██

██████████████████. But you tell him the truth you create—for there are many truths for every fact, and reality can be described to appear as you wish it, while it recedes and is lost amidst the glittering facets of varying perspectives and purposely obscured ends.

From the first, I had tried to make CAPTUS understand that I was his best, his only hope. Only I would listen to him. I was his only friend. This was largely true. ██████████████████████████████████████
██
██
██
██
██
██
██
██████.

██
██
██
██
██
██
██
████████████████████████████████.[1]

---

1 The redacted passages above detail my assessment of how to conduct a successful interrogation. The KUBARK manual notes, in this regard, that "the initial question which a 'questioner' asks himself should be, 'how can I make him want to tell me what he knows?' rather than 'how can I trap him into telling me what he knows?' . . . The assumption of hostility, or the assumption of pressure tactics . . . may make a subject resistant who would have responded to recognition of individuality and an initial assumption of good will."

Today would be different, however. Pressing CAPTUS hard was the best I could do for him now, and for us all.

CAPTUS sat motionless in his salmon suit and, as always, focused on me as I entered, as though only he and I were in the room together. The air was, as always, close, stale, a little too hot and humid. I started my harangue without any preliminary, wanting to shock him and make him understand how important it was for him to answer my questions *now*.

███
██.

██
██
██
██
██
██████████████████████████████.

"We do not have much time," I told him. I spoke earnestly, intensely, leaning toward him, on my knees, locking my eyes on his.

"█████████████████████████████. The situation is changing. █████████
██
██
██
██
██
██
██
██."

I paused and spoke much more softly now, but with complete intensity.

"███
██
██
██
██
██

███
██ ."

██
██
███ .

" ██
██
██ ."

" ███
███
███
██ ."

CAPTUS spoke, but I dismissed his comment. Now he needed to listen. I would allow no exchange at that moment.

" ███
███
███
████████████████████████ ."

██
██
██
██
████████████████████████████████████ .[2]

██
██ .

I left the room, CAPTUS sitting with his eyes cast down, his fingers white from clasping his hands together so hard. Little Guy said nothing to me in the hallway. He could tell I was angry. He was subdued. He compulsively lit a cigarette and found it calming. He remained standing, slightly awkward.

---

2 The redacted passages above describe how I "raised the stakes," as I had put it to Little Guy, the last effort I could make before the case would take a dramatic turn for the worse.

Everyone stayed away from me, sensing my mood. I went to the toilet, just to be alone for a few minutes. It was old. A drip from the hot water faucet had left a brown stain on the enamel of the sink. I sat on the toilet seat, fully dressed, thankful to be out of sight, slowly calming down. After two or three minutes I stood and leaned over the sink a moment, a hand on each side. I cupped water in my hands and wet my face. It was cool and fresh after the stale and close air of the interrogation room. I stared at myself in the mirror over the sink and then looked away, not wanting to think about anything.

GROWN WEARY TOO SOON

*Great efforts were made to hush up for a little
while longer the true facts. . . . But talking about
other people's affairs is so indispensable an occupation
that such efforts are commonly of little avail.*
—Lady Murasaki, *The Tale of Genji*

When I got back to my hotel from this latest difficult session with CAPTUS, I ran my normal four miles through the typically acrid, sickly sweet air and fumes of the city, showered, and ate in the hotel lounge, while reading a book and listening to the live band. My lounge mates were the typical smattering of drunken businessmen on the make, European tourists, locals out on the town, and young but slightly worn hookers. After my dinner, I walked out to the hotel parking lot to my car. Two rather shabby young women with hungry, worn expressions followed me out from the lounge. They were in their early twenties, thin, nice figures, but graceless and tired. I had not seen them in the lounge before; new girls looking to make a buck. They caught up to me as I was about to put the key in the lock, their high heels clicking on the pavement. The homelier of the two placed her hand on the door handle of my car, fixed me with what she wanted to be a sultry look, and asked, "Would you like us to come to dinner, yes?"

The prettier girl spoke no English at all. She smiled hopefully but stood awkwardly, not knowing what to do with her hands, as her companion placed herself between my car and me.

"I will speak for you, for her. We can, she can . . . be with you, if you want. Me, too, but I will speak for her, if you want, at dinner, and . . . after."

I stared, a little taken aback, at what struck me as a slightly bizarre and desperate proposal.

"No." But I did not say it harshly and I tried to convey empathy; they seemed abashed, hard maybe from experience, but at heart young girls, really. It was sad; I was touched. The girl repeated her offer, thinking perhaps that I had not understood, but they left me alone, momentarily embarrassed, once they realized that I knew what they were saying and still refused. I watched them walk back to the lounge to hope for, or at least to pursue, a successful mark later that evening, their heels clicking and their hips swaying now with attractive naturalness. They came to me artificially brash prostitutes; they left me once again two vulnerable young women sustaining each other's confidence. Thereafter, we smiled at each other across the lounge each night when I arrived there from work.

Later that evening I returned to the lounge to read, sitting as far toward the back wall as I could (this is a reflex practice for a case officer; you always want to have everyone in your sight). I was the only one there, ever, reading a book.

The regular waitress, who had come to know me after weeks of the same routine, spoke to me after taking my order. This was unusual. *The locals are assertive tonight; the natives are restless,* I thought.

"We all say that you are 'the spy,' you know."

"You do? Why?"

"You are American. ████████████████████████. You sit alone every night. What else would you be?"

One got used to this in the Agency. ████████████████ we called it playing "spot the spook."

"You think I'm a spy because I sit alone here?" I suppressed a smile. "No, I'm here for the waters."

She looked at me, uncomprehending.

"I read after dinner. I like the music. It's true." I returned to my book, Lucretius's *On the Nature of Things*. The waitress left me alone.

I enjoyed listening to the band each night, watching the hookers chat up the businessmen, who told themselves that the tired women were actually interested in what they had to say, and the enthusiastic tourists struggling with the menu and speaking too loudly, to make themselves understood by the natives. Other nights I went to a bar where men sat in small groups, smoking from a common *cheicha*, their several tubes bending out from the multicolored instruments on a low coffee table before them, sweet smoke scent filling the air. I liked being alone in the crowd, a sentiment I felt throughout my career, wherever I was: the man on the margins, observing the rituals and routines of daily lives.

As far as the CAPTUS case was concerned, however, I was the man in the middle and on the spot. ██████████████████████████████ ████████████████████████████████████. I could see that he was doomed no matter what he did or what I reported.

Bid me bear all toil,
And keep me awake at work through cloudless nights
Seeking not only words but verses, too,
To be bright shining lights before your mind,
That you may see deep into hidden truth.

I put my book down. The music pulsed below me.

██
████████████████████████. I thought of the old DO saw that CTC—the Counter-Terrorism Center, to whom I was reporting on the case—stood for "Check That Cable." CTC had always been a bit of the Island of Misfit Toys in the DO; officers who had had some problem or were relatively poor performers often landed in CTC. It was considered a second-rate division. Then, 9/11 occurred, and CTC immediately found itself the star of the show, the center of attention, overwhelmed with additional resources. ("What are we going to *do* with them all?" was a regular refrain among Agency officers, when the stock solution to the "failures" and "problems" of the Agency in the pursuit

of terrorists was to provide "50 percent more collectors, and 50 percent more analysts." Colleagues and I often responded to this increase in resources by noting that "more was not better. Better was better." But this was a cynic's—"old guard's"—view, unable to oppose momentary political realities.)

The CAPTUS case, as I had come to know it while running it, was shaping up in my mind more and more as a major-league screw-up ▮▮▮▮▮▮▮▮▮▮ ▮▮▮. Yet, many officers had followed his life for years; I hesitated still to dismiss their views as fundamentally wrong. I still wondered, after all the time I had spent with him, if I had not yet grasped the subtleties of the case, which perhaps my colleagues who had specialized on CAPTUS saw in a way that I could not.

Perversely, just as CAPTUS had convinced me that he was, more or less innocently, caught in the middle of the Global War on Terror, the same routine nature of much of the information he provided me had convinced Headquarters that he was dissembling.

But I knew that this was a rationalization. I knew the man. I knew ops. I knew my business. I knew this case. ▮▮▮▮▮▮▮▮▮▮▮▮▮▮▮▮▮▮▮▮▮ ▮▮▮ ▮▮▮▮▮▮▮▮▮▮▮▮▮▮▮▮▮. I knew—I *knew*—I was right, but I was not prepared quite yet to go to the mat about it. ▮▮▮▮▮▮▮▮▮▮▮ ▮▮▮ ▮▮▮▮▮▮▮▮▮▮▮▮▮. And I knew that a formal, collective position was hard to change and that individual or piecemeal criticisms were almost always outweighed by collective inertia and the settled position of the institution.

I sat listening to the music, watching the tired hookers convince the fleshy and pale visiting businessmen that they were sexually iridescent, or at least for the having. Mostly, though, I mulled what to do about CAPTUS, and how to meet what I considered Headquarters' impossible "guidance."

But if the heart's not whole, what struggles then, what dangers must engulf us against our will?

My choices were to run the case as well as one could run it, or to try to challenge the entire case. I knew how that would work out. I would be removed from the case. I would be characterized as a troublemaker—and CAPTUS would be handled by someone who did not question the approach to interrogation that had been authorized, or the foundations of the case ████████

██

██

██

████████████████████████████████. The case would continue, from inertia. ██████
████████████████████████████████. Better this than to have to come to grips with error, delusion, misinterpretation, and group-think. And groups could   not   recognize   group-think.   ████████████████████████

██

██

██

████████████████████████████.

No, malcontents in the DO almost never accomplished anything but destroy themselves. And yet, this was how one proceeded in DO culture for a *normal* operation; our counterterrorism war had changed many rules, and the stakes and our responsibilities had become even greater.

The only way to achieve anything was to work within the system, which of course raised the issues I frequently weighed: When did it become my duty to say no? At what point did doing the best job I could, in the most honorable, legal, and effective way I could, cause me to traduce my oaths and obligations "to the flag" that I served, as Wilmington had so acidly put it when he and I had our tense exchange? I was determined to run the case as well as I could; this was my involvement in our efforts to destroy al-Qa'ida ████████████

██

████████████████████████████████. I would be hard, if I needed to be, while acting honorably. I had been. I did not want to let a terrorist avoid capture or elimination by misplaced tenderness. I had pursued this career to be challenged mentally, physically, and morally. Well, here was the supreme challenge of my career, a responsibility fraught with ambiguity about what was the right course.

The thing we want but don't possess seems far the best; we get it, and beg for something else. . . .

The two hookers who had approached me in the hotel parking lot were sitting down by the band, momentarily alone, looking vaguely forlorn. They stared across the lounge, eyes vacant. They were struggling to remain themselves while, with some visible discomfort, they made the compromises they had to make to get through sometimes callous nights. I watched them for a while, pensive, wondering how deeply they felt, how self-aware they were, feeling compassion for two young girls grown weary too soon.

THE ELEGANT WALK-IN

Inconsistencies cannot both be right;
but, imputed to man, they may both be true.

—Samuel Johnson, *Rasselas*

"The COS wants to see you right away."

I stopped typing, looked at Jack, and followed the COS's secretary across the cramped common room to the other side of the station, into the COS's own cramped office. The CIA is always given the shit spaces in our facilities overseas. I've always thought that this is because allocating work spaces is one of the rare instances ██ ██. Dilapidated and cramped quarters had long since taken on a charm for me. Spacious and nice offices seemed somehow too easy, not *real* enough; surely an emotional legacy, too, of my years living in unheated and moldy garrets above transvestite bars in Paris, while classmates were forging their way up the corporate ladder in Manhattan.

Peter, the COS, had me close the door. Josh, my colleague in the station who had entertained us with nearly unbelievable tales of personal disaster and survival over dinner one night, was in the office with us. He looked serious, slightly high-strung.

"There is a walk-in. I'd like you to take it with Josh."

It was a little unusual for two officers to take a walk-in, but I was the most experienced officer in the station, and Peter had come to trust my judgment, while Josh was very talented, but relatively new to the C/O world. This would be his first walk-in.

"What do we know about him? What's he say he wants to tell us?"

"He says that he has 'important, sensitive information' he wants to tell to 'the appropriate authorities.' That's you. That's all we know. You know the drill. Find out what he has to say. Listen. Offer nothing. Come see me when you're done."

"Okay."

Josh and I left Peter's office and made our way to meet the walk-in.

This was interesting. A walk-in was someone who had come to the office and claimed to have confidential, intelligence-related information. Handling them was, initially, easier than doing developmental work, because a walk-in sought to convey information to the United States, whereas standard operational work was much more circuitous and duplicitous. This would require assessment and good operational skills, but some of the cards at least were on the table from the get-go.

The walk-in was sitting in a holding room, waiting to tell his story. Josh and I would hear and draw him out, to start to vet whether he was legitimate, had information that merited follow-on contact, or was a provocation sent by a hostile service (which could be virtually any foreign service; friends do not exist in foreign relations or in intelligence; there are only moments or phases of shared interests). We also would assess whether he might be one of the large number of nutcases who range from embassy to embassy, peddling delusions and living in a mental netherworld; or whether he was one of the equally large number of hustlers on the make, incredibly trying to scam the CIA and lie his way to some CIA money; or whether he might be one of the also surprising number of off-kilter thrill seekers, who are titillated by touching, if only for a moment, the world of intelligence. Most walk-ins knew less than they imagined, or claimed. Once in a while, though, a walk-in could actually have critical information.

"My name is Cliff," I told the walk-in as he rose from a sofa to meet me in a windowless room in our building, this one with generic wall hangings of pleasant scenes of bucolic America, and furnishings like the lounge in a 1960s dentist's office. I often amused myself by using the throwaway alias "Cliff." Cliff Leach was one of my best friends and my former college roommate. He knew where I worked, though not what I did. For years I had mildly teased him that were he ever detained by a mustachioed foreign customs official and taken to a back room for questioning, he could thank me, but that of course I would deny any knowledge of a Cliff Leach, of any conceivable reason his name might have come to the attention of foreign intelligence services, or that this event had anything to do with me whatsoever. Josh also introduced himself with a throwaway alias.

The man in front of us ████████████████████████████████████
██
██
handed me his card and sat down again, crossing his legs with easy confidence. His clothing and entire bearing were elegant.

"We understand that you have an important reason for coming to meet with us," I began directly.

"Of course. I thank you for meeting with me in such an unusual way," the man said.

The walk-in described his background, speaking with poise and quiet authority. He enunciated his words with care. He dropped many names of prominent individuals with whom he claimed to have worked.

I turned to the business at hand.

"Tell us why you have asked to see us. What do you think we need to know, or would be interested in knowing? Why have you approached us here, now?"

For the first time, he acted slightly self-important, diffident.

"I want you to know that I oppose all that America is doing ████████
██
████████████. I dislike what your government is doing. But I cannot in good conscience keep this information to myself. I feel obliged to share this information with the Americans—with you. ████████████████████████████████

███

███ ."

"I don't want anyone to die, when I have perhaps the means of saving his life. This is true even of those who are not Muslim, even if I disagree with your country's policies. ██████████████████████████████████ . So, I am here."

I had been focused for many weeks on my work with CAPTUS and my team, with keeping our liaison partners happy, reporting the intelligence CAPTUS provided, meeting Headquarters' requirements and demands, and trying to convince them to amend their view of CAPTUS's role in the al-Qa'ida network. But the buildup to war with Iraq was in full swing elsewhere in the world, and drew the world's attention. It was obvious to everyone, inside the Agency and throughout the world, that we were going to invade Iraq, whatever the administration claimed, or whatever it said at the United Nations. The impending invasion came up in casual conversations with locals and foreigners all the time, the moment they learned that one was an American official.

"███

███

██████████████████████████████████ ."

The elegant walk-in provided information about the activities of individuals planning to harm official Americans in the Middle East that, if true, could save the lives of many of our fellow citizens.

I asked the walk-in to provide additional details about how he had learned this information. He did so.

Josh and I pressed him to substantiate what he was alleging.

"This is highly precise information, and few men can possibly know it."

He was not at all ruffled by our skepticism and he explained how he knew the information.

"This is how I can know, and do know," he explained, reviewing how he had come to know of this threat information. "Now, I am here, telling you."

The other walk-ins I had handled in my career had been a scruffier, more desperate bunch. ████████████████████████████████████

███

▐███████████████████████████████████████▌.

This man was poised and confident. He spoke in logical paragraphs without need of any assistance.

What he told us was dramatic information, if at all true. Most walk-ins claim to possess much more mundane information. This elegant man could possibly save many hundreds of American lives and prove of vital importance to our military planners. A successful officer might encounter one such case in a thirty-year career—*if* what he was telling me was true.

The meeting lasted about an hour. I listened throughout with interest, but was cool and noncommittal.

Peter was interested in Josh's and my briefing of the walk-in's claims, of course, but he was even more noncommittal than I had been to the walk-in himself.

"He dropped a lot of names," Peter said, clearly skeptical. "I think he's making a lot of unlikely claims."

However, for several years just prior to my involvement with CAPTUS I had been deeply involved in the issues the walk-in described.

"No, not really, Peter," I said. "I worked this stuff. The events and individuals he cites check out. I know of some of the events. I don't know him, but the events he describes correspond to events as I remember them."

Peter raised his eyebrows, impressed both with the elegant walk-in, whose plausibility I had just significantly bolstered, and with me, for having known these issues.

"Okay. Well, let's see. Write it up. Let's check out this guy's bona fides."

We began an urgent effort to verify what the man had told us, to determine whether he was who he claimed to be and could know what he claimed to know. We had to decide whether he was a provocation or a "dangle" to confuse U.S. intelligence authorities.

The man had told us that he would be back in the city where I was working ███████████████████████, but had business elsewhere in the world meantime. Josh and I wrote "IMMEDIATE ACTION" cables late into the night after his departure from the embassy ████████████████████████

▐███████████████████████████████████████▌

███

███

███

██. Stan-
dard procedure, I also had him thoroughly traced—his background investigated in our files and in the files of trusted liaison partners from a number
of countries.

We found that everything he had told me about himself checked out. He
was who he said he was, and did what he said he did. He had the access to
places and people ██████████ he had claimed. We could verify that he knew
some of the people he claimed to know ███████████████████████

███

███

███

███

███

███

██████. But what about the claims he had made? I did not know.

THERE IS NO WAY
THROUGH THIS

Me: "Dad, when will we get there?"
Dad: "It's just over the next hill."
Me: "There are no hills."
Pause.
Me: "Mom, when will we get there?"
Mom: "We'll be there in no time."
Me: "There can't be no time."

Josh and I were scheduled to meet the elegant walk-in again ██████ ███████████. I continued my normal work on the CAPTUS case.

My wife, Sally, and my kids, Spencer and Margaux, had no idea where in the world I was. I had not spoken with them, or heard from them, in many weeks. They thought I might be in France, because I had told them as I left Washington that I was flying to Paris. This was true—it is always best to lie by telling the truth. But, of course, from Paris I flew on, and on, and on.

I hoped that Sally was coping all right, and not too tired from having to carry all the load of parenting alone. She had been doing better, little by little. I did not know what to do to help much of the time, but in any event, I was now on the other side of the earth and could do nothing. I had no news of them whatsoever. I arranged to send them a letter from time to time, nonetheless, without saying where I was. I wrote about one of my escapes out of the city. Unmentioned, of course, was even the slightest allusion to CAPTUS, assassins, walk-ins, or my veiled disputes with a narrow-minded and duty-bound Headquarters.

The muezzin called to prayer over the noise of the medina, his voice a wavering and nasal trill wafting above the alleyways. . . .

Later, a man with two camels approached me, yet another hustler. I told him I wasn't interested. "But, why are you in a hurry? We have a saying: 'Men in a hurry are already dead.'"

I drove in the desert this afternoon. To keep myself company, I started to sing all the songs I sing to you guys at bedtime, in particular "Edelweiss," "When Johnny Comes Marching Home," and "Take Me Out to the Ballgame." This made me think of you and made me miss you, sad for a moment that I was here, driving through the desert alone, instead of singing bedtime songs to you. . . .

These are unusual, demanding times. You know that I am here on short notice, for what will turn out to be months. I'm using the desk of an officer who was sent on a special assignment for six months. Yesterday, one of my colleagues left for thirty days, just as I have been called here. Other TDYers are coming and going all the time. The public sees a few headlines, that is all, but we are all working very hard. An unusual time. The families affected by all these urgent assignments are called on to work hard, too. So, hang in there. You are helping our country, too, by filling in while I am away, and we can all feel proud. This is our time to serve, as did Granddad Martin in the RAF and as did Grampa Carle in the Marines. It is making a difference!

I did not put in the letter that the ever-present swarm of children had started to hound me the moment I descended from my car, and were trailing me even during my brief exchange with the man with two camels. The urchins pleaded for *zakat*—alms—arms extended, palms up, practiced forlorn expressions knitting their brows. This endless begging had at first struck me as simply a normal part of a Third World landscape. As a Westerner, I was an irresistible mark. I had encountered clouds of young beggars everywhere in the Third World.

I kept walking, as one must to avoid being overwhelmed, one amidst millions. But they had come to irritate me now. Enough. I stopped to engage them, to amuse myself with a characteristic, small act of sardonic subversion, a refusal to submit, even in the knowledge it was futile.

"Listen. Put your hands down. You want to grow up to be good, strong men, don't you?"

They were surprised that I was paying them any attention. My question challenged them. They became momentarily respectful.

"Yes."

"Then you must never beg," I said. "You can never be a man if you beg."

They stared at me, silent for a moment, then let me walk off, disappointed that I had given no *zakat* and mildly alarmed at my non sequitur. But I was exasperated that one of the admirable pillars of the faith—*zakat*—charity, had degenerated into pervasive begging. All the scholarly explanations for the poverty, fatalism, and lack of opportunity that surrounded me, true as they were, felt bloodless and insubstantial after having been beset week after week by endless numbers of grimy and street-smart twelve-year-olds manipulating my sympathy for money.

I entered a small café-restaurant for lunch but was obliged to go to the back, up a stairway, to a small room with a window looking out onto an empty, walled-in deck. For weeks, during Ramadan, my non-Muslim colleagues and I had to eat our lunches out of anyone's sight, to avoid an incident. The restaurateur was polite and apologetic. I told him I understood, but still I had been put in my place. I started to resent that I was obliged to eat in back rooms, out of sight, for a faith that was not mine, because others decided that my beliefs, or their lack of, made my practices unacceptable, or an offense to morality.

Nigeria had arranged to host the Miss World pageant at the same time I was dealing with the elegant walk-in. But Nigeria and its pageant were far,

far away from where I was, physically and mentally. It was incongruous that the pageant came to my attention at all, given my current concerns, but it appeared to offer a disturbing insight to the issues the attacks of 9/11, and our ensuing counterterrorism responses, had brought to the public's attention.

Nigeria has long suffered from north-south tensions, violence between ethnic groups in the north that are Muslim and the politically dominant Christian south. Disputes over allocation of oil revenues are involved. Tribal and ethnic rivalries are involved. The artificial and arbitrary borders drawn by distant colonial masters are involved. And Muslim-Christian tensions are involved. Samuel Huntington and other geo-strategists have pointed to Nigeria as the western end of the many-thousand-mile "Arc of Conflict" between Muslims and non-Muslims, which cuts Africa, the Middle East, and Asia in half, running along the zone where the Muslim-Arab world rubs against the Christian and Animist world. From Muslim northern Nigeria clashing with the Christian and Animist south, to Muslim north Sudan clashing with Christian and Animist south Sudan, north-south, Muslim-Christian, ethnic strife had been endless, and violent. Huntington's argument about a "clash of civilizations" was powerful, with few equally compelling descriptions of broad trends in global political dynamics (although, like almost all holistic explanations of events, it tended to err by underemphasizing specific regional and cultural particularities). The State Department, the CIA, and the Department of Defense had all long paid close attention to the explosive religious and ethnic tensions in Nigeria.

The Nigerian government sought to host the pageant precisely to showcase the country's modernism and its move away from being a corrupt, violent, Third World backwater, defined by religious, ethnic, and colonial divisions. A female journalist in a prominent daily in Lagos wrote an editorial in the run-up to the pageant, praising the poise and accomplishments of the contestants, implying that they were fine representatives of opportunity and progress, and then commenting lightly, and positively, that the women were so accomplished that surely Muhamad would wish to marry one of them, were he still alive.

Ludicrously, but lethally, the Muslim leaders in the north of Nigeria angrily denounced this as a blasphemous slander of the Last Prophet, outrageously perpetrated by an infidel, and a woman to boot. At this point thousands of Muslims promptly took to the streets and public spaces in the north and along border areas with the Christian and Animist south, seized several hundred Christians, placed tires around their necks, doused them with gasoline, and burned them alive. In this way, they defended Muhamad's honor and the peaceful purity of Islam.

I learned of these awful acts of zealotry and ignorance within a day or two of Josh's and my meeting with the elegant walk-in, during my latest solitary excursion out of the city. I had spent the night in a hotel and after breakfast approached the prim and decorous middle-aged matron at the reception desk to check out. She looked like someone my grandmother used to have to the house for tea after the Sunday sermon when I was growing up forty-five years before.

"S'bah al-hair," I said. Good morning.

"S'bah al-Nur," she replied. Good morning.

She helped me change money, mail a letter, pay my bill. I turned the conversation to the news about the riots and death in Nigeria. The receptionist had not heard. I explained the terrible events and described the editorial that had catalyzed the rioting, characterizing it as "moderate, innocuous, even positive about Muhamad."

"Can you imagine killing people for that?" I remarked. "Can you imagine that over two hundred people have been burned alive, gasoline thrown on them, then set on fire, or have had their throats slit in Nigeria because of a beauty contest? It's frightening."

I admit I was probing to see what her reaction would be. The other people with whom I had raised the topic all had retreated into what I had experienced as the standard Islamic-totalitarian-cultural torpor and orthodox, unthinking responses or they feigned ignorance; or they were ignorant of the events; or they evaded expressing an opinion, instead replying in non sequiturs about the weather or the cultural richness of Islam.

The receptionist, though, swallowed the bait.

"Oh, I don't know. That's not good, to say that. You have to respect our religion."

She had become rigid, disappointing me with her small-mindedness and, it seemed to me, controlling her rising anger.

The Muslims I spoke with never ceased proclaiming, with some vehemence, how tolerant Islam is and how "Western media" were running an "orchestrated campaign" to besmirch it. "Islam means peace!" they told me over and over. I had heard the claims of tolerance made in response to bombings, assassinations, and riots, but had yet to observe any Muslim demonstrations *against* such violence. Yet, I had not anticipated that the receptionist would blaze up from what I imagined was an event that we would both lament and leave it at that.

I repeated, taken aback, that the supposedly incendiary remark was good-natured, even positive in its characterization of Muhamad, and that even had it not been it was astounding and wrong, "based on a remark, for people to go out and burn other people alive in the name of 'faith' and 'peace.'"

The receptionist was having none of it, and the conversation started to spin beyond my intention to elicit a response, but not get into a heated argument. She found any reasoning or discussion on the issue to be itself blasphemous and it just added to her anger. She searched momentarily for some way out. She did not wish to be impolite, or to argue with a foreign client. She pursed her lips and stepped back slightly from the counter. But there was nothing to discuss. Her eyes dilated a little.

"Those people should respect our religion. It is not right not to respect and follow our culture. That is wrong."

Her take on her religion was to sanction burning people alive with gasoline because some non-Muslims wanted to admire pretty girls, and because one writer said the women were so impressive that Muhamad would probably want to marry one.

I remarked that I could understand disapproving of something, but "surely one could not kill people who thought differently, over a *beauty contest?*"

"What they [the people supporting or organizing the beauty contest] did was"—she searched for a word—"wrong." She clearly wanted to say "immoral." "They must respect our religion and culture."

Foolish, or refusing to let someone implicitly sanction burning people alive, I persisted. "But you can't kill people for acting in some way you don't agree with. Suppose the non-Muslims said it was an outrage for men, especially men in clerical robes, to wear beards? And that people must kill them unless they shaved their beards off? That's no different than killing people for watching a beauty contest. No one may do that. One religion can't force its views and practices on the entire society. That's not right, and it's frightening."

The receptionist was heated up, struggling to remain under control, but unable to agree to such outrageous statements, so offensive to Islam.

"They should not ignore Islam. Of course people became angry. That was *wrong* to . . . not to listen or respect Islam. They were . . . they do not respect our customs."

Finally I bit my tongue. I had offended her, when I had intended to learn her thoughts on what I imagined to be a common tragedy. Then I had sought to reason and found myself arguing a matter of faith, where argument was futile and positions immediately polarized. For her, the journalist's article and her client's rudeness became secondary, and justified violence against people who had nothing to do with the incident and who did not share her faith. There was nothing to discuss. Whatever differed from revealed Truth justified, well, murder.

The exchange made me suddenly miss my wife, because unlike the receptionist she always tried to think for herself. Sally believed that the way to "get on" in life, as she would put it, required subjecting every opinion to challenge, from whatever authority it came.

I changed the subject. I asked for help packing some trinkets I had bought. The receptionist called a busboy to come over. She forced a smile and started to change money for another hotel guest.

"*Choukran*," I said to her. Thank you. She nodded coldly.

The receptionist had depressed and alarmed me. I walked out to my car, musing that tolerance is so often viewed as a betrayal of principle. Multifaceted truth breaks into pieces against the hard certainties of true believers and conventional minds, whether Nigerian "necklacers," hard-eyed, middle-aged Muslim matrons, or unthinking bureaucracies and their executors, willing to destroy men in misguided pursuit of abstract objectives.

Yet tolerance can betray itself. It comforted the West's own "right thinking" to imagine that the jihadists were fringe extremists, who had perverted mainstream currents of Islam. Condemning individual acts is easy and avoids the explosive—perhaps insoluble—social dilemmas that come from rational analysis and open discourse about any faith. Condemning jihadists avoids passing judgment about beliefs. But tolerance, which is fundamental for a diverse society that prizes inquiry, can have the by-product of intellectual and moral relativism, which dulls thought and creates its own taboos against critical analysis of the implications of any belief.

The very concept of civil society is incompatible with a totalitarian religion. But if the jihadists represented a distilled version of broadly shared beliefs, if men burned blasphemers alive, if bearded bombers were the champions of a prim matron's faith, then one was confronted with the awkward, the perilous, obligation to acknowledge that some religious or philosophical views were incompatible and irreconcilable with the fundamental liberal values of Western civilization.

I was disheartened, at having provoked an argument, at the receptionist's intolerance and anger, and because I could see no way to find common ground with her—with anyone. I stood at my car and looked absently around me, back at the hotel. I searched my pocket for the key.

I headed back to the capital from my trip, driving all day along largely empty roads. I was in a good mood, the air was clear, and I kept myself company by singing wistful, even philosophical tunes my father used to sing, like "The Wayfaring Stranger" and "Johnny, We Hardly Knew Ye":

> While goin' the road to sweet Athy, a-roo, a-roo
> While goin' the road to sweet Athy, a-roo, a-roo . . .
> With your drums and guns and guns and drums
> The enemy nearly slew ye
> My darling dear, Ye look so queer
> Johnny I hardly knew ye.

The sky loomed clouded and dark on the road ahead as night fell. I drove into the clouds. Fog covered the road and obscured my view; rain began to fall. The rain became heavier. I had to turn the windshield wipers on high, but it was still hard to see ahead through the rain on the windshield. The rain became so hard it made clouds as it bounced off the road. It grew so incredibly heavy and pounded so hard on the windshield, it fell so thickly, that I could not see the road. I slowed down to barely ten miles per hour and moved over to the edge of the road. My headlights lit nothing, the light dissipating into the black void ahead. The rain was astounding, disorienting; it blocked all vision. I could not see anything. The windshield was a rushing blur of water. Suddenly, a couple of miles straight ahead, colossal lightning bolts started to explode, their tentacles filling almost half the sky. I was driving right toward them. They left red afterimages on my retinas, which pulsed before my eyes in the dark as I blinked, only to be flashed over by the next lightning bolts, and replaced with new afterimages of red, tentacled lightning bolts inside my eyes.

It started to hail, pea-size hailstones panging, then machine-gunning, then smashing the hood, windshield, and roof. The rattle and smashing were deafening, disorienting. The lightning bolts started to explode directly ahead, now very close and approaching me as I felt my way forward on the side of the road. There were no headlights or cars in either direction. I was completely alone in this extraordinary maelstrom. I had never been in a storm like this in my life, suddenly come out of nowhere. The lightning bolts' explosions thundered through the car, totally drowning the sound of the car's motor, and the clattering bashes of the rain and the hail. I didn't want to drive into the colossal lightning, striking directly in front of me, and I didn't want to pull over and try to sit out the storm; I thought it unwise to stop in such violent chaos.

There is no way through this, I thought. I decided I had to continue on, somehow to drive through the storm, but I was able to only crawl forward. It was pitch black outside now, except for the cloud of bouncing rain lit in my headlights, glimpsed through the wildly waving windshield wipers. I could not even make out the road ahead.

"Oh, my God!" I gasped as the sky suddenly blasted in a sharp, cracking thunderclap, the detonation rocking the car, all the car windows filling with a blinding burst of white light. A lightning bolt jagged down into a tree directly to my right, not thirty feet from me. The tree threw up a huge gush of sparks and blew up, splitting into pieces, and shooting brilliant white fireworks in

every direction—up into the air, out toward the car, down to bounce off the
ground. The flash blinded me, then total darkness replaced the painful blast
of white light.

I kept on, the destroyed tree falling behind, lost in the darkness and turmoil, my unseeing eyes like saucers, slowly rolling through the phenomenal
downpour, thunder and lightning ripping around me, my headlights useless,
the hail battering the roof and windshield in a tremendous, roaring din. What
a storm!

The storm finally passed, after driving through it for an hour, ending as
suddenly as it had exploded upon me. I could see my way ahead again. My
hands and arms untensed on the steering wheel. A few miles on, the road was
dry and the moon came out from behind the shreds of clouds now rushing
backward above the car, to cast the nightscape in eerie gray.

SINCERE,
A DUPE, OR A LIAR?

Seek simplicity, then mistrust it.

—Anonymous

"Jesus Christ. We are really sorry suckers."

The reporting started to arrive from the other individual who had been rendered and who was considered part of CAPTUS's network, while I was working on the elegant walk-in. It was apparent through the neutral and careful tones of the cables that ███ ██ ██ ██ ██████████████████████████████████████. He, the new detainee and ostensible member of CAPTUS's network, probably did know some al-Qa'ida personnel and activities ███████████████████████ ███████████████████████████. This did not make him a critical node of the al-Qa'ida network. This was absurd, I thought.

Jack turned toward me, by now long accustomed to my outbursts at the computer. He started to smile in anticipation.

"Yes?"

"Now we seize retards. This other guy we've rendered—it turns out he's either a superb actor, playing a sort of terrorist's version of the insanity defense, or he's mentally deficient. A retard."

Jack just looked at me, his eyebrows raised in surprised bemusement, initially enjoying my commentary, but then realizing that I was sardonic because I was serious, and disgusted. He sensed I was not in the mood for flippant repartee. I continued to vent my anger.

"██

██

████████████████████████████████. Holy shit."

"Oh, man," was all Jack could say. He stayed out of my way. I returned to my cable writing, silent for a while.

Was rendering this individual called for? Did we need to cast such a wide net on this case and in general in response to 9/11, or were we acting simply, crudely, and without just proportion to our targets' access, knowledge, and putative involvement in terrorism? Headquarters, on instruction from the administration, was proceeding on the view that it was better to err than to allow even the possibility of obtaining valuable information to go unexploited. Americans had died and we would not let this happen again, no matter what. Of course we all were committed to destroying al-Qa'ida and to protecting America. But I had come to feel from my involvement in the CAPTUS case that nuance and judgment were lacking, and that our actions were too often crude and unjustifiable. Lives—American and non-American—were at stake. We would—I would—do everything I could to protect them, but war or not, it was our duty to *get it right*, not convince ourselves and our masters that flailing and callousness about collateral damage was useful aggressiveness. Our rules of engagement lacked nuance and understanding, and had become scandalous.

The elegant walk-in returned. Josh and I met him again. Josh was slightly on edge, trying hard to get everything right, because meeting with assets was new to him still. The elegant walk-in was, once again, reserved and poised. I was pleased to meet with him again; his case was straightforward intelligence work, the kind I had done for many years. It had none of the troubling aspects of the interrogation case in which I was involved.

"I . . . have more information."

What the walk-in then described, if true, was important to U.S. national security. This was good.

Then he explained how he claimed to have obtained it. This was not good.

As with many assets, I was not at all convinced that the elegant walk-in grasped the dangers he was running, or would take Josh's and my cautions to heart.

Nonetheless, the elegant walk-in agreed to do as we asked. I took his explanation of how he had obtained his information to be, perversely, a sign of his legitimacy. It was a typical error of a neophyte. I saw no reason for a fabricator or a provocation to inject such foolish behavior into his description of his activities. A fabricator or double agent would be more likely focused on conveying the disinformation he wanted us to report. But who knew? Perhaps he was an especially smooth double agent.

██.

I was inclined to accept him as a legitimate walk-in. But our formal view was that, for the moment, we had to proceed with the possibility in mind that he was a well-orchestrated provocation or disinformation operation by the ██████ intelligence service. We were faced with a recurring dilemma in clandestine operations: the walk-in had provided unique, important information. But he was the sole source for this information. ██████████████████ ████████. It was risky to rely on a single source. We had to decide whether to disseminate information to our policy makers and war fighters concerning matters of life and death, war and peace, which was critical to save American lives, but which might be a fabrication, and setting up our men, women, and policies for some unidentified enemy operation.

At about the same time that the elegant walk-in appeared, unbeknownst to me, the subsequently infamous source CURVEBALL provided crucial information about Iraq's putative weapons of mass destruction programs, duping the Neocon leaders of our country and elements of the intelligence community, because it comforted the preconceptions and goals of those receiving it, and came to be the pillar on which the justification for the invasion of Iraq rested—despite strong DO opposition and the fact that CURVEBALL was a sole source of critical intelligence. Of course, he was later revealed to be the flagrant fabricator and charlatan that the DO had maintained all along.

Although those involved in the elegant walk-in case and I were unaware of CURVEBALL, the central issue for us in the field was addressing the issue of independent corroboration, and whether to disseminate the walk-in's claims in intelligence reports (the relevant Headquarters desk, of course, was aware of all reporting on the subjects about which the elegant walk-in claimed to have information, and was better able to assess each report). Resolving bona fides and deciding whether information merited dissemination was a standard part of running a case.

The elegant walk-in returned once more to the country where I was working.

"I do not believe that I will be returning here," he told us.

I found that somewhat alerting.

Whatever the explanation, ███████████████████████████ ███ ███████████████████████████████. I had to run the CAPTUS case, Josh had his own responsibilities, and we had officers there, anyway. The walk-in agreed to provide any information he was able to obtain and to do whatever the colleague asked. We arranged for the walk-in to do ████ ███ ███████████████████████████ "ops tests" ██████████████ ███ ███ ████████████████████████. I arranged these steps in my last meeting with the elegant walk-in, as I was increasing the pressure on CAPTUS, and preparing for what I anticipated would be an order for a second CAPTUS rendition. The walk-in had no idea that I was about to leave the country for a while, but ███ ████████████████. If he made the rounds of countries he had described to me as part of his regular business routine, and had traveled to where I was several times in a several-week period, why would he all of a sudden not travel here again? Who knew? There were multiple benign explanations. Almost everything he had told me had checked out. But not every last detail. We had to be paranoid, and believe nothing. This was, simply, sound tradecraft, lest we be diddled. And one cannot afford to be outmaneuvered in intelligence operations, particularly concerning matters of war. So, to the elegant walk-in I bid farewell, with warm thanks for his selfless saving of lives. To Headquarters and the field stations involved, I shared the general interest, but not entirely dissipated wariness, we yet felt.

After the meeting, Josh and I walked upstairs to brief the COS.

"What do you think?" I asked as we passed through the quiet hallways.

"I don't know what to think," Josh replied. I had to suppress my excitement about the case, lest I appear a sucker, and risk losing sight of the dangers of being misled.

"I think he is pretty plausible," I said, going as far as I dared.

We cabled Headquarters and the relevant field stations that we shared the general interest in the case, but that our wariness was not entirely dissipated, not yet.

I never saw the elegant walk-in again. The case moved beyond my need-to-know. I do know that we continued to run him for a while, however, and to try to verify his information. I believe the Agency decided not long after my involvement in the case had ended to disseminate the intelligence reports I had written with the information he had provided ███████████████. To this day, I do not know whether the elegant walk-in was sincere and that we saved lives, was a dupe, or was a liar. I believe the first.

NIBBLING OREOS

There, then, he sat, holding up that imbecile candle
in the heart of that almighty forlornness. There, then,
he sat, the sign and symbol of a man without faith,
hopelessly holding up hope in the midst of despair.
—Herman Melville, *Moby-Dick*

I had the office to myself, with a box of Oreos. Jack was off working somewhere. I sat at my computer, nearly in the dark, pinching my lips with my thumb and forefinger as I read incoming traffic.

The TDYer's question concerning Hotel California, and my subsequent exchanges with Headquarters, had made clear to me that Headquarters' patience was wearing thin, and that operational changes to the case were coming. I had a lot to mull over on my drives to and from the interrogation facility, and evenings sitting in the back of the hotel lounge.

CAPTUS was my world, he was an HVT, but he was one small piece in the Agency's huge effort to identify, track, disrupt, and destroy al-Qa'ida and all jihadists. The institution—the DO and CTC—were running flat out. Pressure was tremendous to "maintain a high-ops tempo." Many were convinced that al-Qa'ida was planning multiple attacks and we could not ease up even a moment. The number of terrorist threat reports coming from the DO was huge; to someone just entering the swirling tides of counterterrorism work, the threats initially appeared almost overwhelming. The images of the World Trade towers and of the fighting in Afghanistan were present realities.

It was natural to accept the standard view: that the United States faced a coherent, growing, pervasive, and imminent worldwide terrorist threat. Our leaders affirmed that such was the case, based in part upon the information provided them by the Intelligence Community. The entire institution looked for, then reported, pieces of this narrative, and therefore believed it. Individuals, and institutions, naturally find information to confirm their convictions and illusions. And 3,000 moldering corpses, following years of lethal attacks abroad against American interests, were powerful arguments.

This was the atmosphere and mind-set in which CAPTUS had been tracked, and rendered. It was natural for an officer in the DO to believe that CAPTUS was the critical player in the al-Qa'ida network that he was presented as being. Of course he was; the Agency would not have rendered him otherwise. The internal traffic and the intelligence collected about CAPTUS by our colleagues—most of whom I knew to be selfless and dedicated officers— had seemed overwhelming . . . I reasoned the same way in my work prior to and after 9/11 concerning Iraq's possession of weapons of mass destruction. I had worked the issue; I had seen the reports; I knew that almost all of my colleagues acted sincerely; I accepted that my colleagues sought the facts and sought to challenge their premises. Except . . . except when positions became ossified and official, and then, to challenge orthodoxy was apostasy. . . . The pressure on an individual officer to conform to the dominant paradigm is exceptionally difficult, and dangerous, to challenge.

To challenge any paradigm requires awareness of its parameters and limitations. Few of us can do this. The DO and CIA, like any bureaucracy, were hard to stop once a direction had been taken; it did not actually think; it moved and fulfilled obligations. Even to have a chance of *noticing* flaws in the operating perspective for terrorist operations would require an experienced officer, knowledgeable of terrorist organizations and capabilities. He would need to be even more knowledgeable of how to interpret and assess raw reporting, of how to read the assumptions and careerism in so much of it. He would need experience and awareness of the innocence of so many officers, and of the pressure on officers to recruit and report. He would have to be cognizant of and experienced in dealing with the desire of officers and the institution to be relevant and players on important issues, which shaped so much reporting; and of the pressure and distorting biases of policy makers—demanding information of the Agency and yet wary of it as hesitant, or clueless, or out of control. And then, even if an officer combined all these perspectives, experience, and insights, and came to a different conclusion about some elements of the U.S. government's terrorism paradigm and operations . . . the result usually played out like my conversation with the prim, matronly hotel receptionist.

██
██
██
██
██
██
██
██.

But I had come to feel dismayed about my case, and the prevailing views about it, and even what I considered instances of careerism in how it was being run. ██
██
██
██
████████████████████████. We had a right to err; we also had a duty to rectify error if we could, in particular when it affected people's lives, even those of our enemies. I found no support for this view at Headquarters. But the reality was that even the possibility of shifting the direction of the case was diminishing. So I could only carry on, doing what I could within the shrinking circle of influence that I had.

██
██
██

███

███

███

████████████████████████████████ .

The only way to change the dynamic of the case would be to succeed in inducing, or obliging, him to answer clearly the small percentage of questions that, for a variety of reasons, he had not answered to my, or Headquarters', satisfaction. In my view, this was highly unlikely to occur, and as far as I was concerned, there were legal and, frankly, moral constraints on how to interrogate someone acceptably.

With these thoughts in mind, the next Headquarters operational cable was not a surprise, but still it made me wince and purse my lips when I read it on the computer screen.

"Goddamn it," I said to no one. I bit an Oreo in half, then tossed the remainder in the wastebasket, irritated with myself for having eaten it. Then I was irritated with myself for having thrown it into the wastebasket. I took another Oreo and stuffed it into my mouth, then felt guilty about eating yet another one. I tossed the whole box of Oreos into the wastebasket, so that I could not eat any more of them. Then I felt stupid and wasteful and that I had acted compulsively. So I picked the box out of the trash and stuffed another Oreo into my mouth as I sat staring at the screen. *CAPTUS is really screwed now*, I thought.

The cable informed me that Headquarters wanted to move CAPTUS to Hotel California █████████████████████████████████████

███

███

████ . Forget about my efforts to establish rapport, ███████████████
████████████ extract information through a human relationship. No, he was a terrorist and we would no longer allow him to play us along. Headquarters' concession to the approach I had been advocating and practicing and, I suppose, to me, however, was to state that it would be unnecessary to send CAPTUS to Hotel California if he very quickly provided the information Headquarters believed him to possess.

I saw Wilmington's hand in this. ███████████████████████
██
██
████████████████.

The situation was perverse. My instructions were at odds with what I knew to be the correct way to interrogate CAPTUS (and just about any detainee).

I decided that the only possible way remaining to keep CAPTUS from being transferred to Hotel California was to be harder than I had ever been with him, on the slim hope that he would speak clearly about the areas he had refused, or been unable, to talk about. It would be my last flimsy chance to protect CAPTUS from a much worse situation, and it would be his last chance to help himself; but I knew this would prove a vain effort to scare him into sharing his last secrets. The clock had just about run out.

I stuffed another Oreo into my mouth, then in exasperation took the box and left it in the common area of the station, so that it would be at least momentarily beyond my reach. If someone else ate them, I couldn't. I did not enjoy the Oreo and wished I had not eaten it.

I DO NOT KNOW WHY
ALLAH HAS DONE THIS

Does there not pass over man
a space of time when his life is a blank?
—Koran, Sura 76

The factotum at the liaison facility's gate received me with his habitual fawning smile. Some days I felt compassion for him. Other days I understood his role, and did not mind it. His manner irritated me this day.

"This guy is a dick," I said to the young officer accompanying me, once he had taken our passports and gone off to inform Little Guy, Big Guy, and Mr. Muhamad that we had arrived.

"What's wrong with him?" she asked.

"Nothing. He's a dick and he's stupid, that's all. I know nothing about him. He's just a dick."

The officer looked at me sideways and thought I had made an out-of-character, senseless, arrogant remark. She let the matter drop. I had nothing else to say. We waited in the reception room just inside the facility gate for the okay to proceed to the interrogation building. I walked out to the car for no reason but to get out of the waiting room. Then I walked back because I did not want to be at my car, and stood in the doorway, looking at the quiet trees. The guards inside the guard booth looked at me, unsmiling, through the tinted glass of their window, then returned to their quiet vigil. They pissed me off.

Once inside the interrogation facility Little Guy and I went over what we intended to accomplish in the day's interrogation. We started our conversation in the holding room and, as was our habit, carried on our conversation in low tones in the dark and dilapidated service hallway. I told him about Headquarters' cable about sending CAPTUS to a much harsher place.

"My superiors may decide not to send him, if I can—if we can—get him to speak about the areas where he has not done so."

"Do you think he can? I mean, he does not seem to know some of these things. He has, I think, answered honestly."

"Yes, yes, I know. I agree. I know. But there are several areas in which, as you know, he has not answered, or has avoided answering. My superiors will not let me allow CAPTUS to avoid answering these questions. And he *must* answer me now, or we will take him away."

Little Guy saw no reason to expect CAPTUS would be able to answer differently than he had been doing. But he nodded his head.

"I do not think he can do this. This is harsh. But, well, we will see, if this is what we must do."

I put my hand on Little Guy's shoulder. He and I had become friends, within the limits of the bizarre work we did together and the constraints of our profession, which made any socialization at all impossible. I trusted Little Guy as an honest and honorable man, and I believe he considered me so. We both doubted that CAPTUS knew what we accused him of knowing, and felt that CAPTUS was, fundamentally, not an evil man. I could not tell Little Guy of the depth of our agreement on this.

"Okay, let's go."

The conditions of this interview were the same as always—chair, windowless room except for the futile transom, the quiet—but I was not my normal understanding self.

We sat down. I looked at CAPTUS and felt pity for him ███████████ ██████████████████████. Was I wrong? Had he misled me? Was he the accomplice to murder that Headquarters—Wilmington and Roger, anyway—believed? No, no, enough. I knew CAPTUS. I knew CAPTUS would be unaware of my thoughts. To him, I was everything now; I was fair, but I was his interrogator. I had no thoughts. I asked questions. I did not believe he could see my inner life or thoughts. But, then, on this, I knew I had briefly engaged in a moment of arrogance. Of course CAPTUS knew me, and had assessed what sort of a man I was. One could do that to some extent in any conversation. The man he saw now, though, was earnest and hard.

"CAPTUS. ███████████████████████████████████████
██
██
███.

"███
██
██
██
██████████████████████████████████████."

I was speaking as intensely as I have in my life, dreadful even to myself. I could feel my adrenaline. ████████████████████████████████
██
██
██
████████████████████████████████████.
██
███.
██
██
██
██
██
██
██
██

██
██
██
██.
    ██
██
██
██
██.[1]

This terrible monologue left everyone motionless.

CAPTUS sat rigid.

Little Guy was distressed, but silent.

Then CAPTUS sat up in his chair, gathering himself. ████████████
███████████████████████████████.

CAPTUS, too, had been thinking a great deal about what had happened to him. He had been working out a philosophy of detention, to make sense of having been forcibly rendered, and stuck in a windowless room, with absolutely no human contact . . . for how long? ████████████████████
██
██
████████.

He looked hard at me, as we sat in silence. "████████████████████
████████████████████████████ . . . ." He continued speaking. Then his emotional strength ebbed a little ████████████████
████████████████████████████, his shoulders slumped, and he slouched back into his chair. The effort had cost him. But the core of his personality remained the same, he remained a man who sought to preserve his dignity, and he had strengthened himself psychologically to cope with his situation. CAPTUS knew the consequences of his words; CAPTUS's answer probably meant that his life would become worse, as I had warned.

---

1 The redacted passages describe how I impressed upon CAPTUS how displeased we were, and what was about to happen to him unless he told me everything he knew about al-Qa'ida immediately.

We both sat there, in our own ways distraught. But I admired him.

I returned to my office after this sobering and draining session, and wrote my reporting cable late into the night. There was nothing to nibble on, so I drank one Diet Coke after another as I wrote, tossing the empty cans across the room into the wastebasket. Several colleagues leaving for the evening poked their heads into my office and asked me to join them for dinner or drinks once I had finished my work. I appreciated their gesture but did not feel like socializing.

"That sounds good. Maybe I'll join you later."

One of the officers looked at me as they left: "Ah, Glenn," she said, not believing me, "he's a loner."

Afterward I drove into the commercial section of town, to the medina and markets. I wanted to walk around the alleys, amidst the throngs of people buying socks, or spices, drinking tea, or simply enjoying the noise and heat and motion. But it was late. The streets and alleys were empty, drab, and dirty with the trash of a day's commotion. The streetlights cast everything in a dim and desolate yellow light. I parked the car and walked for a time, but there was no life and I felt contemptible walking the abandoned alleys alone, when the local residents were in their homes and my colleagues were sitting somewhere laughing over a drink.

I drove back to the hotel and to my seat in the back of the lounge. I have no idea what music the band played that night. Perhaps there was no band. I do not remember. I sat absently watching the young but weary hookers, the slightly desperate businessmen, the vaguely sultry waitress who had accused me of being a spy and who usually liked to linger invitingly at my table, the Latin American band sweating in front of largely empty tables; but everyone stayed away from me, they all looked far away, and I was not really there, even as I sat in my dark corner. But I remember that as I erred through the forsaken medina, a solitary shape, sometimes a stark silhouette, sometimes a shifting shadow, the dark was cold.

Headquarters remained unmoved. ████████████████████
██
██

████████. It was obvious to me that what I reported made no difference; the decisions had already been made.

The instruction came several days later, before I had had time to see whether CAPTUS had responded as we hoped ████████████████████ ███████, that CAPTUS would be rendered again—this time to Hotel California. Judgment, nuance, and measure are easily lost, I knew, in the can-do and machismo culture of the DO and I was now living a distilled moment of this dynamic and perspective. The White House had ordered us to do whatever it took to capture, neutralize, or kill al-Qa'ida terrorists. A narrow mind and hard hand had won out.

Headquarters closed its cable with the standard pro forma, polite salutation and a final instruction:

MUCH APPRECIATE C/O SPORTINK'S EFFORT ON CAPTUS CASE. C/O WILL ACCOMPANY CAPTUS TO HOTEL CALIFORNIA AND CONTINUE INTERVIEW THERE. REGARDS.

PART III

Through ignorance, they often served themselves poison; grown wiser, they serve it now to others.

—Lucretius, *The Nature of Things*, V. 1009–1010

METHANE BREATHERS

Only those who are the true authors of their acts,
which they are free to perform or not perform,
can be praised or blamed for what they do.
—Isaiah Berlin, *Against the Current*

Man cannot so far know the connection
of causes and events, as that he may
venture to do wrong in order to do right.
—Samuel Johnson, *Rasselas*, XXXIV.30

The runway glistened in the cold, damp fog. Distant lights glared as halos in the black. A few isolated men, small dark shapes, stood off on the perimeter, where the dim light was overwhelmed by the night. The nearest building was several hundred yards away. ████████████████ ████████████████████████████ ████████████████████████████ ████████████████. Muhamad chatted in low tones with Little Guy and Big Guy, about thirty yards away. Josh slapped his hands together to stay warm. He and I were working together again. He had the lead this night, as I had had when we worked together on the elegant walk-in case. He ████ ██ had arranged for us to use their runway ██████████████████████████ . He was focused, calm, and professional. It was 2 a.m. We were waiting for our "black" plane to arrive for CAPTUS's second rendition, which would take him and me to Hotel California.

Earlier that night, Josh and I had driven out from my hotel, following directions that liaison had provided, through progressively deserted and ultimately dark and empty country roads, stopping at a nondescript, isolated gate in a chain-link fence. We turned off our car and its lights. There were no other roads, or people, just large scrub bushes fading into the night. The only light came from several buildings hundreds of yards away, inside the facility. Josh and I stood about in the darkness for ten minutes, waiting and largely silent. We checked our watches under our coat sleeves from time to time. I turned up my collar and hunched my shoulders against the cold. At the appointed hour, our contact drove up on the other side of the fence, his tires making sharp crinkling noises in the gravel.

Muhamad gestured us into an ornate but slightly dilapidated waiting room in one of the buildings, underlit by bare, wan bulbs, and unheated. It was freezing. We all kept our coats on. Its scruffy decay reminded me of an Arab version of waiting rooms in which I had spent time in Simferopol, in the Crimea, or outside of Kiev. We all sat awkwardly beside each other on a single long, hard sofa, running the length of the wall. Oriental rugs and a low tea table completed the furniture. Several of Muhamad's colleagues arrived a few minutes later and Muhamad introduced us. ████████████████████████████ ██ ██ .
They were our hosts this night, and puffed themselves up to us in friendly but stilted formality. ██ ██████████████████ . We shook hands all around, smiled thinly at each other, and sat back on the long sofa to drink over-sweetened tea, served from a long-stemmed burnished copper teapot. We had little to say to one another. They did not know what we were doing or who we were and we had nothing to tell

them. After a polite interval of staring mutely at ornate wall motifs, all of us with our hands on our knees, I excused myself, returning to pace slowly up and down the runway, in the dark. Josh joined me a couple of minutes later, also relieved to be quit of the tea room, and we stood silent on the tarmac, looking at and feeling the night. It was impossible not to think of the final, fog-filled airport scene in *Casablanca*; the resemblance was remarkable, but I did not mention this. I thought it would sound artificial and inappropriately light, given what we were doing.

Muhamad somehow found me well off from the nearest building or man, walking alone with my thoughts. He handed me a small packet, with a satisfied look.

"███ ███." I slid the thin packet into the inside pocket of my jacket. █████████████████████████ ██ ██ ██ ██ ██ ██ ███████████.

"So now I can disappear."

He nodded. "Yes."

I'm already half disappeared, I thought. Muhamad returned to his car and stood there with a couple of ██████████████ officers. I walked to the end of the runway, to stare at nothing. My breath steamed when I exhaled, and I put my hands in my pockets.

A small convoy of three or four vehicles emerged from the darkness at the opposite end of the airport from that which Josh and I had entered. It was CAPTUS, escorted by security from the host intelligence service. I was about one hundred yards away from where they stopped. I could see CAPTUS bundled out of the middle vehicle—███████████████████████████████ ██████████, underdressed for the cold, a little hunched over. It struck me that in all the months I had been working the case I had never seen CAPTUS walk before. The security men shuffled him into a building adjacent to the one where I had taken tea with the ██████████ officers. I stared for a moment at the door that had closed after CAPTUS. I felt badly for him.

We continued to wait. I saw Little Guy standing under the small overhanging roof of the waiting room building, smoking a cigarette. Josh went to speak to a couple of our interlocutors, then caught up with me.

"It's coming. ████████████████████████████████████. Ten, fifteen minutes." This was our black plane. I went to our car and got my bag. The distant men on the perimeter moved off the runway. I could just glimpse that they were armed. We moved off the runway, too. Everyone in sight disappeared into the darkness, to attend to unknown tasks.

Shortly, an aircraft appeared out of the sky, very low, very close, and very ████████, and landed with ██████████████████████ a ██████████ ████████, rolling gently to a stop not more than seventy-five yards from me. I had not seen or heard anything until the very last seconds before it landed.

Doors opened. Men emerged and fanned out in bustling, silent, efficient activity around the plane. They were intimidating. ██████████████████████
██
██
██
██
██

████████. A lone black-clad ninja figure came out last. He wore a balaclava, covering his entire face except for his eyes. His jumpsuit was bloused inside heavy boots, and he carried an M-4. He strode toward the waiting room building and was met halfway by one of the locals.

"Methane breathers," I murmured.

"What fucks," Josh said.

I glanced at him, my brows knit. "What?" He did not answer.

He walked over to the lone ninja and the local official and talked for a moment. He gestured for me to join them. He and the ninja walked toward me, leaving the local behind. We met halfway between us on the runway, about forty yards from the plane. Bright light came out of the plane's doors.

To my surprise, the ninja was a woman. Up close, she was petite, fine-boned, with long, dark hair. Incongruous. We shook hands. Josh and the woman were engaged in a testy exchange, which she interrupted to greet me.

"You're the one going with the detainee?

"Yes."

"We'll leave ██████████████████████████████████ [soon]."

She was all business.

Josh and the woman returned to their argument.

"It's protocol," she said. "This is how we do it."

"I don't care if it's protocol. It's unnecessary and we're insulting the ████████.[1] I would be. Why don't you adjust to circumstances? There's no danger here. I've worked all this out with the ██████." Josh was controlled, but direct. The woman took offense. I was bewildered but growing alarmed. What was going on?

"Can't do it. It's protocol. These are our orders. This is how we do it. The station has nothing to do with this." This woman was not budging.

"Who are you?" Josh asked. "I deal with these guys every day. You don't need to do this stuff."

"I am running this operation. It's protocol, designed for everyone's safety. ████████████████████████████████████. There's no discussion about it. I don't care where we are. I run the rendition. As soon as we're done with the physical ████████████████, we're gone."

She looked at me. "Put your bag in the plane."

She ended the conversation abruptly and walked toward the building where CAPTUS was being held, and where several of her ninjas had entered while we spoke.

"What's going on?" I asked. Josh was contemptuous.

"She's a Headquarters fuck. These guys are clowns. She wouldn't know how to drop her pants and take a shit out here if she didn't have her 'protocol' to follow. Her field experience is—these people aren't field officers. They aren't using their heads. They don't know what they're doing. This is supposed

---

1 Josh mentioned the nationality of our hosts.

to be a *black* operation. That's the whole point. That's why we arranged it as we did. ██████████████████████████████████████
██████████████████████████████. But it's not normal with kung fu masters hopping around ████████████████████████."

I understood Josh's irritation now. They had given no thought to adjusting tradecraft to circumstances. ████████████████████████████
███
███
███
██████████████. Bureaucracy at work again—*Check That Cable.*

"That's why we asked, and I arranged," he said, "for everything to be routine, and for our presence to be invisible and nonexistent. ██████████████
███
██████████████████████. That is not alerting. That's why—no one here knows what we're doing or who we are ████████████████████████████
███
██████████████████████████. Ninjas jump out, while a couple of Americans stand around waiting with some guy in chains? That's just how not to draw attention. ██
███
██. That's just perfect. You can bet now that all these guys here will see something pretty unusual has gone on. I wonder if someone might figure something out? ██████████████
███. These clowns should have landed, █████████████████████████ have you and CAPTUS get on
██ with no hint of what's going on."

A minute or two later we walked over to where CAPTUS was being held. One of the ninjas was a doctor, who greeted us just as they were finishing up and taking a hooded and shackled CAPTUS onboard the plane ███████████
███
██████. The doctor, Josh, and I followed. He was good-natured, if a bit hurried and wary of his surroundings. He explained that he had conducted a physical examination of CAPTUS, including a proctologic probe, to verify that the

detainee was in good health, and posed no threat to the rendition squad. ████████████████████████, again so that he posed no threat to the team.

"You ████████████████my guy?!" I asked, taking on the spirit of Josh's irritation. Josh snorted.

The doctor's face was covered with his black knit face mask, but he seemed less intransigent or officious than the woman had been and took my incredulous flippancy in good spirit.

"Sometimes these guys hide stuff there, that's all. Bombs, who knows what. Some of these guys are awful. We have to know before we get him on a plane where lives can be at stake if there's a screwup."[2]

████████████ CAPTUS was onboard. We had reached the side of the plane. ████████████████████████████████. Everything had happened very fast. ████████████████████████████████. Little Guy and Big Guy approached from under the portico of the waiting room building. I thanked them for their help and shook hands. "*Choukran, choukran,*" I said, placing my hand on my heart. The exchange took only seconds. Two more people I would never see again. I noticed that the nearest people and vehicles were already a couple hundred yards off.

---

2 Several public documents are relevant: The KUBARK manual, which I found to be so much a foundational document for rendition, detention, and interrogation practices, instructs: "Subject is given a thorough medical examination, including all body cavities, by the facility doctor." The Council of Europe's Investigation into the CIA's rendition practices, issued summer 2009, asserts that "some accounts speak of a foreign object being forcibly inserted into the man's anus; some accounts speak more specifically of a tranquiliser or suppository being administered per rectum." Also, according to the "Background Paper on CIA's Combined Use of Interrogation Techniques," dated December 30, 2004, which sketches rendition and interrogation techniques for HVT al-Qa'ida detainees, and released to the ACLU under a Freedom of Information Act lawsuit, "a predictable set of events occur. . . . An HVD is flown to a black site [now acknowledged publicly to have included sites in Afghanistan]. . . . A medical examination is conducted prior to the flight. . . . Upon arrival at the destination airfield the HVD is moved to the Black Site . . . using appropriate security procedures. . . . The HVD is subjected to administrative procedures and medical assessment . . . the procedures are . . . precise, quiet, and almost clinical. . . . Procedures include:

a. the HVD's head and face are shaved.

b. A series of photographs are taken of the HVD while nude to document the physical condition of the HVD upon arrival.

c. A Medical Officer interviews the HVD and a medical evaluation is conducted to assess the physical condition of the HVD. The medical officer also determines if there are any contraindications to the use of interrogation techniques."

I turned to Josh.

"Josh."

His face looked hard and etched with fatigue. He was laboring to suppress his anger. We shook gloved hands.

"Okay."

██
██ .

I boarded the plane, followed by the petite ninja woman, the last one in, who did not shake hands or speak with anyone. The lights in the cabin were blinding after the darkness outside. She secured the door and leaned into the cockpit. "Go," she said. The plane's engines immediately revved and we taxied down the runway.

I slid down the aisle and found a seat behind the wing. No one spoke—I gathered that part of the "protocol" was to maintain silence at all times. Everyone pointedly ignored me. ████████████████████████ . I watched the few lights in the darkness below recede quickly behind us and drew the shade.

About twenty minutes into the air I walked back to check on CAPTUS. He was motionless. ██████████████████████████████████████
██
██
███████████████ . The ninjas were not welcoming. They drew a separator across the aisle. The cabin was filled with the roar of the engines. ██████
████████████ I returned to my seat, pulled a blanket over my head, and slept fitfully for what seemed a long time.[3]

---

3 According to the Background Paper on CIA's Combined Use of Interrogation Techniques: "during the flight, the detainee is securely shackled and is deprived of sight and sound through the use of blindfolds, earmuffs, and hoods. There is no interaction with the HVD during this rendition. . . . The procedures he is subjected to are precise, quiet, and almost clinical."

POINT ZERO IS FUCKED UP

La ruse la mieux ourdie
Peut nuire à son inventeur;
Et souvent la perfidie
Retourne sur son auteur.
(The most clever ploy
Can harm the hand behind it;
And often perfidy
Recoils to its author.)

—La Fontaine, *Le Rat et la grenouille*

The sky was leaden, and the darkness descended all the way to the ground. A mist hung in the air and one could not see far before one's vision disappeared into a formless, gray wall of cloud in every direction. I could not believe the murk into which we had landed.

The change of the engines' whine and our descent had awakened me five minutes before from a typically poor airplane sleep. I had the glassy eyes and wild hair, the slightly disjointed motions of just coming to, and had just enough time to glimpse raw, brown, snowy, and immense mountains as we spun in a tight turn and descended sharply. Point Zero.

There was commotion around the jet the instant we rolled to a stop. Our door immediately opened and the rendition squad leader hustled out of the plane. A convoy of 4x4 vehicles drove up within seconds. Bulky armed men piled out of them even before they had stopped. They established security quickly ███████████████   ████████████████████████████ ██.

The security men immediately started to load the 4x4s with packets from the jet. I descended the steps of the plane, wanting to help and to stay out of the way. I asked the rendition squad leader, "Should I take my bag now?"

"No, it's better if you get it once they're done. There's plenty of time." She went back to organizing the luggage and supplies.

I stood by the wing, to the side, and looked around. This was the main part of the airfield, near the control tower. ████████████████████████████ ██ ██ ██ ██ ██ ████████████████████.[1] I felt very exposed. Other than the security men and the 4x4s, there was no visible sign of life, but I could see only a short distance before the mist obscured everything.

██ ███. Men hurried all around me. Various bags and duffels landed with a thud in the backs of the 4x4s.

Within moments the back door of the 4x4 nearest the jet slammed shut. "Okay. Let's go!" The security men broke off what they were doing and hurried to vehicles. The four 4x4s careened to form a caravan. The jet crew was climbing the embarkation stairs to take off. The rendition squad leader was gone.

"Hey!" I shouted, starting to run to the jet stairs. "I have to get my bag. I'm staying!"

---

1 The deleted passage describes what were to me alarming surroundings.

Goddamn it. I sprinted up the stairs and down the plane, grabbed my bag, and ran out. I had taken perhaps thirty seconds. The plane was closing the embarkation door behind me. The vehicles were about seventy-five yards away, lights shining in the growing darkness and mist, moving quickly toward the gate, one hard up against the next.

One of the men who had met us saw me. He raised his arms in a cross over his head. "Halt! Halt!" he called. "Halt! You've got one more ████!"

He was closer than I to the convoy and managed to run up beside the lead driver's window. He crossed his arms again. "Halt!" The caravan stopped suddenly. I chose a vehicle, opened the door, tossed my bags in, and jumped in myself, having half run and half walked in an effort to go fast, while not appearing too much a high-strung neophyte.

"Okay! That's it," I said. The two men inside said nothing. The one riding shotgun held an ████ at the ready. They continued to look out the front intently. The last two men on the ground opened a gate.

"Come on, let's get out of here. We're just sitting ducks like this." The driver's voice was irritated, taut. We started to roll through the gate. We picked up speed into the wasteland around the airport. The men in the vehicle completely ignored me. ████████████████████████████████
██
████████████████████████████████. I glanced back and saw the jet accelerate down the runway and take off, lifting sharply as soon as it was airborne.

The 4x4 started to buck and bump and rock, surging through puddles and twisting to avoid two-foot-deep potholes. A couple of minutes went by in silence, but for the revving of the motor and the crashes of the jeep. There were no people in sight, just buildings every so often. ████████████████
██
██
██
██
██
████████. I stared out the windows astonished as we bounced along and

thought of my college roommate from decades earlier, who through a haze of whiskey used to gaze out our living room windows on the Charles River, declaiming from T. S. Eliot's *The Waste Land*: "All about is stony rubbish and a heap of broken images where no branches grow."

I thought enough time had gone by for the new guy to say something and not disturb some task or danger I did not perceive.

"This place looks worse than Burundi," I said. There was a one- or two-beat pause. No one had even glanced at me yet.

Rain started to fall. Mist formed on the windshield. Then the guy in front of me spoke, staring ahead. "This place is fucked up, man. Point Zero is fucked up." I found that I could not open my window ███████████████ ███████████████.

The land was strewn with football-size stones everywhere. It was a desert-steppe moonscape, ███████████████████████████████. The driver turned the wheel sharply.

"Shit! ████████████████! Look at that!" The car jerked and the tires of the 4x4 passed only a couple of feet from it. ███████████████████████ ███████████████████████████████████████ ███████████████████████████████████████ ███████████████████████████████████████ ███████████████.

"Let's go, let's go! Let's get out of here!" he said, angry and anxious. The windshield wipers didn't work right. The murk and ruins were smeared on the windshield and we could see only distorted blurs of gray and brown out the front of the 4x4.

"Fuck," the guy sitting in front of me cursed.

I found that all my drives on this "road" were like this, although I would travel with men who were less on edge.

REDEMPTOR

Yet all man's life is but ailing and dim
And rest upon the earth comes never . . .
And the deeps below us are unrevealed,
And we drift on legends forever.

—Euripides, *Hippolytus* 191–7

A long while later we rolled to a stop at the station. The security was daunting and impressive. I looked up at a dilapidated building that had seen better days, but then every building I had passed had seen better days.

"He'll need to see the security officer." The driver was talking about me as though I were not there. He turned to me, shouldering his rifle: "You'll need to see the security officer." Then he and Mr. "This-place-is-fucked-up-man" walked up the steps, through the large wooden door, and left me. I watched after them a moment, then looked around at the quiet front of the building and the station's front steps. I hoisted my bag and walked into the front entrance. Like so many places I had been in suffering parts of the world, it was dimly lit with yellowish light from bare bulbs hanging from the ceiling.

Inside, it was bustling with nationals—local employees—and Agency officers. Beyond the ████████ desk and foyer was the dining room, where

numbers of men sat lounging and eating. ███████████████████████
██████████████████████████████████.

I found Cal, the compound security officer, up the stairs and through a
████████████████ door, in a common work area. He was busy, so I sat outside
his office and waited about ten minutes to speak to him. No one paid me any
attention. Men and women in ███████████████████ T-shirts went to and fro.

Cal came out of his office. He was physically . . . quirky, with wild eyes
and longish hair. I told him I had just arrived and was checking in. I was to
learn that Cal looked as though he had just rolled out of bed, whatever time
of day it was. He always moved slowly. I never saw him laugh or become upset.
But he was also more approachable than one would think from the first impression he created. Given his unvarying composure, of course he had been
dubbed "Crazy Cal." He looked at me, eyes wide, one eyebrow cocked, and
said after a moment's silence:

"You'll need some . . . stuff." He walked me to a storage room and kitted
me out. ███
███
█████████████████. I tried it on. "It'll keep you warm, too," he said. Two empty
flaps of material extended down over my crotch.

"It doesn't protect the family jewels," I said, looking down. Crazy Cal
tapped me on the chest.

"It's the pump. It protects the pump."

He handed me some clothes.

"You'll want to wear these. Not good to look like an American." I thought
self-consciously of the Bean boots I was wearing, and of the officers who had
brought me in from the airport ███████████████████████████████
███████████████████████████—they had certainly not looked like the
New England Yankee gone duck hunting that I did.

He issued me a two-way radio.

"You'll need a call sign." He checked a form. "Here. I have one. Your
call sign will be REDEMPTOR. Got it? The guy who had that one isn't
around anymore."

I nodded. "REDEMPTOR. Okay."

He walked me back to the office for the security briefing. It was almost the size of a broom closet and was a wild riot of scattered papers, radios, and boxes, ██ and an overstuffed filing cabinet. He sat, I stood, and he handed me a clipboard with a form to sign, to show that I had been briefed, trained, and issued all the necessary equipment . . . and to cover the Agency's ass in the event I got killed.

I remembered the irritation and disbelief we had all expressed many years before when I went through our paramilitary, weapons training, and certification course. After weeks of firing and practicing how to handle, disassemble, and clean a huge variety of weapons, ranging from 9mm pistols (I prefer the Colt .45 for its power), to ████████████████████████████████████ ██ ██ ██████████████████████████████████ and a range of machine guns ██ ██████████████████████████████████████ after training in planning ████████████████████ reconnaissance missions, ██████████ ██ desert survival techniques, field dressings for wounds, ████████████████ ████████████████ parachuting ██████████████████████████ ████████████████████████████, and on and on . . . we received a briefing from a lawyer from OGC, the Office of General Counsel. He, too, had us all sign forms, like Crazy Cal now. Then, the lawyer had told us, "If ever you are called upon to use your weapon, and someone is killed or injured, you will be responsible to provide yourselves any legal representation that may be required."

We were incredulous, and asked pointedly, "Do you mean to tell us that if we are sent into potentially lethal situations, or combat, and that if we use our weapon in the performance of our duty, or in self-defense, and someone is shot or killed, that the Agency *will not represent us legally*?"

The lawyer went through a little legalistic verbal dance, the gist of which was that the answer was yes.

My mind returned to the clipboard in my hands, and Crazy Cal impassively staring at me. I signed the form.

"Okay," Crazy Cal said. "This is the briefing: ███████████████████
██████████████████████████████. Always take your radio with you. Let us know where you are, ██████████████████████████████████████
██
██
████████████████████. Do not draw attention to yourself as an American. Do not look like an American. ███████████████████████████████████
███. Leave space in front of you when in your vehicle; ████████████████████████. Have 360-degree awareness at all times ██████████████████████████████████
████████."

He stopped. He looked at me, impassive. "Okay." He said it as a statement.

"Okay," I replied. Briefing over.

I found the COS visibly swamped with work. Officers waited to see him, held off by his secretary. His phone rang. The Deputy Chief of Station (DCOS) and small groups of men just in from all sorts of operations tramped heavily into his office and closed the door for crisp five-minute meetings. He saw me after about a fifteen-minute wait. He was distracted and hurried, polite and projecting competence, but preoccupied; I was one of a hundred competing claims on his time, and not the most critical. He saw me for about three minutes. I told him who I was and why I was in country. He was aware of the interrogations of our HVTs, of course, and about the CAPTUS case in general. It was clear that he did not know anything beyond that. That was my job. He told me to see the DCOS, who would take care of me. I saw the COS only in the hallways during the rest of my stay. Too busy.

The DCOS arranged to have an officer assigned to me for security. He told me that we all had to hot-seat the computers in the station—multiple officers would use the same computer on a first-come, first-served basis—as there were far more officers than computers. The ops tempo was very high, resources tight. We worked on a first-come, first-served basis in a common room. I reported to no one. I ran my operation as I saw fit.

"You had your security briefing?"

"Yeah."

"See Crazy Cal or the Chief of Logs for anything you need. Welcome," he said, ending the meeting, and passing through a door directly behind his desk chair into the COS's office before I could even stand up, closing the door behind him.

I collected my gear around me and sat on a bench in the hallway-foyer of the station, completely ignored. Had I sat there for hours I don't think anyone would have paid me any attention. This was a *very* busy station, full of transient TDYers like myself, comets orbiting in and out on irregular schedules, or arriving ▌▌▌▌ as I had, or running ops nonstop. *CAPTUS and REDEMPTOR*, I thought, somewhat dully. I was wiped out.

After a few minutes of rest, I found the common office, a single room with plywood on sawhorse tables, a few laptops, and used Styrofoam coffee cups lying around, called the Bullpen. One of my first cables was to the location that continued to hold CAPTUS's still-absent papers, to renew my request that they be sent to me. The cable was a gesture of hope over experience. I assumed that I would receive the same nugatory responses as before. I now had no one I could even try to send to get them, and in the best of circumstances did not expect the documents to arrive until long after I had handed the case over to someone else. Sending the request both amused me perversely and was the right thing to do, past fustian results notwithstanding.

That afternoon I stepped out onto the landing of the station doorway to watch the dismal dark, fog, and rain. ▌▌▌▌▌▌▌▌▌▌▌▌▌▌▌▌
▌▌▌▌▌▌▌▌▌▌▌▌▌▌▌▌▌▌▌▌▌▌▌▌▌▌▌▌▌▌▌▌▌▌
▌▌▌▌▌▌▌▌▌▌▌▌▌▌▌▌▌▌▌▌▌▌▌▌▌▌▌▌▌▌▌▌▌▌.

A man sat ▌▌▌▌▌▌▌▌▌ on guard duty off to the side, ▌▌▌▌▌▌ leaning against the wall in front of him. One could see only seventy-five yards before the fog shrouded everything. Cars had to use their headlights in the middle of the day, the lights appearing suddenly out of the impenetrable gray. People appeared as dark, bulky outlines against the fog, or faded from view in just a few steps. I would find that this astounding gloom blanketed Point Zero for over a week, rendering ghouls of us all, floating in a death mist. One expected the lowing of a deep foghorn and the creaking timbers of a ghost ship; the fog, though, was often brown.

I stood there for some time, watching the headlights appear, the human silhouettes disappear and emerge, and listening to the gate creak open and closed, as the rain pattered on the ▮▮▮▮▮▮ roof. Every window in the building was ▮▮▮▮▮▮▮▮▮▮▮▮▮▮▮▮; so was the stairwell inside the doorway. People entering and leaving took no notice of me. It was a moist, penetrating cold.

The guard gestured for me to join him ▮▮▮▮▮▮▮▮▮▮▮▮▮▮▮▮ to warm my hands against his space heater. I accepted and sat beside him for a few minutes. We smiled at each other, but I couldn't get him to understand anything I said. He just smiled. I tried some of the local vocabulary I had been practicing, coming up with whatever pretext I could think of to use the ten or fifteen words I had learned: "Yes." "No." "Good." "Bad." "Okay." I pantomimed the question, "Where is the airport?" Nothing worked. He just smiled beatifically, now with his weapon between his legs. Only "thank you" worked. He put his hand on his heart, to indicate that he appreciated my comment and that his heart wished me well. I could just make out a sign in white on the inside of the compound gate, thirty to forty yards away, urging us to be careful and aware at all times.

VARY YOUR ROUTES!
REMEMBER!
AL-QA'IDA HAS PUT A $100,000 BOUNTY
ON EVERY AMERICAN KILLED
▮▮ AN ▮▮▮▮▮▮

THE JIHADI BAR

Oh, you who believe! Wine, games of chance . . . are
nothing but an abomination of Satan's work. Stay away
from them; perhaps then you will be happy.

—Koran, Sura 5.92

An ███████ ratty box with a picture of Usama Bin Ladin on it served as a till behind the bar. I had just put my dollar in for my Diet Coke and was about to sit down, when an officer behind me with a Boston accent said, "What house did you live in?"

"House?" I had no idea what he was talking about. He pointed to my Harvard sweatshirt.

"Yeah, what house at Harvard?" "House" is Harvard's term for dorm. Now I understood.

"Eliot."

"Did you know Mike Kirrane?"

I moved my head back in surprise. Mike Kirrane and I had played hockey together at Harvard. I hadn't thought of his name in twenty-five years. The fellow who had approached me was one of the security officers who would escort me wherever I went. Like everyone in the bar, he was dressed in desert tan combat clothes. There was a pile of equipment against one wall of the bar. We started to talk, leaning on the bar. He and Kirrane both grew up in Milton, Massachusetts. The security officer had gone to Milton High School, the public school in town; Kirrane to Milton Academy, a prestigious prep school there. Growing up, I had played hockey against them both, as my hometown was only a few miles away.

The security officer called over to a sofa. "Hey, Tom! This guy is from Brookline!" A young guy in his early twenties looked up from his beer and came to the bar. Another Bostonian. He introduced himself: "Tom Weston." The name seemed vaguely familiar. I searched my memory, and we engaged in the normal do-you-know chat. He was incongruously young and deferential, surrounded as we were by tired but boisterous and case-hardened men. He said that his mother had gone to my high school, and we worked out to my growing surprise that she had graduated in my class.

"Really?" I said, my eyebrows arching. "What was her name then?"

"Wendy Weston."

"Weston? Wendy Weston?"

"Yeah, that's her."

I was amazed. I was also really tired, a little giddy, and more facetious than I intended.

"Gosh," I said. "Now I remember her. She was good-looking. . . . I think I went out with her. . . . She was really good!" Everyone laughed and I hurried to say, "No, no. I didn't go out with her. I didn't mean that. But I remember her. She was cute."

The security officer from Milton said, laughing, "You might have gone to Harvard, but you aren't very smart. We're all armed, you aren't, and you're talking about one of our guys' mothers." More laughter. "Yeah," he continued. "She was cute. I've seen the pictures of his mother at his house."

Then I remembered a little better.

"Wait a minute. I do remember. I didn't go out with her. But my best friend did. Patrick von Huene. My best friend did go out with her. He took her to the prom, I think. I dunno. But he did go out with her."

I marveled at the circumstance: my past from thirty years earlier, a Harvard hockey teammate, and a girl with whom I had gone to high school and who dated my best friend—found at the end of an astounding trek taken clandestinely, with almost no one in the world aware of where I was, in a bar with weathered security officers. I sat down with the officers and spent the night telling and hearing war stories, a dozen tired men with scraggly beards, drawn features, and fatigue lines slanting down from our eyes.

At Point Zero, you worked nonstop, you slept when you could, or you went to the Jihadi Bar for a drink. There was nothing else to do, everyone was tired, and there was nowhere else to go. The bar was a dump, with run-down everything, but welcoming in the way of a college frat house. One could drink alcohol there, ███████████████████, talk, or just sit. There was a sound system, and a lot of country music, played too loud and sounding tinny. There was no television or radio, just a few plush chairs and sofas, a couple coffee tables, a dilapidated pool table, and the bar, lit by the ubiquitous weak and bare overhead bulbs. ████████████████████████████████████. It looked better and had a warmer atmosphere at night, when the dimness and hour—and one's fatigue—made it feel comfortable. In the day, one noticed the stale cigarette smells, frayed furniture, stains, and the ramshackle, untended feel to the place. There was no staff. The logistics guys stocked the refrigerator behind the bar, and people paid into the metal box till on the honor system.

The security officers commented on their work and told tall tales, like all men in groups or teams. One told a story about the building, which had the recent arrivals among us staring at him, wide-eyed. █████████████
███
███
███
███
██████████. We all wondered what the cellar had been used for, and of course imagined the worst. I passed by it twenty times a day. But I never had time to go look during my time at Point Zero and felt the irony was a little too acidic, in any event, given my own work. █████████████████████████
███████████████████████████. I had little to say during this part of the conversation.

Many predecessors had left their testimonials on the walls, in a variety of hands and pens.

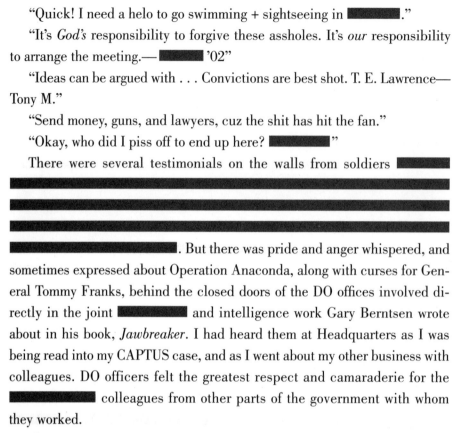

"Quick! I need a helo to go swimming + sightseeing in ███████."

"It's *God's* responsibility to forgive these assholes. It's *our* responsibility to arrange the meeting.— ███████ '02"

"Ideas can be argued with . . . Convictions are best shot. T. E. Lawrence— Tony M."

"Send money, guns, and lawyers, cuz the shit has hit the fan."

"Okay, who did I piss off to end up here? ███████"

There were several testimonials on the walls from soldiers ███████

███████. But there was pride and anger whispered, and sometimes expressed about Operation Anaconda, along with curses for General Tommy Franks, behind the closed doors of the DO offices involved directly in the joint ███████ and intelligence work Gary Berntsen wrote about in his book, *Jawbreaker*. I had heard them at Headquarters as I was being read into my CAPTUS case, and as I went about my other business with colleagues. DO officers felt the greatest respect and camaraderie for the ███████ colleagues from other parts of the government with whom they worked.

The anger was at Franks and Donald Rumsfeld, whose meddling, in the view of the senior DO officers who spoke to me about Afghan operations when the United States destroyed the Taliban regime in 2001–2002, had denied the Agency and the forces in the field adequate support to make Operation Anaconda a success, thereby allowing Bin Ladin to escape, turning what could have been the decisive engagement of the war into a near miss. Some asserted that the issue was higher military's, specifically Rumsfeld's, unwillingness to play a supporting role to Agency field recommendations concerning lethal or combat operations. As a result, several operations in which we had terrorist targets *literally* in our sites were stopped at the last moment, allowing the unsuspecting terrorists to continue their daily rounds, the occasion gone. Opportunities like those come rarely in intelligence work, and our frustration and even contempt was commensurate to the bureaucratic pettiness that put one institution's "control" ahead of effective clandestine operations in time of war. Others expressed anger at Franks's command, characterizing him as an artillery officer who lacked the creativity necessary for senior command of what was fundamentally unconventional or irregular warfare. "Franks was a terrible leader," one senior officer said to me before I started the CAPTUS operation, suddenly sharp in tone. "One of the worst I ever dealt with. Do not look to him for lessons in leadership."[1]

Behind and beside the bar was a collection of old military equipment, flotsam picked up randomly. A number of varied helmets sat on the shelves where one usually sees bottles of scotch and vodka. In a bizarre juxtaposition, I idly handled one in particular while I talked with the security officer about his mother—my high school friend's prom date; it ███████████████████ ██ ██████████████████████████████████.

The last of us went to our bunks about 2 a.m. I noted one more aphorism on the walls as I left the bar:

"The only easy day was yesterday."

Outside the bar, guards pulling night duty stood and shifted from side to side to stay warm. ██ ██ ██ ██ ███████████. All listened and stared out into the thick fog, the silence, and the dark. Beyond the compound walls, at night, no good things made noises or moved.

---

1 I note that I have no personal knowledge of Franks's qualities.

HAD THIS LAND
ALWAYS BEEN SO BLEAK?

The yellow fog that rubs its back
upon the window-panes,
Licked its tongue into the corners of the evening . . .
There will be time, there will be time
To prepare a face to meet the faces that you meet;
There will be time to murder and create,
And time for all the works and days of hands
That lift and drop a question on your plate . . .
—T. S. Eliot, *The Waste Land*

Hotel California lay low in the middle of a brown moonscape. ▮▮▮▮▮
▮▮
▮▮▮▮▮▮▮▮▮▮▮▮▮▮▮▮▮▮▮▮▮▮▮ , every landscape I saw in this country was
a rubble field. I hardly saw a tree or bush my whole time there. The astounding
fog continued to shroud the ground, so that people and objects appeared to
float in a dim dreamscape, looming suddenly into sight, or diminished in the
distance, small islets of hard reality surrounded by the unknown, or un-
dreamed, or unreal, a world without horizon.

███████████████████████████. A security officer, an analyst named Parker who had attached himself to me upon my arrival in country to offer support, and I had taken one of the standard-issue 4x4s from the motor pool to travel to Point Zero to see CAPTUS. I would meet up there with the chief and the psychologist assigned to work with me on my HVT interrogations.

I radioed ahead before leaving the station that REDEMPTOR was on his way.

I gazed out the window as we bounced along, the vehicle rocking violently, and tried to tune out Parker's prattle. The air chilled my fingers through my gloves as we drove, the landscape chilled me as I looked at it, anything man-made lay cold and inert as we passed by. Failed then. Futile now. The landscape on the drive resolved itself into barren, scraggly fields. Once, we stopped by a derelict vehicle to get our bearings. I did not look into it. The helmet in the Jihadi Bar had been enough.

"█████████████████████████████████████
██
███████████████████████████████████."

We pulled up to a discreet guard post.

██
██
██
█████████████████████████████████.[1]

I sat motionless.

The guard gestured for me to show my pass.

"Pass?" I said. "I have no pass." I was in charge of this little contingent, but no one had told me during any of my preparatory briefings and planning that I needed a stinking badge to get in. No one focused on the fact that I had just arrived in country.

The guard was polite but firm. He had strict orders: No pass, no entry. Another guard in the post perked up, a little more interested than before at the commotion. ███████████████████████████████████████

---

1 This passage describes security measures.

███

██████████████. I did not want us sitting there.[2]

The security officer with me knew the guards and started to try to argue our way in. He explained that I was an important officer. Parker, the analyst assigned to me, chimed in, imperious and condescending to the towering, weathered guard. Parker was young, in his mid-twenties, not a field officer, and I would consistently find in the coming days that he overcompensated, trying to play the tough and hard-eyed spy or man of war. The security officer was relaxed but mildly exasperated, a little embarrassed, that we had spent half a day preparing and getting here, and now were unable even to get in.

"Enough, enough," I said after no more than a minute of discussion. "Look, that's it. This guy's following orders. He's right. We aren't going to crash this bloody place. We go back and get me the pass I need, that's all. I'm fine with that."

The security officer agreed. I looked at Parker and he shut up, good-natured and unaware that he was defining himself as a mild ass. So, we turned around and made the ████████ trip through the endless fog back to the compound.

We returned the next day, a security officer, Parker, and me, once again radioing from the compound that REDEMPTOR was on his way, bouncing ourselves over the potholes and rubble ███████████████████████, peering out the smudgy windows of my 4x4 at the desolate landscape. My driver spoke little, while Parker was, once again, a little overeager to project an unearned, hard-bitten swagger.

The same towering and hard-faced local guard met us at the guard post and gate. I had my pass this time and the guard, the driver, and I apologized to one another, he for having been obliged to deny us entry, we for having not come with the proper pass and having put him in an awkward position. He raised the gate, motioned us to a courtyard, and escorted us toward the entrance. It was a nondescript door into a derelict building. We walked easily,

---

2 This passage describes my security concerns at that moment.

but with some tension, for what we were about to enter, and because we did not want to draw attention or, for all we knew, something worse.

As we walked, Parker approached the guard, who was six inches taller than he was. He put his hand on the man's shoulder in a patronizing gesture, then patted it twice and spoke in the tone one uses with a child, or a pet:

"You did the right thing. That was well done! We should inform your superior. You are a *good* guard. A *good* guard!" Parker then walked on ahead, master of his perceived moment, encourager of the simple and pure.

The security officer and I were walking four or five paces behind. "One," my companion murmured to me after he and I had thanked the guard, ██████████████████████████ slightly bowing our heads, "that guy doesn't understand a word of English. But two, he understands perfectly what that little shit said. I bet this guy would just rip Parker's head off and eat it if he got mad. I don't like to be alone around him."

I agreed, but my attention shifted quickly. We had arrived at the Hotel California entrance. I was on.

The music was harsh and incongruous, heavy metal, and it made the frigid building feel even colder, the darkness more ominous, and the ever-present, all-defining browns harder to resolve into recognizable objects when you looked at them. We were indoors, but our breath made clouds as we stood in the chief's office and he went over procedures. He had a pleasant manner.

"No one speaks but you ███████████. Ever. No one speaks. The only noise in this place is the music. ████████████████████████████████ ███████████████████. The doc will intervene if necessary. ███████████████ ████████████████████████████. Your asset appears fine. No one has seen him, except at the processing in, when we examined him. Okay?"

"Yes."

I wondered whether his processing in included another ███████ intrusive body procedure.

"Yes. . . . Oh. He keeps asking for 'Jacques.' Over and over, he says he wants to talk to 'Jacques.'"

"That's me. I'm his friend."

The chief laughed. He thought I was making a joke; this was true, but I was also speaking more than one truth.

"I'll get one of the guards to take you to your boy."

A minute later a guard indicated with a head gesture that I was to follow him. He and I entered the building. He carried a flashlight and a set of keys. It was immediately pitch black. 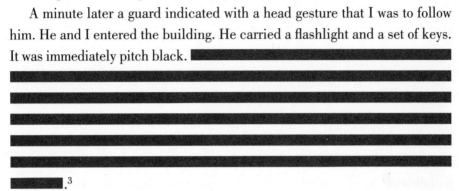.[3]

We turned onto another passage and continued. We turned again. And again. I could not see and was totally disoriented. My eyes clung to the heels of the guard in front of me, rising and falling, the only things I could see.

This is right out of the KUBARK manual and the SERE training I received twenty years ago, I thought as we walked (SERE: Survival, Evasion, Resistance, Escape). As a Career Trainee in the Directorate of Operations I had gone through days of capture, detention, and interrogation training, part of the months of paramilitary training we received. None of it had been relevant to my career for almost twenty years, not since I had spent eighteen months working in the CT office and on ■■■■ Lebanon ■■■■, when we had been trying to free Americans whom Hizballah had kidnapped, tortured, and, in William Buckley's case, killed by torture, simply for the sadistic pleasure of doing so to an American official.

I flashed back to memories from many years earlier of what was around me as we padded through the black, and the frigid air. The interrogation techniques I had experienced were designed to disorient me, to disrupt my circadian rhythms so that I started to feel detached from the world I had always known. Our Office of Medical Services had captured well what the interrogation methods were designed to accomplish:

---

3 This passage describes the sinister inside of Hotel California and making my way through it.

These are designed to psychologically "dislocate" the detainee, maximize his feeling of vulnerability and helplessness, and reduce or eliminate his will to resist our efforts to obtain critical intelligence.

I could not tell night from day, how long any period of time was, even waking from sleep, in the end. Times changed. Temperatures changed dramatically. My food was irregular, or awful, or not enough, or too much. I was forced to stay awake, or my sleep was spastic and interrupted without pattern. The noise was endless and very loud. People screamed and sobbed in other rooms. Fabrics tore in long rips, explosions hurt my ears, and babies cried and cried and cried, wailed and simpered and hollered and cried again. Dogs barked and growled. Hour after hour after hour. Sometimes I had to stand against a wall, with a hood on. For a long, long time. It was hard to do. It was hard to breathe—I felt like I was suffocating. I started to panic. I took the hood off, just a little, just barely over my nose; they put it back on roughly, all the way over my face. I had to contort myself into cramped boxes, in which I could not sit or stand. I was too tired to stay awake, but I was not able to sleep; when I dropped off, a guard woke me. I descended into a world of trauma and dreams, where I was not awake, or asleep, or coherent, or able to think straight. For the first time in my life, I lost the ability to distinguish where I ended, and where the outside world began. I could not tell. I started to lose control of my personality, to inhabit a world in which I was completely isolated, and in which I could not trust my senses. I hallucinated—I saw slimy things, told myself they did not exist, but also told myself I had better stay still so that they would go away. At first the capture and detention training was unpleasant, but each discrete segment was even interesting. At first. But it kept on. It all accumulated on my mind. It never stopped. Nothing existed but the dark, cold, confusion, pain, fear . . . and the slow loss of myself. The only salvation was the moment of sanity when I sat facing an interrogator.

And through it all, *I knew it was a training exercise*. It would last for days, but I knew it would end, and I knew my instructors would do me no real harm.

We stopped at CAPTUS's cell. The guard let me in. I immediately recognized that it was designed according to the old KUBARK manual guidelines:

Cells should be about 3 meters long and 2 meters wide. . . . Cell doors should be of heavy steel with judas port for viewing and separate port for putting food and water into the cell. The slamming of a heavy steel door impresses upon the subject that he is cut off from the rest of the world. . . . Heat, air and light may be externally controlled, but not to the point of torture. . . . Bedding should be minimal—cot and blanket—no mattress. The idea is to prevent the subject from relaxing and recovering from shock.

CAPTUS ███ stirred as the door opened, rousing himself to lean up on one arm and to cast off a single, small blanket.

I sat down opposite CAPTUS and looked at him. I was shocked at his appearance.

I was no longer aware of the loud noise outside. The chair was cold through my pants.

"CAPTUS." He looked at me, not understanding what was happening. My tone was declaratory, matter-of-fact, not imperious.

"CAPTUS, it's Jacques." He continued to stare, his eyes glassy, not making sense of anything yet. I could see his mind starting to work.

"CAPTUS, it's Jacques. I am here too, now."

"Jacques . . ."

He realized now who I was. His circumstances were so disorienting that it took a moment to put someone he knew into this context. I gestured, in a way I hoped was kind, for CAPTUS to take a seat. He rose slowly, hunched over, with a murmured "*choukran, choukran.*"

"CAPTUS, what has happened to you ████? You do not look good."

He tried to dismiss his appearance, responding vaguely and softly, "Your men . . . arriving. No. No men. It is nothing, it is nothing. I do not mind. It is no trouble."

I persisted. "What 'arriving' and 'men'? My men did this?" I found that unbelievable.

"No, no. Yes. ██████████████████████. It is all right."

With some work—every explanation from CAPTUS took work and was a labor, even in better circumstances than this—CAPTUS explained what had happened to him. He said ███████████████████████████████████ ██ ████████████████.

I understood now. I had seen it happen ██████████████████████ ██ ██ ██ ██ █████████████████████████████.

I apologized to CAPTUS, ██████████████████████████████████ ██ ██ ██ ██ ██.

More important, however, in my mind was the *way* CAPTUS narrated this little episode. I knew the facts of the episode he had just explained, and I still had trouble making sense of him. Yet, he had spoken accurately, allowance made for his way of perceiving and describing events. ████████████████ ██ █████████████████████████████████████. The episode strengthened his credibility in my eyes and confirmed that the way I had been describing him to Headquarters was fundamentally accurate: ███████████████████ ██ ██ ██████████████████████████.

I also knew how our business worked. This was the kind of contextual case knowledge that was virtually impossible to put in traffic but was so crucial to running good ops, and to being a good case officer. It was too subtle for the system to digest and accept in formal exchanges.

"CAPTUS. It is cold. Would you like another blanket?"

A noncommittal response.

"I will get you one."

. But we were back at it once again.

As the session progressed I already was finding that what I had argued before was true: We had misread the man; he was not a jihadist or a member of al-Qa'ida; he did not warrant transfer to Hotel California, and doing so would serve no useful purpose.

Wilmington, Headquarters, the White House's Office of General Counsel or its Department of Justice scribes, and much of a fearful and angry public missed a critical distinction when considering the whole issue of using coercive measures in interrogation. The dilemma was, in fact, extensively considered in the various versions of the KUBARK interrogation manuals that had for decades served the U.S. military, and CIA, as guidelines for interrogations, and which I had mulled over in light of my personal experiences, as I had wrestled with what was effective and where I would set boundaries for how I would conduct an interrogation myself: "For centuries," the KUBARK manual deliberated,

> "questioners" have employed various methods of inducing physical weaknesses: prolonged constraint; prolonged exertion; extremes of heat, cold, or moisture; and deprivation of food or sleep. The assumption that lowering the subject's physiological resistance will lower his psychological capacity for resistance: however. [*sic*] There has been no scientific investigation of this assumption.

Just as the KUBARK manual noted, it is easy to stress a man physically and psychologically. I knew this firsthand; it had not taken long to break me

---

4 This passage describes what I told CAPTUS and what my plans were for him.

down. But I also knew—independent of the fundamental legal and moral considerations concerning coercive measures in interrogations—that breaking an individual down did *not* make him more likely to divulge reliable information. Some few men may break from coercive measures. In all cases, however, the decisive factor in a successful interrogation is an individual's personality, and the rapport the interrogator has with the detainee. One cannot conduct a productive, long-term interrogation with a rapport that consists of pain endured and fear engendered.

I opposed much of the reasoning behind, and acceptability of, Hotel California (with rare exceptions). I opposed the reasoning behind CAPTUS's transfer there. I had come to the conclusion that CAPTUS's tangential, inadvertent, and unwanted relationship with al-Qa'ida did not justify a rendition. I had come to disagree with the specific steps taken in the case I was running. I had come to oppose the entire coercive interrogation measures approach. What a fuckup.

The Hotel California chief, the shrink, and I held an after-interrogation meeting in the chief's dilapidated and unfurnished "office" ▮▮▮▮▮▮▮▮▮▮▮
▮▮▮
▮▮▮▮▮▮▮▮▮▮▮▮▮▮▮▮▮▮▮▮▮▮▮▮▮▮▮▮▮▮▮▮▮▮▮▮▮▮ .

We spoke standing up, close together, and in low voices, so that we could hear each other, so that our voices did not carry. All substantive questions were left to me as C/O in charge of the interrogation and the case. I did not discuss them, except to give a general sense of how forthcoming he had been. But we reviewed how the conditions to which CAPTUS was subject contributed to or hindered the interrogation, and made certain that he was in general health.

The chief wanted to be helpful, with the tools he had to offer. What did I want him to do? What was the shrink's assessment of CAPTUS's mental state? Was the psychological dislocation in process? Was he within acceptable parameters of stress? Should the chief increase CAPTUS's level of discomfort and disorientation? Make it colder? Turn up the music? Turn on the lights? Let him sleep, or keep him awake? Give him additional amenities?

▮▮▮
▮▮▮
▮▮▮

[The CIA Inspector General's *Special Review: Counterterrorism, Detention and Interrogation Activities (2003–7123-IG)*, declassified in August 2009, details the authorized "standard" and "enhanced" measures for interrogation. I quote:

> Standard Measures (i.e., without physical or substantial psycho-
>   logical pressure)
> Shaving
> Stripping
> Diapering (generally for periods not greater than 72 hours)
> Hooding
> Isolation
> White noise or loud music (at a decibel level that will not damage
>   hearing)

Continuous light or darkness

Uncomfortably cool environment

Restricted diet, including reduced caloric intake (sufficient to
    maintain general health)

Shackling in upright, sitting, or horizontal position

Water dousing

Sleep deprivation (up to 72 hours)

Enhanced Measures (with physical or psychological pressure be-
    yond the above)

Attention grasp

Facial hold

Insult (facial slap)

Abdominal slap

Prolonged diapering

Sleep deprivation (over 72 hours)

Stress positions

        —on knees, body slanted forward or backward

        —leaning with forehead on wall

Walling

Cramped confinement (Confinement boxes)

Waterboard

In all instances the general goal of these techniques is a psycho-
    logical impact, and not some physical effect, with a specific
    goal of "dislocating" his expectations regarding the treatment
    he believes he will receive.]

The chief's automatic proposal of measures distressed me. I vetoed all the chief's suggestions.

"Not now. Not yet."

I explained that I wanted CAPTUS to see that I was helping him; I noted that CAPTUS responded to my relationship with him. I said that I wanted the chief to give CAPTUS another blanket.

The chief agreed. I saw that the chief was a decent officer, completely willing to follow the instructions of the C/O's running the interrogations. It was just that his job was to use the tools at Hotel California in support of the War on Terror. He was serving his country in difficult circumstances. This was his job. He did not think beyond that.

The psychologist had until now listened silently to the chief's and my discussion, nodding from time to time, his arms crossed high on his chest. I had noticed that he reacted poorly to the chief's suggestions ████████████████

███

████████████████████████. He spoke now earnestly, firmly, to the chief.

"Listen to what you are saying, man! ████████████████. I must remind you formally, that these are human beings in there. I don't like the idea of blanket punishment, simply to make them all suffer. ████████████████████

███

███

██████. Is there a reason to do these things? The detainees are here for a long time. Think of what you are doing with these points in mind."

I was silently pleased at the shrink's intervention. The system of controls and balances was working, I thought. He was here (and so was I) to keep procedures rational and acceptable.

To the chief's credit, he listened to the shrink carefully, nodded his head, and accepted without reserve the shrink's cautions. The Agency lacked a body of experience on coercive measures and interrogation; there was no protocol for detention and interrogation as yet (in fact, there was, but I did not know that). He welcomed the expert assessments and guidance of the case officer and the shrink running the various cases in his charge.

The shrink and I consulted a moment one-on-one after the post-interrogation meeting. He commented in passing that "I'm a psychologist, you know. Not a psychiatrist."

I glanced at him, around us at the facility, then back at him. I did not care. I had been thankful for his focus on the physical and mental health of the detainees. At least momentarily, I had an ally.

"Okay, whatever." I nodded. "Thanks."

When the post-interrogation meeting ended I walked out and stood alone by a window, staring out into the dim and fading light. I still had to drive back to the compound and I wanted to get back if at all possible before dark. I had many hours of work to do once back at the station, writing operational cables, intelligence reports, and taking care of administrative details. Nothing moved that I could see. The landscape was barren under low clouds. What had I become? What had my country become? Had this land always been so bleak?

Parker approached me after I had gazed out the window a couple of minutes, my hands in my jacket pockets and my collar pulled up against the chill.

"What're you looking at?"

"I'm Diogenes," I said slowly, at first not turning. I half smiled and glanced at Parker over my collar. "Got a light?"

"What?"

"Nothing. We gotta get out of here. Let's roll."

YOU NEVER KNOW
WHAT IS WAITING FOR US

Tantum religio potuit suadere malorum.
(So great are the evils to which religion has led men.)
—Lucretius

The days ran together. Organizing an escort. Obtaining a vehicle. Gathering the ▮▮▮▮▮▮▮▮▮▮▮▮ or other relevant officers. The day's interrogation sessions. Returning to the compound as night fell. Writing my reports for hours and hours, into the wee hours every night. I was working on four hours' sleep per night. Everyone worked long hours.

I received instructions that expanded my responsibilities to other operational tasks, designed to pursue al-Qa'ida aggressively and help the conduct of the CAPTUS case. Circumstances permitting, I would become involved with the other individual who had been rendered and who had turned out to be mentally deficient. We all wanted to be aggressive. I was distressed at this development, though, because I disagreed with the assessments made that led to the new operation in which I was to become involved. Strong differences of opinion on operations were common and legitimate; it was a normal part of our jobs to wrestle with decisions where nothing was clear and consequences

223

were great, and to work matters out as best we could. But on this latest operation I disagreed acidly with what we were doing. And I sensed that the other field officers involved shared my skepticism about what Headquarters had ordered us to do.

During one night excursion a security officer and I were discussing where in the world we were. There was almost no way to tell from the little we could see of the landscape around us. It was freezing in the 4x4 and we were heavily bundled up. Parker, once again, rode shotgun.

Parker ostentatiously busied himself with his weapon as we talked. He had done this sort of thing before.

The security officer broke off our conversation and faced Parker.

"What the fuck are you doing?" The security officer was irritated.

"I'm preparing my weapon." He looked at the security officer. "It's always good to be prepared."

The security officer had many years of experience. Parker had sat in a cubicle in Langley and had cracked the books at some university. The security officer was withering. He enunciated his words syllable by syllable.

"You lit-tle shit. Put that fucking thing away, you dumb fuck. It is going to go off and you will kill us all."

Parker looked back at the security officer for a moment, now motionless.

"You never know what is going to be waiting for us," Parker persisted, half defiant, half defensive. But he sat quietly this time, hands in his lap when we drove on.

Officers from Headquarters kept proposing by cable that they come out to assist in the case. I did not need any more Parkers around, who contributed little, did not know the case, did not know what they were doing, were inclined to play the tough guy, and would disrupt what I was trying to do. I declined all their offers of support.

It was enough to deal with the PCS officers at Point Zero. They were solid officers, but they had to address other tasks; none of them knew the case—which was my job, after all; when they did engage on the case they tended to follow standard procedures, without much thought to the CAPTUS case itself.

██

████████████████████████████████████. Not knowing the case, they could not really write up the operational aspects of it with particular discernment, or recognize the intelligence CAPTUS provided. I had long since made this case mine. It was typical for the handling C/O to feel proprietary about his cases. I felt that my handling CAPTUS was especially important, given the unthinking and wrong assessment of who he was and how to handle him.

Advice differed during my time in Point Zero on whether one should go into the city. Crazy Cal thought it was okay. Other officers disagreed and recommended against it.

"There's a $100,000 bounty for killing an American. ███████████ ███████████. They're right here, looking for a moment. ███████████ ████."

I broke my routine now and again and went.

I had started to learn from my first minutes in country that all Americans dressed so as to blend in as much as possible—as had the officers in the convoy that had picked me up at the airport sat in front of me in the 4x4 ██, while I sat feeling clueless and all of a sudden naked. I wore my own local garb every time I went off the compound. But it did not really do much to turn me into a local.

"I look like a clown in this thing," I said to two officers as we prepared to go into town for my first time, as I tried to put the clothing on correctly. I managed only to deform it more. This was a chronic problem for me. Every so often I had to have the employees at the compound fix the way it looked for me. It took them a few minutes of shaping and readjusting. I was embarrassed.

"If I looked any more American in this place—well, I can't look any more American. I look like some kid out of a Rockwell painting, or like some cherubic Irish adolescent just coming out of a pub. All these guys look like killers. I couldn't intimidate a puppy."

With every day, though, I blended in more, as I got scruffier, and at least it was harder to recognize me individually.

It became instantly apparent that road rules did not exist in town. Everyone wove all over both sides of the road. Bikes cut in front of you. Women in traditional dress crossed the street, completely ignoring the cars they stepped

in front of. Men whom you needed to watch, ██████████ were everywhere, on
the road, at intersections, on the sidewalks, at buildings, in cars. Large posters
of the key local leader were plastered on the sides of buildings, on the back
windshields of cars, on walls beside men standing guard, on many road signs,
at intersections, inside buildings; even, in one case, ████████████████████
████████████████████████████████████ so that it hung down like a fanion.

Traffic policemen waved their arms in grand gestures from the middle of
intersections, blew their whistles, and were completely ignored. Everyone cut
everyone else off. The men on the streets all looked old, weathered, and hard.
Women in traditional dress shuffled here and there. It refreshed me to see the
rare modern woman. There were many halt and lame, and many scraggly kids.
Everywhere one saw men who could not walk pushing themselves on little
three-wheeled carts, as I had seen so often in the Third World. Most of the
shops were one-room storefronts, in one-, two-, or sometimes three-story buildings. They sold small retail items: vegetables, soap, bronze pots. I was surprised to see a number of computer shops. Most shop signs were in English
as well as the local language.

I did not know the officers I was riding with this trip. The one driving maintained a litany of distress as he rocked and reared through the streets.

"This place is fucked up. I can't wait to get out of here. You just know
someone is going to get ██████. They're all around us. The bad guys haven't
gone anywhere."

They were both twitchy. "Don't let them do it!" shouted the officer riding
shotgun to the driver at, well, anything he saw. "Move! Move!" I turned
around as the officer shouted, to glimpse a poor cyclist crashing to the ground
in our wake. In my brief experience, I found this crazy driving to be totally
unnecessary, and surely alienating to the locals. The traffic always kept moving anyway.

It was fascinating to observe how people reacted differently to Point Zero.
Some who went into town with me were as nervous as the two officers I ac-
companied my first time. Others were childlike in their wonder at the exotic-
ness of the local wares—rugs, silverwork, leather—and of the people. They
took so long doing things, and were so unconcerned, that even I became ner-

vous. There were many idle men in the city who looked at us intently. The two officers I was with refused to speak or interact with anyone unless they were unable to avoid it. I wondered why they had agreed to their assignments.

I watched out like everyone else, though, and was sometimes tense, too. But I enjoyed the first and my subsequent drives into town, and in general felt calm. ███████████████████████████████████ ███████████████████████████████████ ███████████████████████████████████. I did not tarry. I took appropriate cautions. But I was having *fun*. This was what I had signed up for. I found the experience among the most stimulating of my life. I was invigorated, my senses were heightened, I felt alive and that I was living with a purpose. It was intense. I almost felt guilty to admit to myself how exhilarated I felt from it all.

We ate at a Chinese restaurant, an incongruous place to find in Point Zero. Two cute young Chinese women served us. They looked you in the eye, smiled, and chatted, which was pleasant and striking in the circumstances. They told us that they had believed that where we were "would be a good place to do business," but to their surprise had found it "crazy," apparently not anticipating that Chinese women might find it challenging to establish a business in such a primitive society, where they were memorable simply because we could see them.

I stayed with familiar dishes on the menu, avoiding such offerings as the "wholly braised ovine hoof." In a bizarre, and to me disturbing, episode too reminiscent of how I imagined scenes of GIs in Vietnam, as we started to eat the two girls giggled and capered beside us, the Americans, pretending to shoot enemies with their hands, "Pow! Pow!"

The food was good. But before I stepped onto the sidewalk and back into the world of Point Zero, I looked up and down the street from inside the doorway.

I picked up on signs of underlying ethnic tensions. The ubiquitous photographs of ████████████████████ around town disturbed me. Yet, peer group think and mannerisms are hard to resist, and led me, momentarily, to posture. This manifested itself in an exchange in which I embarrassed myself, engaging in a bit of verbal posing that I heard come out of my mouth, and that was similar to my colleague Parker's little acts of bravura.

"Have you noticed all those pictures of the local leader?" I remarked on one of my subsequent trips in town, with Parker and two other officers. "It's pretty amazing. I'm not sure it's the smartest thing in the world to do."

"I agree," said the local colleague sitting beside me. "I do not think this is good."

"Why not?" asked Parker, at the wheel.

"Because the current winners are acting a little too arrogant, a little too much in your face. It's all ethnic. But they only make up about 10 percent of the population."

"I think it is not very good. It is unwise, not thinking. They should not do it," the colleague beside me in back said, with a slight look of concern.

"What do you think the locals think about it?" asked Parker.

"I think," I said, "they're thinking, 'we'll get you when the time comes, when the Americans go away.' The ███████████ fanatics are as much a tribal phenomenon as anything else."

I denounced the ethnic dynamics and tensions in the country, and added that "the jihadists are, at root, creatures of the goddamned Saudis, with their goddamned Wahhabite Islamic teaching. They finance all this Islamist stuff everywhere in the world."

"Yes, I agree. They are very bad, ███████████," said the local officer sitting beside me. "And the ███████████ [a certain country], too."

"Yes, yes!" I said. "Them, too. The ███████ fanatics were their creatures."

"Really?" said Parker.

"██. Yeah, the clerics and the ███████████████████ [certain country's intelligence service]. The clerics have obliged that their teachings be financed and proselytized around the world. And the intel service are blind bastards. But Frankenstein got away from them. Assholes. Yes, them, too. Some of their intel officers ███████ have asserted to me with a straight face that we Americans don't understand: the ███████ fanatics were a force to make life better for women. They want to go back to the pure Islam of the seventh century. It's frightening. Assholes."

"Yes, yes," said the local officer sitting beside me. "██████████ [the certain country] gets away with all this. America thinks they are an ally. But they are playing a double game."

"You've been reading books," Parker said to me.

Parker and the other men in the vehicle seemed impressed by what I said, the decisive alpha male, on top of the situation, but at last I stopped myself. As we drove along I settled into what the others took to be silent contempt for our adversaries, but was annoyance with myself. I had sat surprised and irritated as I listened to my own performance. My speech and persona had shaded into a mannered machismo. I felt myself conforming to the attitudes and manners around me, part of a vast organism that asked few questions but was ardent to accomplish the mission. This hint of swagger was phony and simple, it was not me, even as my assessments were accurate. Momentarily I had become a louder Wilmington, surrounded by guns and flak jackets.

WHAT SINS MIGHT
ONE NOT COMMIT?

*Pericles: Indeed, I am more afraid of our
own blunders than of the enemy's devices.*
—Thucydides, *The Peloponnesian War*, I.V.143

The situation was deteriorating. Each concrete operational step I tried to take proved impossible for reasons beyond my control. I disliked those I could take. ███. This, of course, frustrated and irritated me, and ███████████████████ in response. But this, too, was no surprise. The KUBARK interrogation manual, and my own experience, had anticipated this and discussed it openly: "Many psychologists consider [that] . . . prolonged constraint or exertion, sustained deprivation of food or sleep, etc., often become . . . counterproductive . . . the subject may become apathetic and withdraw into himself." I had correctly anticipated the evolution of the case, and each operational setback—but Cassandra had derived no satisfaction from her prophesies, and I little from my sardonic asides or efforts to have us all act sensibly.

██

██.

231

"██
████████████████████████."

Frankly, I continued to admire CAPTUS's character in these circumstances.

And yet, he lied. I asked him about individuals I knew he knew. He denied knowing them. I asked him about events I considered uncontroversial and "safe" for him, in which I knew he had been involved. He claimed not to know anything about them. I became very angry with him, despite myself.

██
██
██
██
███████████.

██
██
██
██
██
█████████████████.[1]

I was furious. CAPTUS sat, silent and sullen.

I left him and returned to the chief's office. ████████████████
██. I glowered. I was angry at CAPTUS. I felt badly for CAPTUS. I was angry at the entire situation. And yet, perversely, the issue I had raised was not fundamental.

"Not so good, huh?" the chief said. His attempts to be helpful deepened my anger. I refused everything he proposed, controlling myself.

The whole operation had become sordid. ███████████████
██
██

---

1 This passage describes a specific exchange when I lost my temper because CAPTUS's behavior made it impossible to move forward, to address questions, or possibly to help him.

██████████. Almost everything we were doing to him was wrong. It was stupid, self-defeating, demeaning, and operationally useless to give no choice whatsoever to a person being interrogated, or whom one was trying to manipulate, or whose cooperation one sought. ████████████████████████████

██

███

███

███.

I was living the cautions of the KUBARK manual once again: Use of coercive measures, and pain, had the following consequences: "In general, direct physical brutality creates only resentment, hostility, and further defiance." Worse still, I was angry at myself; the circumstances affected me, too. The "dark side, if you will," enveloped and changed everyone involved in it.

No man willingly will lose his *soul*. For what is the soul but some shred of free will, hope, and dignity? In its psychological and operational obtuseness Headquarters had wanted to humiliate him, to dislocate him psychologically, in the belief that this would break him and cause him to tell all that he knew.

Even terrorists, even killers, define themselves by honor. Fear, honor, interest motivate men. The enhanced interrogation techniques, Hotel California; these played upon fear, and interest. This could be useful. They directly assaulted any man's honor, though, making it more likely that the individual would resist. "It is better to live like a hawk for one day than like a hen all your life," says a Kurdish proverb. We feel this, too, in America. But those driving the CAPTUS case, and the clumsiness of an institution in making decisions that require nuance, considered that terrorists had no honor, deserved none, and could be coerced to surrender what we took them not to have, and what gave meaning to their lives. I found moral clarity in ambiguity, and danger in certainty; Headquarters found this incomprehensible, or dangerous, or weak.

I had been right to establish rapport and to engage with CAPTUS as a man, instead of simply approaching him with a checklist of questions for him to answer. I cannot state forcefully enough how crucial it is in an interrogation, when developing an asset—when establishing any textured and worthy human relation—to sustain and foster the other person's honor, sense of personal independence and control, integrity, and trust. To commit such a delicate, dangerous act as selling out his associates, betraying his oaths . . . or committing treason, an individual must come to depend upon and believe in a case officer as deeply as he has ever believed anything.

Dignity shorn, trust undone, and relationship perverted, the person being interrogated (or convinced to commit treason) has nothing with which to protect his pride and sense of self. Even a terrorist must retain some piece of himself, must in some way still be a man, for him to be potentially a useful interlocutor, or source of trustworthy information. Some men become abject, are totally destroyed, and surrender totally, but they are few. Most require far more subtle and decent treatment. It is both inhumane and operationally harmful to oblige a prisoner to choose between moral debasement and betrayal. An interrogator *can* and must develop a relationship with his prisoner, imbalanced as it will be. Perversely, interrogation and treason, like love, rest upon personal bonds and trust.

Will any man openly accept that he is become Judas? And yet, given a fig leaf, what sins might one not commit?

Parker was at the wheel as we returned to the compound after the latest interrogation session. He was in a boisterous, good mood. I did not have much to say, looking out as we stormed and bashed along, the landscape changing with our motion, benign or ominous depending on how I chose to look at it. He drove much too fast, knocking us in back all over the seat, banging our heads off the roof, and slamming against the doors, as he rammed through deep potholes, our vehicle lurching, yawing, and rearing.

"I like to hear Glenn grunt 'uhh!' and say 'Jesus Christ!' as we go over the holes," he laughed.

"I think Parker is compensating for some low testosterone levels," I said to the officer sitting beside me as we bounced and jangled along.

"What?" Parker said.

"I said," I shouted, to be heard over the rattle and engine roar, and holding onto the back of the front seat as the 4x4 threw me around, "I—think—you—are—a—fucker!"

THERE'S NO TIME FOR
NO "I DON'T KNOW"

*The moving finger writes and, having writ, moves on,
not all your piety and wit can lure it back to cancel half
a line, nor all your tears wash out a word of it.*

—P. G. Wodehouse, *Thank You, Jeeves,*
quoting Omar Khayyam, *The Rubaiyat*

My bunk was in the back of a room reserved for transients, adjacent to the Jihadi Bar. Many tried to avoid being lodged there. Fetid odors wafted into the room from the bathroom doorway five feet from the head of my bed. The door was stuck open. The room was always freezing, and billowing clouds of steam rolled through the bathroom door over my bed whenever someone took a shower. Loud country music, laughter, clinking beer bottles, and cracking pool balls spilled from the bar into the room until 2:30 or later every night. I put my pillow over my head to muffle the sound, and I was so tired I usually fell asleep the moment I buried my head. Once in a while I had to stumble out to the bar, groggy, to say as coherently and nicely as I could through my stupor that I was trying to sleep. The men and women were always abashed and became much quieter. But the compound's kitchen was through the wall beside my bunk, so that the clankings and chatter of the cooks preparing breakfast awakened me every morning before 6 anyway, pillow on my head or not, if by chance I were still in bed. I was sleeping four or five hours a night.

Despite the odors, billowing steam, and successive bar and kitchen rackets, I was satisfied where I was. I've always been quite easy about my work conditions, an attitude that has served me well, since the CIA often ████ ████████████████████████ is chronically crammed into one abysmal space or another. I've enjoyed the hint of adventure and flexibility that these conditions have called to my mind; the romance of imagined fortitude and purpose through material inconvenience. I think I developed this idiosyncrasy during my years of living destitute in an unheated, moldy two-room flat, one floor above a transvestite bar in the Pigalle quarter of Paris. We all find purpose as we may. For a short time, I liked it. Still, what with work and the room's amenities I had slept little and was very tired.

It was midafternoon and I had managed to get onto one of the station's shared computers in the makeshift common office space where I had to work. Usually I had to write up my interrogation and operational reports in the evenings, when the station was much quieter. Officers were endlessly coming and going in the hallway and into and out of the office as I typed. I put my hood over my head so that I could concentrate better.

Running an operation at Point Zero was in some ways freer than anywhere else I had worked. I was left to make my own decisions; I did not have to run cables through a chain of coordination and approval. I had to interact only with Headquarters and relevant field stations. The Directorate of Operations insisted (correctly) that every action be documented in writing and that all formal business pass through cable traffic. In consequence, sending a cable and receiving an answer, even one marked IMMEDIATE, normally took a minimum of ███████████████ hours. Time-critical issues, or issues too complex to be reasonably conveyed by cable, could be addressed on the secure Stu III telephone system. The Stu was not used for day-to-day business, except by a COS; they tended to use Stus far more often—often, for them *not* having a record of conversations and decisions was exactly the point.

I had a long Stu conversation with Ryan back at Headquarters, a good friend, and the desk officer for the operational aspects of the CAPTUS case.

We had spoken so that he could give me an off-the-record description of the atmosphere about the case in CTC: Headquarters continued to take a much harder line than I advocated, and Ryan thought I should know the atmosphere about the operation and, by implication, my handling of the case. Wilmington and I had from the outset clashed on how to handle the case, although never directly. All was couched in collegial terms; in part, this was because Headquarters needed me. Experienced officers were scarce, particularly one willing to disappear from his family on TDY for months, and who were willing and able to conduct an HVT interrogation. Ryan was an ally, so I tried to explain the realities of the case and, perhaps, bring Headquarters around a little. I also tried with Ryan to work out whether I could extend my stay beyond the time frame to which I had initially agreed. I was scheduled to depart Point Zero in a week or two, but I would probably be able to extend if I pushed for it. I had leverage, too: I now knew the case better than anyone; it had become "mine" weeks ago.

I wanted to stay on—I knew what would happen, or would not, when someone replaced me. I had spoken the truth to CAPTUS; he had to speak to *me*. The real problem, though, was that the CAPTUS case would be handled from then on according to largely thoughtless procedures, by PCS officers. No one would take the time with him required to obtain the information he could share. ███ ███████████████████████████████████████. Instead, they would go by the book: ███ ███████████. He could provide critical information; otherwise he would not have been rendered, they would argue. All the standard interrogation procedures would be applied, in one combination or another, to "psychologically disrupt" him: shaving, stripping, diapering, hooding, isolation, white noise or loud music, continuous light or darkness, an uncomfortably cool environment, a restricted diet, shackling, water dousing, sleep deprivation.

███ ███ ███████████████████████████. A case officer would appear, for all intents and purposes clipboard in hand, knowing nothing about CAPTUS or about the past twists and turns of the case, and would ask a series of stock questions.

For this officer, overburdened with too many cases to handle, CAPTUS was a two-dimensional object; the officer's handling of the case could *only* be, itself, shallow. Case knowledge and time are crucial to running any case properly, and in particular an HVT interrogation. Then, the case officer would undoubtedly grow angry ██ ██ ██ ██ ████████████████████████████ and the cycle would spiral pointlessly downward, toward a stasis of rote procedures and miserable conditions, where not providing information was interpreted as proof that there was information to provide—or as the CIA Inspector General's *Special Review* on interrogation techniques would put it, as proof of "the assumption . . . that the detainee was holding back and knew more."

But this circular, narrow, and culturally and psychologically dimwitted reasoning and operational approach did not ask the critical questions about the CAPTUS case and would not obtain the critical answers: Was CAPTUS a terrorist? The answer was no. ██████████████████████████? The answer was no, ████████████████████████████████████. Could he provide critical information? The answer was "nowhere near what we thought when we rendered him." ████████████████████████████████ ██ ████████████████. Did coercive measures make sense? No. Did coercive measures ever make sense? The answer was almost always no. In rare circumstances, one could make a case that they may be called for; but such cases were so extraordinary as to disqualify themselves to serve as the basis for a doctrine of interrogation and legal guidance. Was he willing to be cooperative? The answer was yes, he was. ████████████████████████████ ████████████████████████████. Coercion bred contempt and hate more than it extracted meaningful—or legally acceptable—information. ██ ██ ████████████████████████████████████

██
████████████████████████████████.[1]

I had been hoping to extend my stay and carry on with my work with CAP-TUS; I did not want to lose control of the case and I did not trust anyone else to do it right. But staying at Point Zero to run the CAPTUS case posed logistical complexities. I also was due back in the country where CAPTUS had been held for most of his detention. I had a lot of work left there. I needed to meet with our liaison partners there, in particular with Big Guy and Little Guy. Peter, the COS, had been firm in his orders: He expected me back. I wanted to go back there, in any event. Also, my children were six and eight, I had been away TDY longer than initially planned, and it had been many weeks since I had begun my CAPTUS work. I wanted to see them. There was no way to accomplish everything I wanted to and to fulfill all my obligations. I mulled all these elements while I typed, engaged in the field C/O's eternal struggle to "recruit" Headquarters to the field officer's point of view.

A striking young woman walked past me, dressed in form-fitting ████████ pants, and a ████████████ T-shirt several sizes too small. She wore ████████ boots laced up high, her pants tucked inside them, and had a 9mm pistol in a black holster strapped provocatively on her upper thigh. It swayed seductively in time with her hips. My eyes followed her across the open office space. Each stride was a little self-aware show.

"What's with Lara Croft?" I asked a PCS officer sitting at the computer next to me.

He watched her pass off toward the Reports Office. "Oh, you mean Commando Cathy? Something else, eh?"

"What's with the pistol and holster? She into S&M or something? We're sitting in the most secure place in the country and ████████████████

██

██

she's ready for us to be overrun?"

---

1 The deleted passages discuss the relation of standard "largely thoughtless procedures" for interrogation with the specifics of the CAPTUS case, and my strong conviction that such procedures were wrong, were counterproductive, and perpetuated critical errors in judgment.

The officer laughed a little. "Yeah, she's not the only one; one of the nicest looking, though. She's probably never even left the compound. I dunno; it's exciting for a chick to strap on a gun, I guess."

Commando Cathy was only a momentary distraction, the latest scene from the wonderland into which I had fallen, where hounds bayed at the moon to the tune of bagpipes, ninjas jumped out of planes onto the runway in front of strangers in order to remain clandestine, Chinese waitresses wearing flak jackets hopped about my luncheon table pretending to shoot me amidst their giggles, women strapped on weapons as fashion accessories, and protocol-bound idiots made the rules.

I returned to my typing.

I needed to find Jean, our admin officer, the first of a number of officers I had to see to work out the details of how I could leave the country, and how I might arrange travel back to the States to see my kids and wife after so long. I needed to work out a complicated series of moving parts, and could do nothing without the admin officer's help. I had been looking for her for two days. I could not get a flight without her, and for operational reasons I absolutely had to make arrangements that night or the following morning. I was sure to get stuck in country for a minimum of another week, and more likely ten days, unless I could find her. ████████████████████████████████ ██. Getting a plane dedicated to me was conceivable, but highly unlikely. My personal operational needs were simply part of the general operational pace of a supercharged station. Demand greatly exceeded space, everyone was a priority, weather often socked us in, or kept all planes out, and where our planes generally went was often shut down from fog or snow, or other conditions. Altogether, my travel efforts risked becoming another document saga.

I rose from the computer and walked down the common hallway to her office. Like everyone's, it was a small cubby, converted to serve a larger purpose. She was not around—again. I simply could not find this woman. I thought I would wait a few minutes by her door, hoping that she might appear. It was that or, ironically, get stuck for days where I wanted to stay but had now decided to leave.

Completely plastering the walls around her office were dozens and dozens of schoolchildren's letters and drawings. Some were from six-year-olds. Some were from ten-year-olds. Some from teenagers. I looked at them in growing amazement. Teachers and school systems across America had somehow decided it was a good idea for schoolchildren to write letters and draw pictures to send to us, the CIA, to express support, say thanks, and so on. One tends to imagine that this sort of gesture comes from World War II, or bad movies. It did not, though. It was real. ███████████████████████████ ██. There were letters, and drawings, little kids' crayon pictures of what they thought a spy must look like and do. The letters said things like, "thanks for keeping us safe." Others were drawings—sometimes by mothers—of kids sleeping in their beds, with the caption, "I can sleep safe at night because of you . . ." or "Protect us from the bad guys . . ."

Reading and seeing these letters and drawings—amidst the tired, tense, and dedicated colleagues, urine smells, long hours and weeks, my efforts to accomplish the mission, to make sense of what I was assigned to do, to act honorably in a situation full of increasingly disturbing contradictions or judgmental errors, to keep people safe—was powerful. They moved me much more than I thought could happen. Tears blurred my vision and I choked up. I stood blinking. I was glad that I was alone for a moment. I told myself that I was just tired.

The innocent drawings and expressions of faith, the requests from mothers to protect their children as they slept in their beds, pulled at my heart. It made all CIA officers fathers, as well as sentinels, as well as hard men in a hard business. We are always alone, in our work. We work in areas where the right choice can be murky, or the area or work itself dangerous for yourself or for those in your charge; there are few easy decisions or paths. No one ever knows what we do; what we do is hard and often does not work. There can be a heavy emotional cost. Seeing these crayon drawings and ingenuous expressions of support for and trust in what we do with our lives was more important to me than I would have imagined. It was one of the most vivid, moving memories of my entire career. My children once said to me that they never saw me cry.

I never cried. It's true. I don't, really. I'm a man, an adult, a case officer. We don't cry much. But I have. I did. I did from the wall plastered with school-children's expressions of support and hope for protection.

The one-sided game of hide-and-seek with our admin officer continued. Jean did not show up, so I went to ask Jim, our ███ operations chief, if he knew where she was. Jim spoke with a strong southern twang. He never had much time for anyone, given the daunting series of operational pieces he had to fit together, which he did in a way I always found amazing.

"Hell, I don't know where she is," he said. "We're goddamn busier than a one-armed wallpaper hanger around here, trying to get things done and she's off doing her laundry or sumpin'. Doesn't that woman notice what's going on around here?"

I couldn't leave Point Zero without confirming my flight forty-eight hours in advance. I couldn't delay my departure or arrange another flight unless I could find Jean. I couldn't get to the country where I had initially interrogated CAPTUS, and fulfill my obligations to Peter. It was certain that I would be stuck there another two weeks or more if I could not find the phantom Jean right away.

"Shit, Saturday is her laundry day. You ain't gonna see her until tomorra." I told Jim that some important, critical issues for my work were at play, in part a function of my flight plans. Couldn't he help? No, he could not, but the issue was simple to him:

"Now, I don't want to tell you how to suck eggs, or do your job, or anything like that. But, if it's that important, if you got a mission to do, hell, you do that. Stay and we'll work out getting you on a plane when you're done."

My problem was that my mission called for me to be in two countries at once, and to make arrangements that were impossible to make. I told Jim to cancel my plans for the flight out. Someone else would take my place. I would rearrange my plans for a later date once I found Jean.

The following morning, I canceled a trip out to Hotel California so that I could find her. I searched for Jean all the following morning without success, and ended up sitting around uselessly. It was ridiculous, and by now I was getting pissed off. I told Jim my arrangements were still unresolved, which was starting to complicate his life, too. He had to make arrangements to accommodate my needs, which were hostage to Jean's domestic priorities. Without her approval and coordination with onward points—a task only she could perform—I was stuck there. Bureaucrats can have power, but this was becoming absurd: The admin officer trumped the ops chief and a case officer on an HVT case.

"Her laundry? Her laundry?! Sweet Mother Mary. Jesus, motherfucking, goddamned motherfucking goddamned Christ! Doesn't she know what the hell is going *on* around here?! ██████████! Is she a *complete* dodo turd?" Jim was really irritated now. I was angry, too, but Jim's explosion still made me laugh, which irritated him even more.

I finally found Jean in her room that afternoon. Jean was a heavy, fifty-five- or sixty-year-old woman, with overwhelmed eyes, pleasant but harried, and struggling to keep herself emotionally under control. As she stood in the doorway I could see her small room behind her, piled with clothes on the floor, and flotsam lying about in disorder. It was apparent that she was struggling to deal with conditions at Point Zero, and a huge workload. I suspected that she wanted to be in a regular office job back home with her friends, not with harried officers pressing her to arrange flights at all hours of the day and night. I wondered what in the world she was doing at Point Zero; I figured the money was good and the DO was running all hands on deck, sending whomever, wherever, because pressure on the Agency to be aggressive against terrorists was so high.

Jean simply would not engage with me and refused to hear my tale. Everyone had priorities, she was exhausted and strung out and insisted that she have a little time to herself.

"I am doing my laundry. I won't do it. I am *off* now. I never get out of here. Not here. It never ends. I will see you tomorrow, in my office." And that was that. She closed the door.

As difficult as her position was for me, I understood her. Everyone bombarded her, at all hours of the day. One of the first lessons I learned as a manager was that everyone always had a story that justified immediate special treatment. Dozens and dozens of officers had preceded me with their requests for particular attention. She did deserve some few moments to herself. She was at risk of having a breakdown. She really should have been replaced by someone more suited to a high-ops tempo. But she still obliged me to alter my operational plans on an important case, and to risk the real prospect of getting stuck in country for another ten days or two weeks . . . for the sake of her *laundry*.

Once again, I had to delay my departure and had to inform Jim that I was unable to resolve the conflicts in my plans.

Jean was as good as her word. She saw me first thing the following morning, proving to be efficient and polite, and wearing clean clothes. And after all my efforts to find Jean to make special travel plans, in the end, the imperfect solution to my need simultaneously to continue my work at Point Zero, to travel to the country where CAPTUS had been, and to get back to Washington to see my family was to depart two days later. Jean told me that it was the only flight I could try to take to avoid getting socked in and stuck there for another two weeks or more. I told her to schedule me, tentatively, and I would get back to her.

Just as this little burlesque finished, an earlier one returned for a reprise. The station holding CAPTUS's documents replied to my latest request to have the documents sent to Point Zero for use in the interrogation; of course, the station informed me that they could not spare anyone to courier them to me. The station helpfully suggested that they be pouched to Headquarters. This would take ages and would accomplish nothing useful. I took sardonic enjoyment from having confirmed my expectation and from having catalyzed the same senseless, futile response that had been frustrating me for months.

I was swamped with work. The only way I could possibly leave on the flight Jean had reserved for me would be if I stayed up all night to write my reports and cables. I sat in the heaped chaos of the overcrowded, jury-rigged common office space through the wee hours, once again all alone.

I knew that this was one of the critical moments of my career.

I had often considered during my career how to see clearly in the gray world, where right depends on circumstance, one's perspective, or one's flag; where there are few obvious answers; and where our independence and agency are lost at the same time they are exalted. From the outset, the CAPTUS case presented acute challenges to an officer's sometimes conflicting obligations, in a career of blurred and contradictory moral imperatives in the service of one's oath—to the flag. But through the fog, and the dark, and the noise, methane breathers, and the pressure to act aggressively, and from my oath, I knew, I had known for some time, that I would try to express my fundamental opposition to the premises and conduct of the CAPTUS case, and to state how I believed we were disgracing ourselves in our zeal. I saw clearly in *this* gray world, and I wanted to say "No! Enough!" that night, before I lost all influence on the case.

Slowly the night passed, as I worked, drank coffee, and stared glassy-eyed at the screen. Then, quietly, over a half hour one, two, then several officers started to shuffle around the station. I stood up and walked to a window from time to time. The sun rose, first wan and then stronger, but never warming, and the daily round began again.

Jim found me late in the morning, still typing amidst the cramped chaos of plywood trestle tables, masking-taped wires on the floor, and stale coffee cups. Time was up. He was typically brusque.

"You goin' tomorrow?"

"I think so. I don't know yet, really. Jean sent the notification cable, so I could go."

I needed to head to Hotel California for another session with CAPTUS, and wanted to put off this topic until I returned later in the afternoon.

There was a hint of irritation in Jim's voice. He became a little martial, impatient. He was under a lot of pressure, too, and had little time for one officer's hemming and hawing.

"There's no time for no 'I don't know.' You won't be going if you don't know. You going?"

I had to decide. He was right, of course. I was glad I had worked all night. I had really known I had to go; I had just been trying not to admit it to myself.

"Yes, I'm going," I said, resolving on the spot my plans for Point Zero; my travel through a series of other capitals, designed to get me to the country where Peter awaited my return, in a way that avoided making a beeline to my destination; and my hopes to get home to see my family after so long away.

Jim nodded, tersely satisfied. "All right, then." He headed off.

WHEN TO SAY NO

Atrevíme, en fin; hice lo que pude; derribàronme,
y aunque perdí la honra, no perdí, ni puedo perder,
la virtud de cumplir mi palabra. (I dared, in the end;
I did what I could; I was overthrown, and although
I lost the honors, I did not lose, I cannot lose, the
virtue of honoring my word.)
—Cervantes, *Don Quixote*, II.66

It is not necessary to hope in order to act,
or to succeed in order to persevere.
—William the Silent, Prince of Orange

Overnight, I had written the two bluntest cables of my career. One was an ops assessment about CAPTUS, and the other an ops assessment of the man I had characterized as a "retard." My time was ending, the charge was passing to other hands, and I was determined to do what I could to challenge what I considered a sustained series of serious errors in judgment, and that the case had been kept running through conceptual and analytical error and, like so many cases, bureaucratic momentum.

247

Kidnapping, suspension of habeas corpus, interrogation, "enhanced inter-rogation," the meaning of torture, relations with liaison partners, political struggles in Washington, life and death, war, the safety of American lives—all were in play in the CAPTUS case. I knew from the outset that this was a case in which the normal compromises one makes with peers and with the in-stitution in order to accomplish the mission were unacceptable. I had known from my first conversation on the case with Wilmington that it raised the most sensitive issues of law, duty, and morality, and that on this case as for perhaps no other in my career I had to act according to my sense of right and duty, whatever the institution's positions and the general views of what was accept-able. From the outset, I was not going to go along because the institution had chosen a certain course of action, not when American lives were at stake, and not when de facto kidnapping and torture were possibly the tools with which I would be involved.

The case was a coup and put the CTC office handling it in the big leagues; CAPTUS had the attention of the very highest levels of the Agency and the administration. According to the guiding narrative, the office handling the CAPTUS case had identified a senior al-Qa'ida operative after years of painstaking work involving many CIA officers, in coordination with the FBI and other federal agencies. In a decisive blow against al-Qa'ida and its global network the Agency had rendered CAPTUS—kidnapped him off the street with our own officers—to disrupt his and al-Qa'ida's operations, learn about the plans, intentions, personnel, locations, and structures of the most senior levels of al-Qa'ida and its worldwide network and supporters. It was possible that CAPTUS could provide us information that would cripple al-Qa'ida, and the entire operation had been conducted with decisiveness, care, and dis-patch, and in the shadows. No one in the world, except for the allied services involved in the operation, knew what had happened to CAPTUS. Al-Qa'ida's leaders had probably by now come to fear the invisible lethal hand of the CIA, that silently erased al-Qa'ida operatives from the face of the earth—and where, they had to wonder, was that hand now? *This* was how to wage the Global War on Terror.

I shared these views when I had first been brought into the case. I knew my colleagues. I knew their devotion and care. I saw the painstaking work, done over years, by multiple analysts and case officers, on the CAPTUS case. Like all CIA officers, I was determined to devote myself entirely to destroying al-Qa'ida: I had worked al-Qa'ida and the Afghan problem for years prior to 9/11 and felt that I had known the seriousness of the threat before 9/11, and before ever having heard of CAPTUS. I accepted the standard paradigm uncritically: that al-Qa'ida posed a global threat and was a global organization. That 9/11 was the latest in a series of coherent attacks. Like all officers, I took the CIA's commitment and perspective, from the DCI down to the lowest support officer, as proof that this view was correct. The Agency did not tilt at windmills; individual officers could err in their assessments, of course, but the carefully and endlessly vetted views of the entire institution described and responded to objective reality. And so, as we all do in our various walks of life, I accepted the views of most of my peers, of my institution, and of my government—after all, they worked specific elements of the threat, and often I did not, so of course their views were more likely to describe accurately what was going on—and enthusiastically set out to do my duty. I was honored to have a key role in such an important case, on the premier issue of our day.

But now, sitting alone in the shared office space, covered with the dust of Hotel California, my head spinning sometimes from fatigue, I knew the truth. I knew the file, I had run the case, I saw the flaws in the conventional views, it was I who was confronted with questions touching upon human rights, the law, rendition, detention, interrogation, torture—who had to make the right decisions about these issues, or at least could influence them, *and I had measured the man.* I had thought all the elements of the CAPTUS case through; Headquarters did not think. As with any institution or group of men, a narrative once embraced becomes real, and most people will then reject incongruous or contradictory facts as erroneous, because they do not conform to accepted reality. We are all unconscious victims of multiple distorting paradigms in our lives; I had become aware of the errors in the CAPTUS paradigm, and I was determined to try to right the grievous wrongs it had caused. And throughout my involvement with CAPTUS, as I led the team, shaped the reporting, assessed his motives and veracity, dealt with Headquarters and liaison and overeager analysts and jailors, *the CAPTUS case also had been measuring me,* of what mettle and morals I was made.

People are burned at the stake for challenging deeply held "truths." For a case officer, bucking the system endangers one's career. But lives and honor were at stake in this case. I would not go along with the crowd, not on an issue this important. I accepted that intelligence work, terrorism, and war called for hard decisions, manipulating men, and even sacrificing or taking lives. But I refused to believe that we destroy lives unnecessarily, from error and craven thought, and that we dismiss error, when discovered, with a cynic's shrug. I refused to accept conventional views and practices, not if they were flawed, not if they were fundamental; not if I became aware of how they limited perception, skewed thought, and distorted action. Not if I could help it. I would do what I could to get the CAPTUS case right, to right the errors of perception and commission.

There are several avenues in the DO that one can take to address wrong-doing. One can write a "front channel" message—a cable in normal channels, for consideration by the regular chain of command. One can send a cable to the Inspector General, if there are questions of malfeasance or gross wrong-doing. One can send a cable through the special channel of the Office of Security. One can approach the COS and send a back-channel cable that way. One can file a grievance (although this channel is usually restricted to issues of discrimination or unfair treatment). One can approach the Office of General Counsel, for issues touching upon the law. Any of these was possible; none of them was satisfactory.

One learns in the DO that almost without exception an officer who challenges the institution, or uses one of these channels to challenge some issue, may win a battle but will harm his or her career, and is unlikely to change the underlying practices initially challenged. This was especially true for an operational issue. It would be so for the CAPTUS case, where the issues concerned matters of judgment, not clear malfeasance, and where the issues touching upon law (interrogation methods) had been sanctioned by a careful process in advance, involving the general counsels of various government agencies, and the White House. Who was one officer to challenge the reasoned weight of the executive branch and of the CIA?

I had wrestled for some time with what would be the most effective way to change the DO's perceptions of CAPTUS and how we approached the case. I

decided the most likely way to get the case changed was to work through normal DO channels, trying to use the influence and credibility I had developed
as an experienced case officer, responsible for running the case in the field
for months. Officers up the chain of command would listen to my message as
an insider, part of the team; they would tend to oppose a criticism that was
presented as a challenge to the entire system. If I simply withdrew myself
from the case and the issues, I would have no effect at all. An outsider has no
voice and no influence, especially in the CIA, especially in the DO. So I tried
to do right and to influence decisions from within—as much as I could, without compromising past a hard-to-locate critical line of right and wrong; past
a "No! Enough!" moment. I would accompany my formal recommendations
with face-to-face meetings with the several senior officers, to describe to them
as a peer what was wrong with the case, and how we might rectify our handling
of it.

The cables had to stand out. I wanted to oblige the DO to take notice of
them, to be obliged to take action. They had none of DO cables' de rigueur
collegiality and detachment. Yet, since I had written them as the senior ops
officer responsible in the field for the CAPTUS case, who had operational
credibility, I hoped that Headquarters could not treat them reflexively and
defensively as alien criticisms of DO practice.

The gist of my thinking, arrived at after months of handling the case,
was that:

CAPTUS was not a member of al-Qa'ida. The assessment that led to his
rendition had been wrong. Sending him to Hotel California was a counterproductive and gratuitous use of enhanced interrogation procedures, which
had contradicted my assessment of the appropriate approach to take, and
which punished CAPTUS to no purpose. ███████████████████
███
███
███.

This made our treatment of CAPTUS, quite simply, miscreant. It was wrong
to detain and destroy the life of a man who was not in al-Qa'ida and whom
we had mischaracterized. It was shameful, ███████████████ to persist in detaining him once we had realized these points. Concerning the other rendered

individual for whom I had some responsibility, it was outrageous to detain someone who appeared to be none of the things that had justified his rendition, and who on top of it proved to be retarded. It was an error to seize him, but errors happen all the time and there was no shame in that; yet, it was an injustice not to rectify error when we could.

The situation, as I perceived it, had become Kafkaesque and needed to be put in stark terms: We held a cretin who did not know the information that we rendered him for, in part to enable us to pressure CAPTUS with information from a different source, who also did not know what we had rendered him for, and we then sent them to Hotel California to use coercive measures to get them to tell us what I was convinced, and some colleagues also now recognized, they probably did not know. I could conclude only that we continued to detain and interrogate them because we were deluded, or incapable, or unwilling to rectify our errors.

I urged that we liberate CAPTUS and the other detainee with whom I had been to some extent involved.

It was our *duty* to do so. I said that the DO must act aggressively in our counterterrorism operations but that we must also embody our principles and remedy our errors, not bury them in silence, the dark, and Hotel California.

I left the common office space after Jim's departure and went to see the COS. He was not in the station, so I met with the DCOS. I closed the door, always a sign of sensitive discussions, and directly summarized my views of the CAPTUS case, and of the other case I had been involved in. I cautioned him that my two cables were stronger and more direct than one ever read in the DO, but that the subject was so important I had consciously written them in such an incendiary style. The subject called for it. I urged him to understand that I was a responsible officer; I was not overheated and easily shocked. But the CAPTUS case had gone awry; we were acting in grievously harmful ways—███████████, to the DO, and to our responsibilities. I knew the case better than anyone and we needed to change the premises that drove it and the operational practices we had settled on. I urged to the DCOS that we liberate CAPTUS and the other individual with whom I had some involvement.

The DCOS was controlled and quiet, but showed some surprise at my vehemence. I suspected, as I had anticipated, that he thought I was overtired.

He certainly viewed my comments as different from what one discusses, or how one discusses matters, in normal operational meetings. He promised to take the matter up with the COS. I left the meeting knowing that one needed to have a personal professional relationship with the superior for what I said to be accepted and acted upon. The DCOS and I had not seen each other once since the day of my arrival. He had no perspective with which to evaluate the comments of the wild-eyed and exhausted officer in front of him. I suspected he would send a back-channel cable about the issue to Headquarters; I would have. But I needed the cables to go in normal channels, too. This was why I had seen the DCOS and had spoken so earnestly.

When I stepped out of the DCOS's office, I looked around the foyer, looked again at the children's drawings on the wall, saw Lara Croft cross from one doorway to another down the hall, and passed through the doorway toward the Jihadi Bar. I rounded up my security officer, stepped out the front door, smiled at a local colleague standing outside the door, and in a bantering tone spoke a couple words of the local language as I passed him. He nodded, smiled, and I could see he had no idea what I was talking about. I picked up a vehicle from the motor pool and bounced off through the muted earth tones of the countryside to go see CAPTUS.

A JAUNDICED BLUR
OF WORK AND FATIGUE

A platform or a prison are places,
one high the other low; but your moral
purpose can be kept the same in either place.

—Epictetus, *Discourses I*

My last meeting with CAPTUS was uneventful, the jaundiced end of a blur of work and fatigue. My meetings with him had lost their colors, shapes, and the specific details that gave them individual life. Impressions all ran together and what passed for normal now mixed the grotesque, the banal, and the surreal. CAPTUS and I had slid outside the normal arrow of time and three dimensions in which everyone else lives.

I recall vivid odors, sounds, and emotions, jumbled together and all around me: the jolting, wary rides through blinding fog, while my thoughts, when I had any through my weariness, turned progressively jaded and angry at the hard certainties of institutions and of protocols, and of what they can do to men; the hint of the occult at Hotel California, just beyond my shaded lamp and perceptions; moist, cold air, and noise looming and ebbing, pressing in and fading all around, all the time, from beyond the little circle of feeble light, until nothing but the questions were real, the endless questions . . . and then the black enveloped everything again, and nothing was real and I died each time the light went out; silent colleagues around me, imposing and sometimes daunting by their mournful seriousness, and by their weary, even tragic gentleness, appearing or flitting or fading in my periphery as shades from another world, or were they menservants to a silent, unguent Mephistopheles waiting just beyond my sight?; the earnest, decent, slightly overeager chief greeting me as I left the fog and entered the darkness, whose formal procedures defined his intellectual limits, replaced his moral sense, and affirmed his sense of justice.

Back at the station the lights shone bright, the fog burned away, eyes focused intently, and men and women acted rational. But I had the feeling that my cables usually were like the lamp I carried at Hotel California: It cast weak light for a few feet but was lost to the gaze of those looking at what they expected to see, who saw power as strength and nuance as apology, and who were convinced we were exorcising a demon, in a perverse triumph of fear and delusion over muddled reality.

Two episodes stood out from all these desolate trips. Once, we came around a little bend in the road, not far from our destination. We found ourselves face-to-face with an unexpected man standing on the edge of the road holding an ██████. He was as startled as we were. ████████████████████████ ██████████████████. We came to a sudden stop, so that we found ourselves in a momentary, tense Mexican standoff from about thirty feet. After a moment we realized that, surprised though we were, he was one of our allies, doing we knew not what. ████████████████████████████. We drove on past the man, who quickly dropped behind us, around the bend, and out of sight.

"What the fuck," commented our security man at the wheel, in surprise, fear, and relief.

But even at the moment, and often since, I have wondered: *Did this really happen?* It was so fleeting. In ways and at moments we often cannot discern, conviction, perception, and imagined memory are as real as facts. I kept these ruminations on heuristics to myself.

The other recollection that stands out from my trips to meet with CAPTUS was as I sat half daydreaming in the back of the 4x4 as it lurched over the potholes and rocks on the "road," staring idly out the window at the bobbing landscape. About a hundred yards off to my right I saw a young boy, perhaps ten years old, picking his way through a field, going from one apparently non-existent destination to another, and seemingly unconcerned that he was walking in a minefield. There was no one else I could see anywhere, and there was nowhere I could see where he could be going. His journey seemed pointless and he appeared oblivious to, or unconcerned about, the dangers all about him. I was amazed.

"What is that kid doing?" I asked no one in particular. Parker shrugged, but said nothing.

I thought of a Baul lyric I had heard years earlier: "Your life is a precious bridge of marble, but unfortunately it does not reach either shore . . ." This kid, too, quickly faded into the distance behind us, as we carried on. I kept this thought to myself, too.

I had lost the power to offer hope. There were no friends to anyone in my business. Much had gone wrong. But I had often told junior colleagues, when they became frustrated, that our job was to identify problems and then try to fix them. Problems *were* the job. We were hired for our judgment. I had worked to act honorably, to fulfill my oaths—as had my colleagues—and to embody the spirit of our laws. The echoes, and victims, of 9/11 spread across the world, and America's righteous wrath—and sometimes unreason—was fully as deep as, and infinitely more powerful than, Bin Ladin's Islamicist nihilism.

On my last approach to the compound, returning from my last meeting, I thought again of my call sign: REDEMPTOR. REDEMPTOR. I didn't know about that. But no one ever does, and there is no final judgment, and we never reach the end of the marble bridge.

YOU LOOK LIKE A GHOST

A face looked down in the gathering day,
And laughing spoke from the wall:
"Ohe', they mourn here: let me by—
Azizun, the Lucknow nautch-girl, I!
When the house is rotten, the rats must fly,
And I seek another thrall.

"For I ruled the King as ne'er did Queen,—
Tonight the Queens rule me!
Guard them safely, but let me go,
Or ever they pay the debt they owe
In scourge and torture!" She leaped below,
And the grim guard watched her flee.
—Rudyard Kipling, *The Last Suttee*

I was now standing on the tarmac of Point Zero's airport. The wind was stiff, the air fresh, the sun wan.

The long vistas in all directions were heartening. It was the first time since my arrival that I had had any sense of physical grandeur in anything I had seen, and now, as I departed, I glimpsed what had inspired and conquered men for millennia. Around me were men long experienced on lonely airstrips in forsaken corners of the world. I took a deep breath; the cold air invigorated me. Eight of us were leaving Point Zero, heading for onward points and new assignments.

Jim, the chief, had driven me out from the compound and was chatting with a colleague. We had some time to kill before the plane arrived. I amused myself by gazing at the massive mountains on the horizon and enjoying the first sunshine I recalled in ages. A large aircraft sat not far from us.

"Hey, Jim. Can I go take a look at that?" He thought a moment, weighing whether he could trust a clueless officer out of his sight. "I won't touch anything."

"All right."

The controls in the cockpit were all marked with taped instructions. I enjoyed a momentary crazed "Far Side" impulse to commit an absurdist's prank and to shift the descriptions on the control panel around, so that "flaps" would be taped below the "landing gear" control, or "fuel discharge" below "altitude" or some other foolish combination. A gentle, puffing, springlike breeze blew into the cockpit through an open window, the sill wet with the raindrops and condensation remaining from that morning's shower.

When I bored of that I walked around and scanned the airfield.

Crazy Cal was chatting with another passenger a few dozen feet behind me. I walked toward the exit and the runway. "Don't go beyond the gate! Don't go out there!" Crazy Cal shouted to me as I got to within thirty feet of it. It was the first time I had ever seen him animated. ██████████████████ ██ . I stopped and stared dully at where I must not go. I had hardly slept in five days. The world around me was a kaleidoscope of impressions, one after another, merging together and breaking apart, my eyes open too wide, my perceptions passive; linear thought was hard.

I idly mulled that the airport was surrounded by mountains and that this would make it hard to defend. I wondered who was up in them. I wondered whether the British encampment, over 150 years earlier, was anywhere near where I was.

About a half hour passed.

The plane arrived without my seeing or hearing it, even though I thought I had been looking. *I really must be out of it*, I thought. Things just appeared before me.

The eight of us gathered our bags and waited for the arrivals to deplane. I stood gazing vacantly across the strip, when one of the guys who got off the plane came over to me, smiling.

"It matches," he said, indicating my clothes. I was a little distracted and wondered why this guy was talking to me and what he was talking about.

"It does? I'm always very careful. Presentation and appearance are very important." I thought he had said something about my blue and green ski jacket, and answered in what I thought was the same wiseass and inappropriate manner. Sort of weird. Maybe this guy was on edge about arriving at Point Zero.

He said something else. I didn't get it and wasn't paying him any attention. I started to shuffle dully toward the plane. He repeated it, with a smile of recognition and familiarity: "It matches. The scarf. The colors go with your jacket."

What was this banter? I turned my attention from the mountains and boarding the plane and focused on what he said. It was true; I hadn't thought of it before: My scarf, which was wrapped around my neck and rose up to my mouth, was off-white, with a green pattern on it, matching the green piping of my jacket.

I looked the guy in the face and focused on him consciously. I knew him! That's why he was talking to me out of the blue. It was Ryan, my replacement. He was good-naturedly ragging on me about going native and playing at intrepid man of the desert. The last time he had seen me, months earlier, I was in a suit, as always. In a rare instance of logistical efficiency—surely a random event—the Agency had arranged it so that my replacement arrived on the very plane I was taking out of there.

"Hey, Ryan!" I said, shaking hands. "Sorry, I was zoning out a little. The scarf? No, no. You'll want to get one at the compound as soon as you get there. You'll need to wear it. It's not a good idea to be recognized as an American. We are supposed to be incognito, not be recognizable as Americans. Really." I had forgotten I was even wearing it.

"You'll want one of those hats, too. ███████████████████████ ███. They all wear them. I left mine at the compound for someone else to use."

A flicker of doubt passed in Ryan's face. He thought perhaps I was being a wise guy, or playing at tough war-fighter. His smile was slightly frozen, with a hint of hesitancy. I had forgotten, too, that I had a beard, and that my appearance and dress had been so changed by my location.

"It's true. You'll want one. They can help at the compound. ███████████ ██████████████████████████████████████ but you'll get one as soon as you get there. You have to wear it ██████████████. Very stylish. You'll find this place amazing, an *unbelievable* shit hole."

"All right! Let's load up! We gotta move!" Jim called from beside the loading ramp. I had only a couple of minutes.

"Listen, Glenn, I have an open mind on work," said Ryan. "I think you make sense. I'm coming out here without any ax to grind. I'll take it any way you or Headquarters wants. I don't go the hard-guy routine in work, usually. You'll have to work the office when you get back. I suggest you make the case in a cable."

Ryan was referring to a long Stu III conversation we had had a few days before. I was challenging Headquarters on how to run the case. It was a big deal and it was an awkward moment for me to be pulled out. Ryan and I really needed to talk shop. There was so much I should brief him on. It was kind of Ryan, actually, to readily seek guidance from the guy he was taking over for. Normally we are all pretty proprietary: Once a case or issue is yours, it's yours and you tend to avoid ceding the degree of control that comes with consulting others, especially your predecessors, who are knowledgeable of the work and may want to take the case in a different direction than the one you want.

The other seven passengers were hauling their gear and themselves into the plane quickly. Jim stood by the door, hands on hips.

I gestured with my head and Ryan and I wordlessly walked a few dozen feet away from the bustle around the plane, to where we could talk openly, unheard by others. Everyone around us was visibly more on edge and hurrying, not as tense as when I had arrived in country—we were protected by the berm—but still anxious to load up and leave an exposed location.

Our conversation was hurried. I noticed that Crazy Cal and Jim and the few who had arrived were getting ready to mount their vehicles. Jim wanted to close up the plane, get it airborne, and get off the runway.

"Don't look to the guys stationed PCS here, Ryan. No disrespect to them. But you gotta do it yourself. They don't have the manpower or the expertise. I don't see it. It can't happen. It has to be you. And don't let any more god-damned 'experts' come out from Headquarters to offer their advice and play at tough guy, so they can get a trip out here. Just shut 'em down. I've denied travel to a bunch of them. It's much better. Ask them what you need to by cable, or by Stu."

There was no more time. Jim and Crazy Cal had signaled to the pilot and were getting into their vehicles. I hadn't even expected to have these two minutes to brief him and to try to get him to see the case my way.

"Gotta go."

"Okay."

We shook hands.

"Oh, man," Ryan said, in compassionate dismay, "you look like a ghost."

I stared at him dully, sunken-eyed.

"Oh? No, I'm the REDEMPTOR."

Ryan looked at me, bewildered, a trace of concern in his eyes that I was speaking alarming gibberish.

"It's my call sign."

I turned, climbed into the plane, and sat in one of the four seats with a window, looking out the left side of the plane. Ryan had already jumped in a 4x4, for the ride back to the station. The engines started, we pulled out onto the runway, and in seconds I felt the peculiar floating sensation of the takeoff. I looked down on the mountains beside the airstrip as we gained altitude.

The inside of the plane roared.

"We're going to make a quick stop in ███████!" the copilot shouted to me as he passed into the hold directly behind my seat. I looked out the window with great interest and lost what little sense of time I had through my fatigue.

My mind came back into the plane when we started our descent. The flight had taken only an hour, a trip that would have taken men many days through hard country in times past. They could not have done it at all at this time of the year.

I had the floating sensation again as we came down. The runway looked surprisingly well tended and modern, the airport buildings in good repair. It all seemed modern almost, like a suburban high school from the 1970s, nothing like the dereliction and ruin of Point Zero. We were down quickly and within seconds pulled up to the main airport building. Three 4x4s were lined up, engines running and lights on. A few men in civilian dress stood in a rough row. There were no other signs of life or movement, just a soft breeze, lightly hazed-over sunlight and quiet, broken by the engines' drone.

███

███

███

███.

The men all boarded the plane and loaded various packages onboard in seconds. As soon as the men were on, the copilot called out, "Okay, let's move!" I gestured to one of the men to sit down beside me. The plane was rolling forward before he could do so.

"Thanks." We shook hands and the plane was airborne seconds later. Another impressive performance by my colleagues. We rose fast and swung north. We passed two or three hundred feet over what looked like a tent village

███

████████████████████████████████████. Then we were gone. The desolate airstrip was behind us.

My seatmate told me this was his second time in country. "I was here a year ago." "Oh? In December?" "Yeah." "You were really one of the first, then." "Yeah." I nodded, my eyebrows raised. One of the ███████████████

██████████████████. He was burly, about thirty, mild-mannered, laconic.

The plane roared on. Everywhere I could see looked desolate.

I was very tired. The drone and roar of the engines made me drowsy. Below, the landscape turned into solid, deep snow, endless steppe without the slightest sign of human life. My ██████████████████████ seatmate fell asleep in minutes. So did I, two U.S. government representatives on the frontier of American influence, leaving for a time to others the tasks of interrogating, or hunting, those trying to destroy America.

A couple hours later the shifting tone of the engines awakened me once again. We were only one hundred feet above the ground, about to land. The ground was covered in deep snow, the runway in half-cleared areas, with swaths of slush all around. I was surprised: I had anticipated something backward, small, and shabby. Now I was looking at long runways, numbers of Boeings on the tarmac, large hangars, snowplows.

The plane turned into its slot plowed in the snow, pivoting on its axis, then stopped. The pilot cut the motors. This time, the hatch on the side of the fuselage opened and we exited down the stairs. I followed my ████████ ████████ seatmate down the stairs.

"Hey, good luck."

"Good luck. See ya around."

Standing at the bottom of the stairs with a welcoming, confident smile was Reggie, a colleague I had known since the very beginning of my career and had last seen months before in the Headquarters cafeteria over breakfast, each of us benign and banal, sipping our coffees and eating our muffins at the beginning of the day. He was at least ten years my senior, but I had always found him unpretentious and unconcerned with rank. He was just a nice guy who was also competent. One of the better men and officers I had known in the Agency.

"I get off the plane on the edge of the planet, and the first person I see is you!" I laughed. "What are you doing here?"

Reggie laughed, too. "Welcoming you. What do you think?" We shook hands. It was obvious that he had a lot to do, so I moved out of the way as he oversaw the unloading of the cargo and shipping the dozen of us off to the various hotels he and his assistant had reserved for us. Watching Reggie do his job, chatting occasionally with him and the other arrivals, I thought that we were a very small outfit; during the previous several weeks I had crossed paths with three officers with whom I had worked over the years, in three different parts of the world, and now I had run into another one in the back of beyond. But I knew that we were everywhere, too, despite our size, working in dozens of other posts I had passed through.

A moment later Reggie's mood darkened suddenly.

"You, sir. Come here. Now."

The man to whom Reggie spoke had been on the flight with me. He walked the few steps to the back of the plane where Reggie stood over some of the packets that had just been unloaded. The friendly bustle around the plane stopped and all the men stood motionless, hands in pockets. We had all tensed. Reggie was angry, and loomed more imposingly than a moment before.

"What are you doing? You know you may not bring weapons here."

"What? Oh. I didn't know."

Reggie was angry.

"You didn't know? Here's what will happen, unless I succeed in doing you a favor: You will be confined to quarters, you might be arrested by the local authorities—they have zero tolerance for anyone with any weapon—and we all may be thrown out of the country. If we're lucky. And then your real trouble will begin." Reggie looked around the motionless men. "All of you will give to me now all weapons and any related equipment you have with you. Then you will accompany me while I secure this with my security people. Do you understand?"

"Yes, sir."

There were a couple of minutes of chastened luggage rustling, as Reggie closely watched the men separate their booty from their bags. I receded a little farther toward the snowbanks.

A couple minutes later Reggie and I walked to the waiting vehicles. The wind had picked up and was blowing snow horizontally in huge gusts. Darkness enveloped us as soon as we left the plane side. Reggie had returned to his jovial self as quickly as he had become stern a moment earlier.

"Jackasses. They didn't know? They didn't know like we're in Miami right now." I got into one vehicle, Reggie into another. "Hey," he said, smiling and shaking my hand, "good to see you. Welcome to the edge of the planet."

My vague preconceptions about the city where we had just landed were completely wrong. The city was large, with broad, clean boulevards, well-situated and numerous trees, modern and well-tended buildings. . . . Women were stylishly dressed. They wore very short skirts and lots of makeup, over-doing and confusing excess with attractiveness. The hotel lobby was bright, spacious, modern, and welcoming. The hotel had a good restaurant. There were fashion boutiques, buses, television, traffic. . . . I was back in civilization. It was a shock. A colleague told me that once he had spoken with a Russian *Spetsnaz* officer who had told him that the Russians had posted a sign one saw when entering into ███████████████, the country I had just left, that said, YOU ARE NOW ENTERING THE EIGHTH CENTURY.

The following morning, back at the airport, a sign caught my attention while I waited for my onward flight. It was written in English, but like so many signs one sees in non-English-speaking countries, it was almost incomprehensible. It said, more or less:

welcoming travelers:
    must to be to ask of friendly traveling people that is to make so closely with awareness rules all formalized carrying bags. you not must to do, very friendly noted, such items as allowed forbidden to take in the internals of the craft with selves. charges will to be to make, if is size superfluent, or if is items larger of permit required leave. electron items allowed not will. too gracious to be cappted tipped.

And beside that:

passenger dears
    your formalized carrying bags larger than perrmit required authorization we take to send in all directions.

I picked up a *Wall Street Journal* and *International Herald Tribune* in the ████████████ airport during the first of a number of transfers, barely twenty-four hours after I had flown out from ████████████████████████ ████████████:

Journal: A grenade attack in Kabul injured two U.S. soldiers and an interpreter who were riding in a jeep. . . . Al Qaeda reactivated some camps in eastern Afghanistan and new volunteers are heading there for training, a U.N. monitoring agency said.

Herald Tribune: Two U.S. soldiers Wounded in Kabul Grenade Attack . . . one with injuries to the eye and the other to the leg. . . . It was unclear how badly their Afghan translator was hurt. . . . The assailants, ethnic Pashtun Afghans, were arrested. . . . Mohammed . . . was arrested with at least two grenades in his pocket. . . . The attack Tuesday was the latest in a series of sporadic attacks on U.S. soldiers in Afghanistan. . . . Fifteen U.S. servicemen have been killed in combat or hostile situations in Afghanistan since the U.S.-led anti-terror campaign began last year.

VICTIMS OF DELUSION

Certainly he scored it, bold, and black, and firm,
In that Indian paper—made his seniors squirm,
Quoted office scandals, wrote the tactless truth—
Was there ever known a more misguided youth?
—Rudyard Kipling, *The Man Who Could Write*

A piercing high-low alarm tone sounded throughout the office. We all had to crouch under our desks immediately. This is to protect us to some extent from any flying or crashing objects if anything bad were to happen. This was the first time I had had to get under my desk.

Years earlier, when I was serving overseas during the first Gulf War, we had to evacuate the office one evening due to a report that someone, presumably Iraqi agents, was going to blow it up. It was a festive occasion then, all of us making flippant, wry remarks. The air was chill and the squares and streets were stunning with their twinkling lights. Then, as I was walking past a beautiful hotel, all the lights in the area went out simultaneously. I had a momentary shock. Was the evacuation more serious than we were taking it? In the end, the blackout was unrelated to the Gulf War, nothing happened and we went back to our offices. This time, none of us felt festive. We took the threat seriously and did not mind the petty indignity of hiding under a desk.

We all had to wait there until the loudspeaker announced "all clear." It had been only a drill.

I had returned to the station and the country where I had interrogated CAPTUS for a rushed few days of cable writing, meeting with liaison, and tying up the loose ends of a complicated case. As usual, each day I worked until my colleagues shut the station down, about 9 or 10 p.m. Peter, the COS, had asked me to write up an overview cable of my work before I left. I agreed, but told him I had written the overview cable from Point Zero and did not know what to add in a cable from here. I put it off.

Near the end of my last day Peter came back to my desk again, in a bad mood because other people in the office had not done what he had expected of them. I had not done the wrap-up cable. I was at a loss, and I also did not want to rub Washington the wrong way more than I already had in my blast cables from Point Zero.

Peter expressed his frustration about various matters and then asked, "Have you done the cable?" It was not the moment to go into an explanation or rationalization for what he could interpret as only my inaction.

"No, I've been writing some pretty important reports all day." He looked expectant, as though he was turning a little of his exasperation to me. "And I don't want to piss off Headquarters by sending in yet another cable that disagrees with them."

"Let me simplify it for you," Peter told me. "It's your work. It happened here. It is appropriate to do a wrap-up cable *from here*. I don't care what Headquarters is pissed off about. It's late. You leave tomorrow. Do the cable. Got it?"

I looked at him. His eyebrows were slightly raised. "Got it. I'll do it." I did it. He was not especially irritated with me; more, my not having done the cable was an end-of-the-day example, after an afternoon's worth of them for Peter, of how nothing goes as it should and of how the boss can never quite get his staff to accomplish what he would like. He did not want to hear a story; he wanted his subordinates to do what he asked. I was surprised, however, that he had not seen my two cables. I assumed that he had been too busy to focus on my case and that, in any event, as he said, his responsibility was his station, not what I had written many thousands of miles away, out of his charge.

I arrived at the office at 7 the following morning to fine-tune the cable. Peter was in a much better mood. He asked me to write another quick cable. Done, even though my time was short; I had to be out of there by 9 a.m., and our commo guy—communications officers, of either sex, are invariably called commo guys—came in at 7:40 to tell us we had to log off because "I have to bring the system down."

"You were supposed to do that at 0700. What you're telling me is that you were supposed to be here at 0700, but you weren't." The commo guy laughed. Peter looked at him. He did not laugh. "Next Friday, come in at 0700." The boss's day was starting as bosses' days do.

I went into Peter's office to summarize my cable and brief him on my work before my departure. Peter had not focused on my departure date. "You're leaving today? In an hour?" He became very friendly, expressing his best wishes, making suggestions about what I could do back in Head-quarters, suggesting people I should talk to about my next assignment. I was touched.

A few minutes later the daily staff meeting began, the whole office gathering just as I had to leave. Everyone smiled, shook my hand, wished me well. I felt true warmth and friendship, that I was a liked colleague and friend. I was moved to feel their goodwill—earned goodwill—toward me. A select, elite brotherhood. Jack, my officemate during my stay, and I shook hands last.

"You've got your office to yourself now," I said to him.

"Given your fetish about urinals, I was going to give you a pot to piss in as a going-away gift, but then I figured you'd need a stool to stand on to use it, so it wasn't worth it."

I laughed. "Jack, this is your first tour, and already you have grown to be a fool."

I would have cherished such a pot.

Then I was out the door, hurrying to the hotel to check out and to catch my plane.

Traffic to the airport was light. The driver was chatty. I did not really feel like chatting. The Chevrolet Lumina felt very big and luxurious. "I'm not ac-customed to American cars anymore," I said. The sun broke through the rain clouds as we arrived at the airport. I had time to read a couple of pages of *Le Figaro*, then we embarked.

We took off just a few minutes later. Clouds quickly obscured any view. Other passengers were eating, or reading, shoes off, absorbed in their lives, comfortable in their routines. The flight back to Washington was long, requiring a couple of changes of plane. The in-flight films held no appeal to me on this trip, nor did the book or *Figaro* I had with me. Much of the time I spent staring blankly out the window, peering into the clouds and, eventually, the ocean miles below.

My work on the CAPTUS case had been one of the supreme challenges of my career. It had begun to change my views about the terrorist threat to our nation, and made me aware of grave conceptual errors in our counterterrorism structures and practices. A woman across the aisle was wiggling her stocking-footed toes. A child beside her played with his earphones and station buttons. I tried to spot some detail on the ocean but could not make out what I was looking at. I knew, though, that if only we descended low enough I would be able to see it surging, currents flowing, whitecaps endlessly foaming, rolling, and disappearing back into the waves.

As I looked at the ocean I could not see, I thought about my decision to write my last cables in Point Zero trying to set the CAPTUS case right and stating "No! Enough!" We all shape our actions, and our convictions of what is acceptable behavior, in relation to the norms around us. There are the Ten Commandments, of course, the Golden Rule, millennia of religious precepts and civil laws. These give our societies our sense of right and wrong. But, day to day, our understanding of duty and honor, of how to behave, is bounded and defined by the prevailing beliefs and behavior of those around us. We then, according to our personal lights and moral compass, fit our behavior within this imperfect circle. Some will be punctilious about the rules; others will let them slip; but almost all of us define right actions and right thinking in reference to the bell curve of behavior and belief of those around us. So, only slightly more than a generation ago, it was acceptable to shun those who broke the color line and fraternized with someone from the opposite race. So, until recently, it was acceptable, and even expected, that men should condescend to women and exclude them from meaningful professional activity. Some push the limits of acceptable behavior: my father who advocated sex education at a time when it was illegal to say the word "pregnant" on the airwaves, or those who moved to desegregate groups that refused entry to blacks, or to Jews. But, almost without exception, the parameters that obtain wherever we are bound what we consider acceptable behavior.

But what happens when we are confronted with exceptional circumstances touching on individual rights and social obligations, when what is "normal" and "expected" has shifted to accept, well, abominations? What do you do if you are in a laughing crowd that is about to lynch someone? What do you do if you are assigned, on penalty of death for desertion or dereliction of duty, to guard Jews being marched to the gas chambers? What do you do if, like many people I have lived with overseas, your country is destroyed, hundreds of thousands have died in weeks, you have no hope of opposing your enemy, whose regime *is* an abomination, and your death is almost certain if you try? What do you do if you are assigned to interrogate someone whom you believe to be a terrorist, and are instructed to use "enhanced measures" if necessary to obtain information that could save the lives of your fellow citizens, measures that the authorities to whom you have sworn service and who for your entire life have represented order and justice have determined are acceptable, but have not defined beyond the standards of "pressure" and of imagined efficacy, and which transgress law, tradition, and what your nation is supposed to represent?

Only heroes, or saints, or monsters can challenge the very order in which they live, their leaders, and the apparent course of events and history. We read about them, or sing their praise, or tell nightmare stories about them, because they are so rare. A hero like this comes only once a generation. The rest of us do the best we can, almost always within the circle of prevailing behavior, pushing against the boundaries if we are unusually strong.

I had flown out at the beginning of my assignment as enthused as one could be to be part of the Agency's counterterrorism work. I had worked the terrorism target, as we called it, for years (although not exclusively) and I accepted the nature of the threats facing us as presented piecemeal by my institution and our leaders, inferred but unanalyzed as a series of threats, operations, and public warnings amounting to a global jihadist opponent. The 9/11 attacks were no surprise to me; I had been involved in our effort to stop Bin Ladin and had known that al-Qa'ida had been killing Americans, for years. My first extensive experience living in Arab societies these past months had, to be frank, confirmed the preconceptions I had taken with me based, I thought, on a reasoned assessment of the threats facing the United States. I shared the "clash of civilizations" paradigm. I inclined toward the conventional wisdom and pervasive view that Islam was "fundamentally 'other,' with core values incompatible to those of the West," as I put it in a letter to my family, and that jihadists were the frontline warriors in a millennial struggle. I shared the dominant narrative about 9/11 and the other Islamic-based terrorist attacks, that viewed the Islam-West struggle as the defining dynamic of the post–Cold War world. I felt that, as I wrote my wife, "the hope then becomes that the power of Western values themselves will undermine the obscurantism of Islam, before Islam undermines the fragile practices of tolerance and individualism that are the West's triumph and raison d'être."

The number of terrorist threat reports is stunning when one first gains access to them. From all over the world, every day, from human sources, communications intercepts, liaison reports, from learned classified analytical pieces, the avalanche of reporting confirms its validity by its quantity.

The work done on the CAPTUS case, over years by many skilled analysts, was impressive. The Agency, the FBI, and other agencies had compiled a huge amount of information, which our analysts concluded tagged CAPTUS as a senior member of the al-Qa'ida network. Upon assuming my responsibilities on the case, I naturally took the collective assessment to be correct. I knew from many years' experience that regular review of operations is an integral part of DO and DI procedures. CAPTUS was what we believed him to be, or my colleagues who had worked on his case would not have concluded that he presented a grave danger to U.S. interests.

I had been the chief officer responsible for the CAPTUS case for months, however. I was living a specific operation intensely, not reading cables and taking them as accurate-because-written, as so often happens when a report has a SECRET classification on it and has been acquired clandestinely. It is a case officer's job to know the soul of the target.

Slowly, progressively, first in dismay, then in anger, I had realized that on the CAPTUS case the Agency, the government, all of us, had been victims of delusion. Our premises were flawed, our facts used to fit our premises, our premises determined, and our fears justified our operational actions, in a self-contained process that arrived at a conclusion dramatically at odds with the facts as I came to know them, that projected evil actions where there was, more often, muddled indirect and unavoidable complicity, or nothing much at all. These delusional ratiocinations were all sincerely, ardently held to have constituted a rigorous, rational process to identify terrorist threats. The entire edifice was like Ptolemy's Theory of the Spheres. We built epicycle upon epicycle, circle upon circle, and all the facts fit to explain the motions of the heavens, orbiting around the earth. It was astoundingly impressive, observation substantiated theory for 2,000 years—and it was all wrong.

I concluded that we had, fundamentally, been spinning in self-referential circles. Each step taken in the case was because we saw the world through the prism of our fears. I started to use a phrase that I would subsequently use as the Deputy National Intelligence Officer for Transnational Threats in numerous briefings and speeches, "the closer you look, the less you see." I started to wonder what else in the Global War on Terror we might have so egregiously misunderstood or done wrong.

I came to this conviction first by discovering that the facts of the case I had been working, and had come to understand firsthand—which no one else had done—clashed with the assessment reached over years of collective effort of the nature and conduct of al-Qa'ida; then by concluding that my institution—as so often has been the case—had projected American cultural norms on a situation and a man where they were largely irrelevant.

Finally, we had been interrogating a man who had disappeared from the face of the earth, for whom habeas corpus did not exist, using methods that entered the gray areas where lawyers argued, justifications were theoretical, but men remained flesh and blood. Doubt and uncertainty define most intelligence operations. Case officers are hired because we thrive in and can see clearly through ambiguity. But this case, this situation, involving men's lives, approached one of the supreme, "exceptional circumstances touching on individual rights and social obligations, when what is 'normal' and 'expected' has shifted to accept, well, abominations." I grew concerned that our fears were coming to define our character. I constantly weighed at what point one must affirm, "No! Enough!" The assignment demanded that I second-guess every decision and action and get them all right, or speak up if I thought we had not. I had tried to do so. That was how I answered Wilmington's hostile challenge from so many weeks earlier, "Which flag do you serve?"

A passenger walked past me in the aisle and brought my thoughts back into the plane. I pulled down the window shade. The jet engines, as always, cocooned us all in a loud drone and whistle. I was surrounded by passengers but, as always, I was alone. I was always alone. The child across the aisle from me was sleeping now. I had crossed the Atlantic countless times over the years. It was always the same. Yet each time the ocean below had changed, too, whether I could see it or not; and so had I. I reached for the blanket to pull it over my head, but decided I did not want to. I closed my eyes.

I descended from the plane in Washington weary, troubled, but proud. I had entered the Agency to grapple with exactly the kind of insoluble dilemmas, on important issues, that defined the CAPTUS case. I had worked hard to accomplish my mission and to discharge my responsibilities honorably. My job was to collect intelligence on terrorism and I had done so. I had forcefully challenged accepted conventions, conceptual flaws, and dishonorable compromises of principle in the case, and attempted to rectify them.

The customs doors closed behind me and I walked toward the large group of people standing behind the barriers, waiting for loved ones. My seven-year-old daughter, Margaux, with her shining chestnut hair and cute pageboy haircut, saw me first and ran over to me. We hugged and her first words were, "Daddy, you're so bald!" My wife, Sally, and my nine-year-old son, Spencer, came over a moment later. As Sally and I hugged she whispered in my ear, "You've put on weight."

Beyond the doors I was a man of the shadows, who weighed souls and manipulated men, an interrogator fighting terrorism. A hug and a whisper had transformed me back to a father and a husband, fighting early middle age.

WHAT A POOR BASTARD

We shall die in darkness and be buried in the rain.
—Edna St. Vincent Millay, *Justice Denied in Massachusetts*

What, to the strong, was one man
more or less in a crowded world?
—*Wall Street Journal*, December 22, 1989

The drive home from Dulles was a revelation. Our car was quiet. The roads were smooth. Cars drove slowly and sometimes ceded way at intersections and rotaries. All the streetlights worked. There were trees everywhere and the streets were clean, the shops well lit. My neighborhood had neat homes, tended lawns, calm people strolling the sidewalks, softly blinking streetlights, cars signaling before turns. Women walked alone, or with friends, smiling and at ease. It was stunning to see how orderly, prosperous, and safe America was.

Sally still became exhausted at the end of each day, and had to be careful about what she ate, but she seemed to have managed all right. She was doing as well as she could. The kids had been a lot to handle at the same time that she tried to regain her health and spirit. Our kids seemed, from what I could tell, unaffected by all the turmoil of the past several months. They stormed around, said cute things, and at times acted petulant. The big event in Sally's and the kids' lives was managing to drag the Christmas tree they had bought through a large snowstorm into the house.

A week after my return from Point Zero, Sally, the kids, and I drove up to Boston to visit my eighty-two-year-old parents. My father had played competitive hockey through age seventy-five, had been acting chairman of the town school committee for many years—pushing for one of the earliest sex education programs in the country—and enjoyed swearing at machines, which he insisted on not learning how to use. He did not so much swear, though, as cuss, his worst epithet being "Jumping Jesus!" My mother was wheelchair-ridden, but held her chin with a jaunty, appraising air, and *e-nun-ci-ate-ed* all her words *im-pec-cab-ly* in her Brahmin accent. As a child she had studied dance under Isadora Duncan, and she had been Miss Brookline and acted before the troops during World War II. My parents still lived in the family home, a fourteen-room Victorian house walking distance from Fenway Park, with a wraparound porch, stained-glass windows in the front hall and master stairway, and a Masonic rising sun carved on the lintel over the front porch. I was the fourth generation of my family to have lived there—all the generations lived there together when I was growing up—and, sadly, surely the last.

After the initial bustle of greetings, and of Spencer and Margaux running up to the attic to bring down old toy rifles, Lincoln Logs, my grandfather's World War II air warden helmet, and the billy club he had been issued as a deputized law officer during the Boston police strike of 1919, and of the kids hiding in the "telephone room"—a walk-in closet under the main stairway where we had the phone when I was growing up—I settled down in the living room to chat with my father and mother. A fire crackled in the fireplace, a bas-relief of the Devil blowing on the flames visible at the back of the hearth.

"I always like watching the Devil through the flames," I said as I sat beside the fire.

"No, dear," my mother said to me in a recurring exchange. "That is not the Devil. That is Aeolus, the Greek god of wind." She had always been slightly offended at the idea that there could be a devil in her house. Who in his right mind would put the Devil in someone's hearth, of all places? We both smiled, intransigent.

Heavy drapes separated us from the music room, where we had had two pianos and other instruments when I was growing up, and my aunt Joyce—more like my big sister than an aunt—had practiced voice an hour or two a day. My mother's other sister, Alexandrine ("Aunt Sandra," pronounced AHnt SAHndra, as in "open your mouth and say AHHHH"), now seventy-three and living once again in the family home, came in and sat down to listen to the Wandering Nephew. Sally went off to the butler's pantry to make her ritual cup of tea.

"I haven't heard from you in months, Glenn," my mother said, looking me in the eye. Four generations of family portraits on the walls looked me in the eye, too. I glanced at a photograph of my grandfather, with whom I had grown up, taken in 1917, standing in his lieutenant's uniform. His own grandfather had been a lifelong friend of, and shot buffalo with, Buffalo Bill, and my grandfather had sat on his knee one day when Buffalo Bill visited the house. My grandfather had received a shooting lesson from Annie Oakley during that visit, too.

"No. No. I was away for a long time."

My mother raised her chin ever so slightly.

"I assumed as much. Traveling a lot, I suspect. Anything you can tell me? I love your stories."

Her eyes sparkled. For many years, I had been writing or telling my parents about my adventures with the silverback mountain gorillas in eastern Zaire, or with gypsies at the base of Mount Olympus in Greece, or with sullen locals in a small-town bar on the Pacific coast of Costa Rica. My mother frequently consulted the Rand McNally atlas beside her chair when she received my letters. It had been printed in 1940 and contained a good map of "Hitler Occupied Europe." The window beside the bookshelf—all the windows in the house—still used the blackout curtains from World War II.

"Well, I had a lot of work in Europe. It was good to get back there. I was able to go up to the top of the Zugspitze, in Germany." I then described my trip to the cable cars, the wind at the picnic tables at the observation café at the top, and how well I did using my German. "I was still able to get by after all these years; *was kostet das? Haben zie ein zimmer? Ich muchte Bröt, bitte. Wo ist die Bahnhof?*" My mother enjoyed my tales and was proud that my German was still so serviceable.

I had not been to the Zugspitze, or southern Germany, for five years.

As I always found when I returned from overseas, most people I interacted with had little real interest in where I had been or what I had been doing. I simply left their frames of reference, or interest, when I went away. Someone I had not seen for a while might ask, "Where have you been this time?" I would answer, and after two or three sentences the person usually would respond, more or less, "Neat. Did you see the Notre Dame game last month, while you were away?" and that was the end of my months, or perhaps years, somewhere beyond the horizon. Or, if they were interested in public affairs, they might mention a speech the president had given on terrorism, or domestic security. Then the conversation would revert to old patterns, and my months or years spent wherever I had gone simply did not exist.

Sally and I left our kids with my parents one evening and went to a dinner party at the home of one of my old college roommates, Sam Carr. That we could enjoy an evening out together was a sign of how much Sally had recovered physically and emotionally. I was quietly happy, and relieved, to see this. I often fretted that she did not realize how much her efforts and struggle moved me, how much I was coming to understand the strength of character and body it took, how much I hoped to help, and struggled myself to know how.

Sam was a true representative of the Brahmin class, with ancestors who arrived on the *Mayflower*, and others who served as officers on General Washington's staff. I had teased Sam that I, too, had direct ancestors who had fought in the Revolution, five of them, in fact; only, four of the five had been Loyalists who fought for the British. I told Sam that I would set aside justice and still be his friend, even if he continued to refuse to compensate me for the properties that his ancestors had expropriated from mine. When we arrived at his property, we drove through the gate, past the gardener's house, rolled past the greenhouse, and two hundred yards farther on parked and walked into their large home, passing into a book-lined salon with French windows that looked out to a field and a wood separated by a stream running through their land.

About a dozen former classmates and their spouses attended the dinner: lawyers, doctors, people in finance. Waitresses dressed in black skirts and white blouses made the rounds of the drawing room, discreetly serving hors d'oeuvres. Baroque chamber music played in the background.

Sam's wife, Margaret, greeted us warmly.

"Sally! It's so good to see you. What can I get you to drink?"

My stomach tightened. Sally's smile froze. I am not sure if she looked apprehensive, or if I projected my apprehension onto her features.

"Oh, I'll just have sparkling water, thanks."

"Really? No. A glass of champagne, perhaps?"

I felt even more on edge.

"No, thanks," Sally said, polite as ever. "Sparkling water, please."

I was relieved, and disturbed. This was going to happen over and over, forever. There was no escape, but then, there never is.

Margaret was an exception to my typical experience with my friends and acquaintances, and always enjoyed questioning me about my work overseas. She knew that I had worked on Iraq and Afghanistan over the years, and mentioned this to the small group of guests sitting and standing with us. Naturally enough, the conversation turned to 9/11, our recent invasion of Afghanistan, and the hunt for Usama Bin Ladin.

One of the other guests, an ophthalmologist, was an attractive thirty-five-year-old woman in a cocktail dress cut slightly too low. She wore a demure beret in her blond hair, like a halo above her clear face. She looked down at me, as she stood with a drink in one hand, lightly touching the arm of a sofa with the other. I was sitting in front of her, on a small chair, separated from the sofa, one hand inside the other on my lap.

"Why can't you find Bin Ladin? I mean, come on. You work for the State Department. What are all of you doing? We have to get him."

She shifted her weight to one leg and lightly placed her hand on her hip. I looked at her for a moment in silence.

"Well, I understand," I answered. "But the area along the Afghan-Pakistani border is huge, and really, really rugged. I mean, it's hard enough to find my own kids in my townhouse when we play hide-and-seek. We're talking about an area as big as Texas. It's really hard to do."

The woman was having none of it.

"I know what I'd do. I'd solve the problem."

"Oh?"

"I'd grab some guys out there, the ones where we think he is, and I'd make them tell me where Bin Ladin was. You can make people talk. You know the CIA can do that sort of thing. They should, anyway."

I had just come from a black, windowless, freezing cell, where for months I had been the Interrogator, the Hand of Judgment. Now I sat in a paneled room overlooking a bucolic estate, surrounded by refined men and women in designer clothes, being stared at with appraising eyes and genteelly berated for not torturing our enemies enough, whoever they might be. *I am in the same place I was a week ago*, I thought. *I never have gone anywhere.*

"But we can't just grab anyone and expect him to know where Bin Ladin is," I replied, in what I hoped was a measured voice. "Most people there don't know anything. The few who do, do not want to give him up. It's a cultural thing. And we can't just make someone talk."

"They killed 3,000 Americans. They aren't civilized. It's not like we should be reading these people their rights. They deserve no respect. They deserve nothing. And then, if we can't find him, I have a simple solution to the problem of finding Bin Ladin, anyway."

"You do? It's not so easy." I wished that Sally, or Sam, or Margaret would change the subject. I did not want to give puerile answers to insipid observations that irritated me. But everyone seemed content with the conversation and, with me as the lone Washington official, wanted to listen to my supposed insights.

"Yes," she said. Her forceful confidence reminded me a little of Wilmington, back at Headquarters. "I'd just nuke the whole place. Kill 'em all. That'd get Bin Ladin."

"But there are millions of people there." My voice was flat, but I hoped not disdainful. I wanted neither to fuel the discussion nor antagonize the woman on a subject about which she knew nothing, but had made up her mind. "You can't just kill millions of people, none of whom but maybe two hundred or something have anything to do with Bin Ladin."

The ophthalmologist was indifferent. "They attacked us. They are hiding the guy. So they're guilty. He is evil. Nuke 'em." She seemed to mean it, too.

I almost remarked that barely thirty miles from where we sat, our forebears—

at least Sam's and mine—had hanged or stoned people to death for witchery, after having wrung confessions from them by "dunking" them—drowning them under controlled conditions—and that we all now shook our heads in condescension about such collective insanity and fanaticism. My attractive and educated dinner partner was coldly suggesting that we kill an entire population, so as to exorcise one demon. But I bit my tongue.

"I suppose that might kill Bin Ladin," I replied, raising my eyebrows.

The CAPTUS case had enhanced my sense of solitude, of detachment from everyone around me. Were CAPTUS and I—two "inmates" from the asylum, captive and jailor—the only two sane men alive?

Barely a moment had passed. Margaret at last came to my rescue.

"It's all just so interesting," she interjected. "I mean, I don't think we'd want to bomb—use a nuclear bomb on so many people. I'm sure the government knows all about what to do. Or don't they? But, Bin Ladin is just so *awful*. I think it's very hard." She looked at me and rose, smiling. "I'm glad to know that people like you are working on it." She raised her voice. "Let's all find our seats in the dining room. Our dinner is ready."

On the drive back to my parents' house, Sally told me not to get so worked up.

"Why do you let some noo-na bother you? They are ignorant. You know the truth."

I did not answer for a moment. There were no streetlights on this road. Christmas lights twinkled in the windows of the homes we passed, small points of light amidst the swirling snow in the sharp wind and formless dark. I nodded, half convinced, half cynic. I wanted to avoid talking or thinking about or reacting to any of the conversation, or about the shades it had conjured, of which the attractive ophthalmologist in the low-cut dress had never dreamed, but of which she was certain nonetheless.

I enjoyed driving at night, feeling the steering wheel cold through my gloves; it was solid and gave me a sense of control, the tires crinkling in the snow, all sounds muffled. The solitude made me feel safe.

"I guess."

I glanced at Sally out of the corner of my eye. Sally had done all her drinking in the dark, out of sight, a secret crisis that was slowly destroying us. At last, in a series of painful revelations, I had learned what had been happening, and sometimes I knew what to do. Sally's—our—recovery became possible once I recognized, and she acknowledged, the truth. We could handle the truth, or at least try.

I looked back through the windshield, the headlights casting a narrow beam of light into the dark. Countless snowflakes shone an evanescent moment before us, captured just an instant in their anonymous flight, before disappearing back into the enveloping black.

"I guess. Yeah. I know the truth."

Ryan had responsibility for CAPTUS now, in Point Zero, while the CTC desk carried on as before. I had hoped to see Keith, the branch chief, to talk about the two cables I had written as I was departing the station, and to try to change the direction of the case. I was dismayed to learn that Keith had changed positions, and moved to another branch. I did not even see him, as he was away TDY. His position was unfilled. I had no memorable discussion with Wilmington, either, who was always very busy, or out somewhere. I was unable to engage with him, but did not want to anyway. We knew each other's views. He obviously had no interest in seeing me. Our conversations were superficial. He had moved on to other operational issues. CAPTUS? Being handled by the branch. No problem. Thanks for your help. For the higher offices, for all that CAPTUS was a high-profile case, the higher offices referred operational issues back to the branch, which knew the case.

I looked for my two cables. No one knew anything about them. Point Zero had never sent them. They did not exist. The COS or DCOS had obviously decided that they were too incendiary. My views were not collegial and, had they been transmitted, would have raised awkward issues about CAPTUS, Hotel California, and CTC's handling of the case, over a long period of time. A single C/O who challenged *years* of DI assessments and DO operational practice was usually viewed as someone almost by definition bizarre and to be silenced, probably unfit because he was unable to meld with the team and how professionals did their jobs. Who was one officer to challenge the collective views of dozens of officers and offices, from both branches of the CIA, over years of careful review? Who was I to challenge the foundations of an *entire program, ordered by the president*? I regretted not having sent them to myself, back channel, even though one was not supposed to do that.

All in all, CAPTUS, who had so consumed my life, viewed from the urgent, overworked atmosphere of CTC and the CIA, in the context of the aggressive GWOT, was just one case—albeit an important one—but one that no one would want to have complicate the larger operational issues of how to conduct counterterrorism operations, while following the White House's guidance on rendition, detention, and interrogation. There was a saying in the DO: On major issues, one should let "kings fight with kings." The issues raised by the case I had handled were issues for kings, such as the DDO—the senior operations officer in the CIA, or the DCI, or members of Congress, or the Office of the Vice President, or the White House. I had had my differences with Wilmington; CAPTUS was rotting in a dungeon; but most everyone in the DO would consider that any officer out in the field, or down in the bowels of the organization, who challenged Agency and U.S. government practices, to be a fool embarked on a fool's suicidal errand. The men running the country suppressed anyone who challenged them on these issues, even the most powerful officers in the government. A smart officer, a good officer, did his job and left philosophy in the classroom, law to the Office of General Counsel, and politics to our most senior masters. And that way, he would keep his head.

That summer, President Bush issued a statement in observance of United Nations International Day in Support of Victims of Torture. The statement said, in part:

> The United States declares its strong solidarity with torture victims across the world. Torture anywhere is an affront to human dignity everywhere. We are committed to building a world where human rights are respected and protected by the rule of law. Freedom from torture is an inalienable human right. . . . Yet torture continues to be practiced around the world by rogue regimes whose cruel methods match their determination to crush the human spirit. . . . Notorious human rights abusers . . . have sought to shield their abuses from the eyes of the world

by staging elaborate deceptions and denying access to international human rights monitors. . . . The United States is committed to the world-wide elimination of torture and we are leading this fight by example.

I found this speech infuriating. I knew what we were doing; our actions soiled what it meant to be American, perverted our oath, and betrayed our flag.

Lawyers could argue that our actions were legal. But I had lived what we were doing. I knew otherwise. Our actions contravened the Geneva Conventions, the Convention against Torture, and the U.S. Constitution, whatever ratiocinations administration lawyers had tried to spin. At work, one did not raise these issues, or question one's orders. Not in any conversations I had, or heard about. These issues had been resolved. Do the job, or find another.

A month later Ambassador Joe Wilson's article "What I Didn't Find in Africa" was published. Joe had been, essentially, my first boss twenty years before in Burundi. He argued, of course, that the rationale for our invasion of Iraq had had little to do with the facts about Saddam's ostensible weapons of mass destruction programs. I paid special attention to Joe's article, as I knew Joe, had worked with his wife, Valerie Plame, many years earlier, knew that his article was fundamentally sound, and of course recognized that the article would catalyze a heated polemic all around.

I had lunch with a senior DO colleague around this time. For years, he had been heavily involved in our Iraq operations. We had known each other for a decade and spoke openly with each other. Of course we spoke of Iraq and Afghanistan, and the War on Terror. Joe's article was just beginning to make waves. I told my colleague that Joe's article was simply one example of an almost infinite number of crude distortions of intelligence and perception concerning terrorism and Iraq. I said I had come to be appalled at how the administration, and the CIA, so grotesquely mischaracterized the threat from al-Qa'ida, rolling all terrorists together as though they posed one enemy, rather than a broad range of challenges—even going so far as to assert the fundamental identity of and associations among al-Qa'ida, Hizballah, the narco-traffickers in Latin America, Mexican "coyotes" along the U.S. border, Saddam (who was secular!), Palestinian suicide bombers, and on and on, in a frankly lunatic mishmash. I alluded to the CAPTUS case as representative of how distorted perception had led to mortifying error.

My colleague nodded. I was not telling him anything he did not know. Hundreds of people in the cafeteria around us created a loud background babble. No one could hear us even at the next table. It was hard to understand anything amidst all this noise, even when listening. The thought occurred to me—surely I was not the first to have it—that I was sitting in the middle of a ziggurat.

"I know, I know," he began, holding his fork and knife above his plate as he spoke. "I was involved early on in the planning for the Iraq invasion. This was Seventh Floor stuff. We went around the table, discussing specific tasks we would need to accomplish to support the invasion. This was long before the invasion. Way before it. We hadn't even started to deploy troops to the theater yet. When it was my turn to speak, I said that I had worked the Iraqi target for years, and everyone needed to understand that Saddam and al-Qa'ida had nothing to do with one another. Totally different problem sets. I said that we could not justify invading Iraq by citing the al-Qa'ida threat, because al-Qa'ida was not there, and had nothing to do with Saddam. No one said much of anything. We continued the planning. It was clear that we were going to war."

My colleague was dispassionate as he spoke. I slightly shook my head, although what he was telling me was no surprise. We all knew Saddam and al-Qa'ida had nothing to do with each other.

"So, then, a month or so later, we have our next big meeting. Same issues: planning the invasion of Iraq. It came my turn to speak again. This time I said that I had also worked proliferation issues for many years—this was the whole 'Saddam has WMD' thing; if we were concerned about the biggest threat from weapons of mass destruction, then we had to focus whatever we were doing on North Korea. Saddam posed little threat. Then I said that we also needed to consider the likely consequences of invading Iraq. We would probably cause the country to break apart, and for what? Al-Qa'ida wasn't there, Iraq posed no significant problem from a weapons of mass destruction perspective. We would create new problems for ourselves by invading. The assessment we were basing our actions on was divorced from the facts; we couldn't accomplish what we claimed as our objectives; and we would create problems we probably could not solve. So we needed to make this clear to the White House. I finished, and the meeting carried on as before, planning the invasion of Iraq."

Here, my colleague paused, took a bite from his plate, and smiled slightly.

"After the meeting, as I was coming out of the conference room, one of DDO's senior assistants walked with me down the hall. 'Some advice from a friend,' he told me. 'Say what you want in the meetings. It's your decision. But you are doing yourself no favors. The decision has been made. Either one is onboard, or, well . . . No one can change this. The only effect of what you say will be to harm yourself. Be careful.' Then he walked away. So I thought, 'Fuck it. I'm done. I won't have anything to do with it.' I arranged my new assignment not too long afterward."

Two years later my friend and colleague Ryan, who had replaced me in Point Zero, sought me out. He was leaving CTC and the Agency, moving on to a different part of the government. I had not seen Ryan for over a year. This was to be a parting. We went for coffee in the Headquarters' cafeteria.

"Glenn, I know you had major differences with CTC about the CAPTUS case. I know your views. I'm out of here. I wanted to tell you something before I left. When I went out to Point Zero to take your place, Wilmington and the office gave me one order: 'Keep the case going. Do whatever you need to do, but keep the CAPTUS case going.'"

"I know."

"But there is something else I wanted you to know. You were right. You were right, Glenn. You got the case right. I came to see that. I wanted you to know. That is something to take with you. That is not something one can say in here, really; it undoes the whole fucking thing. But I wanted you to know I respected you for what you were doing. It took courage."

I have not seen Ryan since.

A little more than three years after CAPTUS's rendition, I came out of one of DCI Tenet's daily five o'clock meetings, the most senior operational and substantive meeting in the Intelligence Community on the conduct of the

Global War on Terror. Mark Lowenthal, the ADCI—the Assistant Director of Central Intelligence for Analysis and Production—had also attended and we walked together down the carpeted hall of the Seventh Floor, where the CIA's most senior officers had their offices. Mark was a friend whose candor, judgment, and wit I particularly enjoyed. One of the subjects of discussion at the meeting had been what the White House wanted to do about the detainees we were holding in various locations around the world. This was most definitely a White House issue, not a CIA one. As always, there had been no resolution. I knew, however, that in particular Under Secretary of Defense Douglas Feith was one of the main obstacles to resolving the problem. In a series of meetings held to resolve the detainee problem, Feith regularly became incensed at the positions of various elements of the government, notably the State Department, which urged that Guantanamo and our various detainee sites be closed, and most of the detainees liberated or tried. Almost incoherent with anger, he accused the representatives of the other agencies of asserting that the administration had broken the law with its policies toward detainees. "Are you accusing us of breaking the law? We did not break the law! We did not break the law!" he would shout over and over, furious. He invariably paralyzed the meetings. Feith was widely viewed among my colleagues as a dangerous zealot, who inhabited a world of his imagining. But in these meetings he was a guilty queen: "The lady doth protest too much, methinks."

I told Mark that I had handled one of the HVT cases. I told him—I could speak frankly to Mark—that I thought we had, in effect, gotten everything wrong, despite all our efforts, that we had been acting on delusions, and that I was deeply concerned about it all. More important than that, though, was what happened after that, and to all of the detainees, at least the HVTs.

"These guys are kept in abominable conditions. ███████████████
███████████████████████. They don't exist anymore. What is this? We can't do that. The White House can't just keep these guys *forever*."

"I know," Mark agreed, frustrated, resigned. "But they don't know what to do with them. The White House doesn't know what to do with them."

From what I could tell, the administration both did not care about holding our detainees without habeas corpus forever, and did not want to acknowledge what, based on their vehement and ruthless infighting in the government, even they knew was criminal policy. If the "torture memos"[1] were found to be illegal and were rejected, then the policy's architects were as guilty of subverting the law and our process of government as a detainee was naked at rendition.

As an HVT, the CAPTUS case had been particularly tightly held. To my surprise, also in 2006, the case leaked to the media. I know the FBI investigated how this had happened, but I believe they never found out. For the record, I did not leak the CAPTUS case, or any other bit of information, to anyone, at any time, ever. I do not know how CAPTUS leaked.

In 2007, I retired from the Agency after nearly twenty-three years as a case officer. The CAPTUS case was my last significant operational assignment. I served my last years after the CAPTUS case as Deputy National Intelligence Officer for Transnational Threats, a senior, but non-operational assignment.

In 2008, I chatted with a former colleague. As old-timers do, we shared war stories. He had worked CAPTUS, too. He mentioned to me, to my real dismay, ██.[2]

"Collateral damage," Wilmington and others might say.

"What a poor bastard," my security officer would say.

In 2009, while lining up "Beltway Bandit" contract work with the Agency, I needed to renew my security clearance. The Agency's Office of Security declined to renew it, the legacy of the disastrous phase that was capped by my having forgotten my bag.

Finally, not long ago, I learned that CAPTUS had been, at last, released.

---

1 The "torture memos" were written by John Yoo, a political appointee in the Justice Department, to provide legal cover for the administration to authorize the CIA to use enhanced interrogation techniques. It was the central one of these memos that Wilmington cited to me as authorization for my interrogation of CAPTUS.

2 The redacted clause describes the evolution of the CAPTUS case.

AFTERWORD: DELUSIONS, CONSEQUENCES, TRUTH

One step at a time. One day at a time. Speak the truth.
Hide nothing. Admit failing and forgive it. Seek help
from others. It is good to lean sometimes. Never give up.
And then, you can even contend with demons.

—Truths I have learned with my wife

The CAPTUS tale is darker than I have been allowed to tell. Under the guise of "protecting sources and methods," the CIA has imposed numerous redactions and elliptical phrases on my manuscript. These have eliminated or softened harsh facts about what our government has done in the pursuit of terrorists, rounded edges of wrongdoing, and obscured the corruption of our institutions and of our system of government caused by the rendition, detention, and coercive interrogation of terrorists or terrorist suspects. To oppose these policies risked one's career. To write about them challenges a governmental *omertà*.

The Agency initially redacted about 100 pages of the original 250-odd pages of my manuscript. I have written this book literally a dozen times over to meet the professed sources and methods concerns of the CIA. For two years, amidst legitimate issues, I have had to fight redactions of such egregious threats to national security as when I wanted to say that someone spoke "with authority," or that "the fog was brown." I quoted T. S. Eliot, and they redacted that. Tastes vary, I know. Perhaps the Agency was striking a blow against obscure snobbery. I could not write "kidnap" in a certain sentence, even though I was quoting a previously published, CIA-approved book. I was not allowed to write that I "assumed" that a certain individual would act "innocent." I was not allowed to mention—ever the Harvard man—that at one point I discussed "the Bible, the Koran, and heuristics." In one spot I was not allowed to make the explosive revelation that CIA Headquarters, several colleagues, and I all . . . "disagreed." The Agency redacted such sensitive national security terms as "rot" and "shit hole." The Agency and I engaged in months of argument because they repeatedly refused to allow me to mention a U.S. government . . . urinal. The Agency censored passages on seduction—and they the sizzling romantic secrets of a WASP. At one point I was not allowed to note that I "vented my anger." The Agency censored that I considered someone "a gibbering fool."

It is clear that various elements of the CIA and executive branch, even after the departure of the Bush administration, are concerned about the implications of drawing a picture of the rendition, detention, and coercive interrogation policies of the United States while waging the Global War on Terror.

I share these concerns, which is why it is my duty to bring to public attention my firsthand knowledge of how these policies and practices debase the men and women and institutions involved with them, fail in their objectives, and even threaten our own freedoms.

Forlorn and narrowly focused as the CAPTUS narrative is, it illustrates broader actions, arguments, and policies of the CIA and the government during the Global War on Terror. Three critical elements emerge.

Delusions

The CAPTUS case depicts that our government has been deluded about the nature and extent of the threat of jihadist terrorism. These delusions guided the policy makers of the Bush administration in waging what it characterized as the Global War on Terror, bounded the Intelligence Community's assessment of the threat from jihadist terrorism, and shaped a trusting public's conception of the depth of the dangers of "global jihad" confronting the United States.

I initially shared the Intelligence Community's, and what after 9/11 came to be the Bush administration's, standard view of the jihadist threat as coherent, structured, global, imminent, and nearly existential. Frankly, these became largely the views of the Office of the Vice President and his Neocon colleagues in the executive branch. The White House itself appears to have been conceptually inert in elaborating what came to pass for the strategic framework of the Global War on Terror, or overmatched in the policy debates by those advisers who zealously knew their own minds, and who confused nuance and distributed power with weakness.

The CAPTUS case disabused me of the coherent, structured, global, imminent, and nearly existential threat perspective. The facts showed that the Intelligence Community paradigm, and the White House Global War on Terror, were literally delusional.[1] I found that CAPTUS was not the critical member of al-Qa'ida we had convinced ourselves he was, and I found something far more important: that the closer one looked at al-Qa'ida, the further it receded and the smaller it was. I learned that we attributed excessive importance to the concrete threats we detected—and there are real threats—and threw a host of unfortunates, zealots, and a few real terrorists into dungeons, for fear that they were demons, and might kill or enslave us all. I found that we chose to sacrifice our own principles in the hunt for the few terrorists threatening us. This was a Faustian bargain; the Devil's ways could not make us any safer than had we retained our soul.

Analysts within the Intelligence Community (IC) who specialized in terrorism analysis, and the Office of Terrorism Analysis (OTA) of the CIA, tended (with many caveats and exceptions) to present al-Qa'ida and jihadists as coherent, global—"linked" was the operative jargon—growing, and perhaps even an existential threat to the United States and the West. This paradigm took shape in the early 1990s and dominated terrorism analysis. This perspective focused by definition on terrorist reporting,[2] which in relative isolation from other factors—economic, social, historical, psychological—tended to present an alarming and coherent narrative of threat. Clearly this perspective

---

1 Delusion: a persistent false belief held in the face of strong contradictory evidence.

2 For example, operational reports from the field that a terrorist individual or group was planning to do something.

comforted and shaped the view of the Neocon strategists in the Bush administration, who once the World Trade Center towers collapsed, finally consented
to pay attention to the threat of Islamic terrorism and quickly married this
perspective to the Neocons' geostrategic objectives for the Middle East, which
included finishing with Saddam Hussein once and for all.[3]

Analysts with broader mandates, however, in general what are termed in
the IC "regional analysts," tended to relativize the power and coherence of
the various Islamic terrorist groups. Terrorists and terrorist groups were assessed as phenomena within the larger social, economic, technological,
cultural, and religious forces affecting individuals and societies. This perspective, by definition, placed their role and importance in a much richer context. "Links" among various Islamic terrorists were not considered prima facie
proof that terrorists in Indonesia, Yemen, and Morocco were therefore part
of a "global movement." My experiences provided strong evidence in support
of this broader perspective and assessment (while my subsequent work on the
National Intelligence Council reinforced and deepened the assessments I had
reached during the CAPTUS case).

The OTA perspective was ascendant for many years. When a terrorist incident occurs, or issue arises, logically, OTA (and now the National Counterterrorism Center, known as NCTC) takes the lead. Regional analysts, experts
on Islam, and others play secondary roles. By definition and bureaucratic procedure, therefore, policy makers receive reporting and analyses of terrorist
incidents that tend to overweigh the incidents' true position in the larger context of trends and issues in a given country or region.

In addition, after the horror and the "intelligence failure" of the September
11 attacks, the pressure to pass on to policy makers almost all terrorist threat
reporting became nearly irresistible. It is safer to warn and have nothing happen than to assess that a report need not be passed on to policy makers, only
to learn that another attack actually occurred. Psychologists have demon-

---

3 The Bush administration, from January 2001 until September 11, 2001, had three foreign
policy priorities: confront the rise of China, taken to be hostile to U.S. preeminence; build a bal-
listic missile defense system; destroy Saddam Hussein. The Clinton administration's grave concerns and deep focus on the threat of terrorism were taken as a small-bore issue, unworthy of a
superpower, and diverting U.S. attention from its true strategic interests.

strated that the very act of analyzing threats and future scenarios—in this instance the assessment of the terrorist threat and specific kinds of possible terrorist attacks—increases among experts the perceived likelihood that such threats and attacks will occur.[4] Of course, policy makers will take the views of experts as more likely to be "right" than the views of non-experts, thus validating the biases developed by the experts in the act of analysis.

Policy makers post-9/11 have been awash in endless "streams" of terrorist threat reporting.[5] Terrorist threat reporting almost always appears to increase post any terrorism disaster. The reporting in turn formed the policy makers' perceptions of what appeared myriad, pervasive terrorist threats. Of course, policy makers also felt obliged to respond to these reports, lest an attack occur on their watch. The dynamic of "streams" of reports shaping a sense of pervasive threat, leading to vigorous preemptive counterterrorism actions, was hard to resist with 3,000 Americans incinerated or decomposing in lower Manhattan.

---

4   See in particular Richards J. Heuer Jr., *Psychology of Intelligence Analysis*, 3rd ed. (Washington, DC: Center for the Study of Intelligence, Central Intelligence Agency, 2003), especially Chapter 12, p. 149; but also the work of Dr. John Ioannidis, who has found disturbing cognitive bias and distortion among medical researchers, and the hard-to-resist pressures to conform to dominant paradigms of thought. See David H. Freeman, "Lies, Damned Lies, and Medical Science," *Atlantic Monthly*, November 2010.

5   The concept of "streams" of reporting is a malign consequence of the Bush administration's and the Intelligence Community's responses to the 9/11 attacks. The term was, to my knowledge, not used before 9/11. At least it was not in vogue inside the Intelligence Community. It implies to the layman that there are numerous, concordant sources of information, providing regular reports on a given threat or subject. But the term is largely meaningless. There are intelligence sources and reports. Some are reliable; some not, some unreliable but accurate, others reliable but wrong. There are rarely "streams," and no experienced intelligence professional whom I know found the term to mean anything. Were there a "stream" of intelligence, the information in the "stream" most likely then would have been substantial enough to act upon, rather than merely allude to in public. The concept and expression endowed the confusing, sporadic, contradictory, and on occasion critically revelatory process of collecting, disseminating, and acting upon clandestine information with an aura of competence and awareness that policy makers were only too happy to weave into the narrative of threat they presented to a public that had to trust its leaders in time of danger. In fact, the stream of intelligence exaggeration has sometimes misled senior intelligence officials (I have observed it happen), scared many citizens for years, and provided officials a way to appear to substantiate their assessments and policies, and to sound like dynamic, courageous leaders. Worse, those using the term were often sincere, duped by the illusion of professional assessment implied in the term "streams of intelligence," and confirmed in their preconceptions. There is nothing so dangerous as a sincere ideologue, whatever the object of his devotions.

The perception of increased threat after a disaster, embodied in the apparent (and probably numerical) increase in threat reporting, is a deep-rooted, atavistic phenomenon. Wildebeests at a watering hole know as they drink that there are crocodiles somewhere under the surface. When a crocodile suddenly pulls a wildebeest below the water in a terrifying rush of splashes and thrashing, in panic all the more fortunate wildebeests thunder up the embankment to safety, aware all of a sudden of a grave danger before them. After all, they all just saw one of their own devoured. Yet, the danger is no greater than before and, if only wildebeests could think, they already knew about it. They cannot reason themselves past the alarm of having seen one of their own pulled down to his death. They must do something to protect themselves—how could their lookouts have failed so miserably?—and so, up the embankment they rush.

Humans imagine themselves masters of their emotions, their perceptions servants of their reason. But humans, and the institutions they create, are also ruled first by unconscious, instinctive drives; the difference being that we wear the mantle of "civilization" and reason as we scurry away from the watering hole. We may have dominion over all the earth, and every creeping thing upon it, but we have not dominion of ourselves, and often are unaware of why we act and feel as we do.

Neither the Intelligence Community nor policy makers resisted or were aware of their herd behavior, or the bureaucratic exaggerations and limitations on perception. And so, prudence, fear, institutional bias and limitation, passing judgment up the chain of command, all conspired to foment more fear, a sense of greater threat, and cruder policy responses, than an independent and cold assessment of terrorist threat reporting warrants. The administration, abetted by parts of an Intelligence Community unaware of its cognitive biases and psychological reflexes, led us thundering up the embankment.

There are evildoers who killed many of us, and who merit cold excision from the world of men. I did my best to make it happen. But our own atavistic reflexes and errors are the deepest failure of 9/11, not the attacks themselves, because although we sometimes must suffer the deeds of others, we always must be responsible for our own.

These are organic consequences of how terrorism analysis is conducted within the IC. Nonetheless, many officers and components of the IC opposed the "global movement" perspective and strove to give greater local, regional, religious, political, and sociological nuance to the IC's analyses of Islamic terrorism. Tragically, OTA's paradigm about the overarching framework of Islamic terrorism dominated, but also proved distorting and alarmist, while the Bush administration considered any challenge to this perspective, and the administration's consequent GWOT, to be proof of political hostility or insubordination. When faith, fear, and death combine, they sacrifice nuance first.

I learned something else important and must be explicit: The contention that enhanced interrogation techniques [sic] provided critical intelligence and saved many lives is flat wrong. Close review of most specific claims of critical intelligence obtained from rendition, detention, and enhanced interrogation techniques shows that, in almost every case, the "intelligence" obtained was faulty and subsequently discredited or suspect, or of secondary importance. The after-action assessments have mostly, albeit very quietly, found that we obtained little of critical benefit.

Some who have asserted that enhanced interrogation techniques provided critical intelligence and saved lives, like former Director of Central Intelligence George Tenet, are honest victims of their institutions. They, as I had, believed that the entire institution would know what it was saying and would tell the Director the truth—or would know how to recognize the truth. But the internal assessments of the interrogation techniques and programs fed up the chain of command were like the proverbial "self-licking ice-cream cone." To protect the administration, the CIA, the rendition, detention, and interrogation programs, and the officers involved, the assessments "found" that the counterterrorism and interrogation programs justified the premises that had engendered them. The institution and its leaders also fell victim to the perennial problem in the intelligence business: that one usually finds what one is looking for. I saw the reporting. I worked the cases. I wrote many of the reports myself. I know the culture. One simply does not write an assessment that says, in effect,

Our assumptions were wrong, our policies flawed, the results obtained paltry, misleading, or harmful to our own interests.

Instead, one writes something like,

We responded vigorously to a grave threat. The measures were carefully reviewed. We have had significant successes in protecting our nation. Our officers are selfless. We continue to refine our actions, to respect our obligations, to uphold the law, and to fulfill our mission.

Others who assert that enhanced interrogation techniques provided critical intelligence and saved many lives, like former vice president Dick Cheney, are either sincerely misinformed (although the IC concluded and reported years before the end of the Bush administration that enhanced interrogation had provided little breakthrough intelligence), persist in their delusions, are protecting from criticism the policies they have advocated and the men who made them, or are incapable or unwilling to acknowledge grievous error. This group, more than any I saw during my decades in intelligence, or than any that I heard about from colleagues whose experiences extend decades before my own, sought any shred of information that justified their preconceptions, and took differing views as proofs of disloyalty. But what senior leader has ever acknowledged, even recognized, in matters of war, peace, torture, and the rule of law, that they understood little, misunderstood much, did almost everything horribly wrong, killed thousands needlessly, and cost the nation boundless treasure?

In a number of ways, the least delusional of the protagonists in the Global War on Terror versus global jihad dynamic have been al-Qa'ida and all the fellow-traveler jihadists whom al-Qa'ida inspires. They have accurately identified Western values, and the United States as the West's champion and heart, as existential threats to their theology and way of life. Yet they are utterly deluded in imagining that they can exorcise the demon of Western thought and life through physical violence—or in any way at all.

The rise of the individual, based upon the growth of knowledge, is the single, irresistible dynamic driving human history, across epochs, geography, cultures, and institutions, and despite religion. Al-Qa'ida's very existence, and its leaders' theological ratiocinations, demonstrates the rise of individual thought and agency that al-Qa'ida's leaders decry as the root of decadence and that is the center of Western civilization. Yet, Usama Bin Ladin and his acolytes have eaten of the apple of knowledge (in the form of literacy, mass communications, the decline of traditional authority figures and references), their eyes were opened, and they can never again cover their nakedness, try as they may, until they return to dust.

Progressively, then, as I lived the CAPTUS case, I came to realize that our leaders, our Intelligence Community, and our public have been deluded into exaggerated fears, reinforced by institutional and perceptional bias; that enhanced interrogation techniques do not provide critical information that could not be obtained from more acceptable, conventional interrogation methods; and that our jihadist enemies have deluded themselves that they know what they are doing in anything beyond a tactical sense, and have a solution for the social and theological "ills" that so exercise them.

Consequences

The CAPTUS case reveals how our rendition, detention, and coercive interrogation policies have corrupted our government's institutions, eroded our society's most deeply cherished values, undermined our system of laws, and, in any event, do not work. My initial reaction to the beginning of my first briefing for the CAPTUS case was "We don't do that." The "that" was, make no mistake, what all men not deluding themselves or others with sophistry would in familiar conversation call "torture."

Defining torture is quite difficult. I wrestled with this conundrum throughout my handling of the CAPTUS case. In fairness, the entire administration and executive branch struggled hard to define it clearly, and the CIA was always aggressive in demanding clear legal guidance from the most senior legal bodies in the government. One truly enters the "gray world" when attempting to define what is acceptable in an interrogation, what is legal, what is necessary, and what is torture.

The "hallway" characterization of the legal guidance we received during my tenure on the CAPTUS case was that coercive measures did not constitute torture so long as the physical and psychological effects were not "severe," "lasting," or "permanent." I always found that argument spurious concerning physical pain, and would have nothing to do with it. Going back decades to my own SERE training and interrogation experience, however, I at first accepted the efficacy and acceptability of measures that disrupt and disorient a prisoner psychologically, for brief periods. I had been trained that our experts had determined that these measures could induce cooperation in a prisoner.

As I became involved in the CAPTUS case, however, and my own experiences came back vividly, I realized that believing psychological dislocation was an effective and legitimate interrogation method was yet another delusion. It was easy to disorient and disrupt one's psyche and sense of self. It had happened to me with shocking speed. But even in that "psychologically dislocated" state, I was no more likely to share information than had it not occurred. I became angry in my misery, that was all. Could one more readily fool or manipulate a "psychologically dislocated" individual into revealing information? Not in my personal experience, either as a person subjected to coercive interrogation measures or as the interrogator of CAPTUS. Already, decades ago, the infamous KUBARK manual had explicitly noted that coercive methods bred resentment and a decline in cooperation, rather than induced revelations. I concluded, to paraphrase the Duke of Otranto, that torture is worse than a crime, it is an error.

Yet, when I read the legal support for our instructions—the now infamous Department of Justice "torture memo"—it was simply transparent that the justification was a "do-what-you-want" card that swept away in one executive note extensive American and international jurisprudence and proscriptions against torture. I had been immediately concerned about torture, but my concerns grew deeper as the case progressed; I became alarmed about our institutions of government.

As I stood gazing out the window of Hotel California at the bleak landscape, making a sardonic reference to Diogenes's lamp, I started to fear that the CAPTUS case was symptomatic of an even deeper crisis than the involvement of the United States in torture. I became acutely uneasy that the CIA and all of us were being subjected to a de facto usurpation of constitutional and executive powers, rationalized with de jure, self-authorizing flimflammery (gussied up by casuists as the "theory of the unitary executive"). It was shocking to learn that the president's advisers informed him that his orders superseded our laws. We were becoming—in secret and out of sight except to the few of us involved in the "dark side, if you will" of the Global War on Terror—no longer the government of checks, balances, and law that has defined us as a nation, and which I had proudly sworn to "preserve and protect." Even more alarming, it was apparent that our leaders believed that they were doing right. The landscape I gazed at was bleak indeed.

We denounce these procedures as totalitarian in other countries. We oppose them. I feared that I had become part of what constituted elements of a de facto American junta. The thought was so outlandish that for a long while I doubted my own perceptions. It simply could not be true. Finally, when I mentioned these concerns, most looked at me as though I were wildly exaggerating for effect, a crackpot, or a partisan. No one could take seriously that such a term might be applicable *in the United States.* "We have to do whatever is necessary to protect ourselves from a grave threat" was one immediate response. But I had learned—I had lived—that our assumptions were wrong, our fears exaggerated, our actions harmful to the society, laws, and values we sought to protect. "Americans do not do that sort of thing" was the next stock reaction to my concerns . . . just as I had reacted to Wilmington at first, when I said "we don't do that." But we did, largely in secret and the dark, the measures taken and laws traduced justified by our leaders and their followers, as juntas do, as necessary responses to grave national danger.

Truth

Finally, the CAPTUS case begs the question: What should be done to dispel the delusions we have believed, and to repair the harm to our society and government caused by coercive interrogation and the corrosion of our laws?

The U.S. Intelligence Community became aware of the threat posed by Islamic terrorism many years prior to the September 11, 2001, attacks. DCI George Tenet increased the resources and focus devoted to counterterrorism by orders of magnitude in the years prior to the 9/11 attacks. From the mid-1990s on I, like countless others in the IC, was drawn into our efforts to neutralize, detain, or kill Usama Bin Ladin and his acolytes. CTC had been a backwater; after 9/11 it became the center of all attention. Suddenly officers coveted CTC assignments, following the old dicta that promotions come from assignments where the bombs go off, and where policy makers focus their attention. The Agency took substantial measures to enhance the professionalism and specialization of counterterrorism officers.

These trends increased after 9/11, and are manifest in the recommenda-tions of the Bush administration, to increase the number of counterterrorism analysts and field officers by 50 percent, and of the 9/11 Commission, to create the Department of Homeland Security, and especially the National Counter-Terrorism Center (NCTC)—the two signal organizational responses to the "failures" of 9/11 and the threats from Islamic terrorism.[6]

Whenever there is a "failure" or a "flap," the CIA must demonstrate to Congress and the public that it has identified the problem behind the failure and will address its causes. This almost invariably takes the form of an insti-tutional reorganization—as though a new box on the flow chart, or new pro-cedures, will banish the misperceptions and errors in judgment that are almost always the underlying causes of intelligence failures.[7] The defect in this clas-sic response to disaster is that no one can institutionalize better judgment. Bureaucratic reorganization and new procedures designed to rectify past er-rors give the appearance of motion and soothe anxieties, but almost always actually slow institutions down, while the employees remain as flawed (and dedicated) as before.

Perversely, the specialization of our counterterrorism officers and offices throughout the Intelligence Community in response to the threat of Islamic terrorism has in some ways made matters worse. Just as our instinctive reflexes noted above distorted our perceptions, our counterterrorism institutions and officers see terrorist threats as looming larger than they do, because the coun-terterrorism perspective has narrowed. These assessments of threat in turn appear to justify the specialized focus on and resources devoted to them. It is as though we have built an institutional telescope and can now see only a larger threat than we would if we took our eyes away from the eyepiece and looked at the broader view—as our substantive generalists can and must.

---

6 The other signal responses to 9/11, of course, are the Patriot Act of 2004, which addressed the legal framework of counterterrorism work, and the creation of the position I filled briefly as head of and then as Deputy National Intelligence Officer for Transnational Threats (responsible for terrorism analysis).

7 In addition, one must acknowledge, though never accept, that sometimes our opponents simply succeed through no fault of our institutions or men and women.

It is an error to isolate counterterrorist offices from the larger regional analytical offices in the intelligence, foreign policy, and national security establishments. It is an error to overspecialize our counterterrorism offices and officers—as creating NCTC has done. Each step diminishes perspective, lessens insight, and impairs judgment.

The Department of State's Bureau of Intelligence and Research (INR)—a small office of a few dozen officers barely known to the American public—tends to produce deeper and more policy-useful analysis than the far more richly resourced CIA. Ironically, INR benefits from its paucity of resources. INR officers must be generalists as well as experts, which forces a broader perspective on them often denied to their more specialized CIA counterparts. INR can address only critical, strategic issues (or at least try to address them), rather than attempt to provide comprehensive and highly focused analysis on all conceivable issues. In consequence, INR is less likely inadvertently to hype what are secondary issues through an institutionally engendered cognitive bias.

There are remedial steps to this self-created problem of narrow perspective, hyped threats, and deluded perceptions about the real terrorist challenges facing the United States and Western values.

Our counterterrorism analysis and operations would have a more measured perspective about the trends and nature of Islamic terrorism, and would be less likely to delude themselves and policy makers, if terrorism analysts were incorporated as important parts of regional analytical offices, charged with broader regional, sociological, and political analysis, rather than separated, isolated, and placed on an institutional par (and rivalry) with regional analysts. During my tenure as DNIO for Transnational Threats (i.e., terrorism), I often cautioned my colleagues to "beware the questions you ask, for you will receive answers to them." Our counterterrorism structures post-9/11 too often have queered the questions we ask, and the answers we give, about the terrorist threats facing us. The organizational changes noted above would give a broader and more accurate perspective to our counterterrorism analysis, operations, and policies, producing probably greater strategic coherence and success. At least, it would be more difficult for policy makers to find justification for their policies in distorted expertise.

Almost all individuals and institutions involved in coercive interrogations strictly followed guidance that had received the repeated approval of the highest bodies in the U.S. government. Prosecution would not rectify the errors committed, but it would fray our society. Punishment metes out no justice.

We do not need more laws. The laws are only as strong as the men who interpret and enforce them, and the social compact that embraces them. As I lived the CAPTUS case, I saw that a few of our leaders, in their insularity and sanctimonious certainty, corrupted the laws and started to corrode our social compact. We can take actions, however, to diminish such men, and that reaffirm our society's commitment to our principles, our institutions, and the rule of law.

The U.S. Congress should hold public hearings on the coercive interrogation programs of the United States. All involved should have immunity, except for a refusal to speak the truth and to tell what one knows. The hearings would be an American version of the "Truth Commissions" that did so much to heal South Africa of the decades of apartheid.

I am not naive about what would happen: Behind courtly smiles, some members of Congress, pundits, and interested citizens would cast doubt on the impartiality, integrity, and trustworthiness of those who criticize or lay out what enhanced interrogation is. They would express concerns about weakening national security by what they would characterize as a distorted account of practices that in their version saved lives and safeguarded the republic. They would note that no attack has occurred since September 11, 2001, and would attribute this to the courageous decisions taken by our leaders in a time of war—when in fact enhanced interrogation has had *nothing* to do with the lack of another successful attack on U.S. territory. They would worry that discussing controversial practices will strengthen our enemies. Statements would be made indirectly that those speaking out are neither patriots nor strong enough to protect the public from ruthless killers. Some politicians and pundits would state that they know who are "real Americans"—who would not include critics of enhanced interrogation techniques. Off-stage, disturbing reports would surface about the integrity, impartiality, courage, and character of various individuals testifying. In the struggle for influence and power, one always seeks to destroy a messenger perceived as hostile to one's interests, to discredit the message, and to divert attention with counterclaims. The average citizen, pulled in opposite directions by authority figures, on subjects the average citizen cannot know firsthand, would be confronted with a sterile "he said, she said" polemic and would usually accept the views expressed by the political leaders with whom he or she identifies. Everyone would decry the character assassinations and unsubstantiated assertions; all would deny engaging in them; those whose power base and interests were threatened by the truth about enhanced interrogation would make sure they happen.

What good, then, a public hearing that ruthless politics is sure to distort and sully? The facts. The facts. The facts in conflict with our laws and our principles. In the end, despite innuendo, fear-mongering, misleading assertions, and probably a variant of Swift Boat character assassination, the facts will out—and will make it harder for leaders to corrupt our system of laws, checks, and balances when a new crisis pressures them to shake off the fetters that bind our power but guarantee our freedom.

Knowledge of the truth strengthens a nation, and may strengthen its laws, more than punishment. An evil known can be avoided in the future. Yet, it is difficult for a society to protect itself against actions taken in secret. The executive branch should not be allowed to hide matters of law and principle behind arguments of "national security" and "operational sources and methods."

Those most responsible for having subverted our laws against torture are the small number of senior officials who drafted the legal rationalizations for the coercive interrogation methods, and the governmental officials who ordered them to do so. They were the highest legal officials and policy makers in the country, to whom the CIA turned for guidance, the ultimate guarantors of our system of laws, checks, and balances. They did not err; they committed willful, if deluded, acts of subversion. Yet, the punishment for the policy makers who traduced their oaths should consist of public shaming and lasting disgrace, nothing more. This is especially true for those lawyers who perverted the spirit of our laws by writing justifications that undermined centuries of blood, struggle, and sacrifice for a constitution that guaranteed habeas corpus, for everyone, wherever our flag held sway, even for our enemies, whatever their practices, and that established a government of laws, and not of executive orders. We would be a stronger nation for it.

The United States must have a robust, aggressive, and subtle intelligence service that operates in the "gray world" with all the tools necessary to defend or advance the national interest in the ruthless interplay of states and competing interests. Rendition, detention, and interrogation all have their legitimate places among the methods used by our national security establishment, as does protecting sources and methods of intelligence collection. The Clandestine Service is clandestine so that it can function successfully. The public has no "right to know" intelligence activities, sources, or methods, and should not have one. Coercive interrogation methods, however, have no place among the methods used by our national security establishment. No threat justifies institutionalizing these practices, or subverting the numerous laws against torture that the United States subscribes to and often champions.

Upon reading this book, some will call me a torturer. Others, perhaps, a hero. Colleagues whom I respect have told me that they believe openly discussing our failings in the conduct of the Global War on Terror—and, they have told me, writing this book—would "aid and abet" our enemies. Other colleagues have quietly urged me to tell the sordid truth to the American public. My critical colleagues make a profound error: Our flag has long been a rallying point for the oppressed and a symbol of freedom because it embodies public debate, draws strength from acknowledging our failings, and then makes them good. The weak and the guilty flee their acts, or hide them behind claims of "sources and methods" and "national security." The strong and honorable take responsibility for even their failings.

One cannot gainsay what happened in the CAPTUS case and in the Global War on Terror. I know what we did. I did it. Yet, in the end, the way to contend with the demons and harm to our country that this story reveals is what I kept telling CAPTUS: Tell the truth. If we are strong enough to do so, our fears may not possess us once again, and we may avoid becoming the demons whom we claim to oppose, as well as victims of delusion. *Fahimt*?!

INDEX